A BOO

Elizabeth Goudge was born in we[...]
and educated at Grassendale School, Sou[...]
bourne, and the Art School of Reading
University. The author of several novels and
books for children, she has also written a
biography of St. Francis of Assisi and *God so
loved the World*. Among her best known novels
are *Green Dolphin Country* (filmed as 'Green
Dolphin Street'), *The Herb of Grace*, *A City of
Bells*, and *The Scent of Water*.

About this delightful personal anthology of
prose and poetry, Miss Goudge writes: 'This
book, one-sided and limited because con-
ditioned by my ignorance and limitations,
contains what I myself find comforting, and I
am not only comforted by the great forms of the
world, the glories of the Bible and the remembrance of saints and heroes, though they are
pre-eminent, but by comic rhymes, fairy tales,
verses that set me remembering birds and bees
and creatures of all sorts. It comes with good
wishes to anyone who may read it.'

ELIZABETH GOUDGE

A BOOK OF COMFORT

An Anthology

COLLINS

FONTANA BOOKS

First published in Great Britain by Michael Joseph Ltd., 1964
First published in Fontana Books 1968
Eighth Impression November 1974

For Jane Franklin

CONDITIONS OF SALE: This book is sold subject to the
condition that it shall not, by way of trade or otherwise,
be lent, re-sold, hired out or otherwise circulated without
the publisher's prior consent in any form of binding or
cover other than that in which it is published and without
a similar condition including this condition being imposed
on the subsequent purchaser

© 1964 Elizabeth Goudge
Printed in Great Britain
Collins Clear-Type Press
London and Glasgow

PREFACE

The request to make an anthology with the title 'A Book
Comfort' made me ask myself, What *are* the sources of
comfort to which we turn in what Saint Augustine, in a
passage quoted in this book, calls 'our mortal weariness'?
The answer is that our existence is as light with comfort as
it is weighted with weariness. The sources of our comfort
are legion, and cannot be counted, but if we attempted the
impossible and tried to make a list most of us would place
books very high indeed, perhaps second only to faith, for
reading, is not only a pleasure in itself, with its concomitants
of stillness, quietness and forgetfulness of self, but in what
we read many of our other comforts are present with us like
reflections seen in a mirror. If the light of our faith flickers
we can make it steady again by reading of the faith of the
saints, and hearing poetry sing to us the songs of the lovers
of God. In the absence of children we can read about them,
and in the cold and darkness of mid-winter look in the mirror
of our book and see flowers and butterflies, and spring passing
into the glow and warmth of summer.

And so of the making of books there is no end, and of the
making of anthologies there seems particularly to be no end
because we are all anthologists. The collection and hoarding
of bits and pieces is basic to all animals, from the squirrel
with his nuts laid by in a hollow tree for comfort in the dark
days to the anthologist with his oddments stored up in his
memory for a similar purpose. Anthology-making is there-

fore essentially selfish, like self-preservation. Indeed it *is* self-preservation, for where should we be in our bad times without the treasure stored up in our minds? It is also, like many selfish activities, highly enjoyable, with the advantage of literature over nuts that it can be shared without personal loss to the hoarder.

But the sharing can cause trepidation as well as pleasure for what is treasure for oneself is not always treasure for other people. Their hoard would have been very different and they will think yours an odd mixture. I am aware that this anthology is so. It contains some of the great poems of the world, and others that have little literary merit, but the latter are included because it would have been like turning one's back on a friend to leave them out. My gratitude is great to all the writers of the poems and prose passages quoted in this book because they wrote them, centuries ago or only a few years ago, to be our comfort and delight today. Time has nothing to do with comfort, and in no instance are these extracts dated. I am also grateful to authors and publishers alike for permission to include them, and to the publisher of this anthology for giving me the opportunity of making it.

CONTENTS

7

I. WE ARE COMFORTED WHEN WE CONSIDER THE GLORY AND WISDOM OF CREATION, AND BOTH BY THE SIGHT AND THE REMEMBRANCE OF ALL CREATURES OF THE EARTH

1 IN THE BEGINNING

In the beginning was the Word, and the Word was with God, and the Word was God.

The same was in the beginning with God.

All things were made by him; and without him was not anything made that was made.

In him was life; and the life was the light of men.

And the light shineth in darkness; and the darkness apprehended it not.

The Gospel according to St. John

Doth not wisdom cry? and understanding put forth her voice? . . .

The Lord possessed me in the beginning of his way, before his works of old.

I was set up from everlasting, from the beginning, or ever the earth was.

When there were no depths, I was brought forth; when there were no fountains abounding with water.

Before the mountains were settled, before the hills was I brought forth:

While as yet he had not made the earth, nor the fields, nor the highest part of the dust of the world.

When he prepared the heavens, I was there: when he set a compass upon the face of the deep:

When he established the clouds above : when he strengthened
the fountains of the deep :
When he gave to the sea his decree, that the waters should
not pass his commandment : when he appointed the
foundations of the earth :
Then I was by him, as one brought up with him : and I was
daily his delight, rejoicing always before him;
Rejoicing in the habitable part of his earth; and my delight
was with the sons of men. . . .
Blessed is the man that heareth me, watching daily at my
gates, waiting at the posts of my doors.
For whoso findeth me findeth life, and shall obtain favour of
the Lord.
But he that sinneth against me wrongeth his own soul : all
they that hate me love death.

The Book of Proverbs

2 THE SUN BY DAY,
THE MOON AND STARS BY NIGHT

SUN, MOON AND STARS

The pride of the height, the clear firmament, the beauty of
heaven, with his glorious shew;
The sun when it appeareth, declaring at his rising a marvellous
instrument, the Work of the most High :
At noon it parcheth the country, and who can abide the
burning heat thereof?
A man blowing a furnace is in works of heat, but the sun
burneth the mountains three times more; breathing out
fiery vapours, and sending forth bright beams, it dimmeth
the eyes.
Great is the Lord that made it; and at his commandment it
runneth hastily.
He made the moon also to serve in her season for a declaration
of times, and a sign of the world.

From the moon is the sign of feasts, a light that decreaseth in
    her perfection.
The month is called after her name, increasing wonderfully
    in her changing, being an instrument of the armies above,
    shining in the firmament of heaven;
The beauty of heaven, the glory of the stars, an ornament
    giving light in the highest places of the Lord.
At the commandment of the Holy One they will stand in their
    order, and never faint in their watches.

          The Apocrypha The Book of Ecclesiasticus

CANTICLE OF THE SUN

Oh, Most High, Almighty, Good Lord God, to Thee belong
    praise, glory, honour and all blessing.
Praised be my Lord God, with all His creatures, and especially
    our brother the Sun, who brings us the day and who
    brings us the light: fair is he, and he shines with a very
    great splendour.
Oh Lord, he signifies us to Thee!
Praised be my Lord for our sister the Moon, and for the stars,
    the which He has set clear and lovely in the heaven.
Praised be my Lord for our brother the Wind, and for air and
    clouds, calms and all weather, by which Thou upholdest
    life and all creatures.
Praised be my Lord for our sister Water, who is very service-
    able to us, and humble and precious and clean.
Praised be my Lord for our brother Fire, through whom Thou
    givest us light in the darkness; and he is bright and
    pleasant and very mighty and strong.
Praised be my Lord for our mother the Earth, the which doth
    sustain us and keep us, and bringeth forth divers fruits
    and flowers of many colours, and grass.
Praised be my Lord for all those who pardon one another for
    love's sake, and who endure weakness and tribulation:
    blessed are they who peacefully shall endure, for Thou,
    Oh Most High, will give them a crown.
Praised be my Lord for our sister, the death of the body, from

which no man escapeth. Woe to him who dieth in mortal
sin. Blessed are those who die in Thy most holy will, for
the second death shall have no power to do them harm.
Praise ye and bless the Lord, and give thanks to Him and serve
Him with great humility.

  St. Francis of Assisi Translated by Maurice Francis Egan

AN OLD WOMAN SPEAKS OF THE MOON

She was urgent to speak of the moon : she offered delight
And wondering praise to be shared by the girl in the shop,
Lauding the goddess who blessed her each sleepless night
Greater and brighter till full : but the girl could not stop.

She turned and looked up in my face, and hastened to cry
How beautiful was the orb, how the constant glow
Comforted in the cold night the old waking eye :
How fortunate she, whose lodging was placed that so

She in her lonely night, in her lonely age,
She from her poor lean bed might behold the undying
Letter of loveliness written on heaven's page,
The sharp silver arrows leap down to where she was lying.

The dying spoke love to the immortal, the foul to the fair,
The withered to the still-flowering, the bound to the free :
The nipped worm to the silver swan that sails through the air :
And I took it as good, and a happy omen to me.

                                        Ruth Pitter

          How sweet the moonlight sleeps upon this bank !
          Here will we sit and let the sounds of music
          Creep in our ears : soft stillness and the night
          Become the touches of sweet harmony.
          Sit, Jessica. Look how the floor of heaven
          Is thick inlaid with patines of bright gold :
          There's not the smallest orb which thou behold'st

But in his motion like an angel sings,
Still quiring to the young-eyed cherubins;
Such harmony is in immortal souls;
But whilst this muddy vesture of decay
Doth grossly close it in, we cannot hear it.

Shakespeare The Merchant of Venice

THE STARLIT NIGHT

Look at the stars! look, look up at the skies!
O look at all the fire-folk sitting in the air!
The bright boroughs, the circle-citadels there!
Down in dim woods the diamond delves; the elves'-eyes!
The grey lawns cold where gold, where quickgold lies!
Wind-beat whitebeam! airy abeles set on a flare!
Flake-doves sent floating forth at a farmyard scare!—
Ah well! it is all a purchase, all is a prize.
Buy them! bid then!—What?—Prayer, patience, alms, vows.
Look, look: a May-mess, like on orchard boughs!
Look! March-blooms, like on mealed-with-yellow sallows!
These are indeed the barn; withindoors house
The shocks. This piece-bright paling shuts the spouse
Christ home, Christ and his mother and all his hallows.

Gerard Manley Hopkins

NIGHT

Mysterious Night! when our first parent knew
    Thee from report divine, and heard thy name,
Did he not tremble for this lovely frame,
    This glorious canopy of light and blue?
Yet 'neath a curtain of translucent dew,
    Bathed in the rays of the great setting flame,
Hesperus with the host of heaven came,
    And lo! creation widened in man's view.
Who could have thought such darkness lay concealed,
    Within thy beams, O sun! or who could find,

Whilst fly, and leaf, and insect stood revealed,
    That to such countless orbs thou mad'st us blind!
Why do we then shun Death with anxious strife?
    If light can thus deceive, wherefore not life?

Blanco White

NIGHT

Swiftly walk over the western wave,
    Spirit of Night!
Out of the misty eastern cave,—
Where, all the long and lone daylight,
Thou wovest dreams of joy and fear
Which make thee terrible and dear,—
    Swift be thy flight!

Wrap thy form in a mantle grey,
    Star-inwrought!
Blind with thin hair the eyes of Day;
Kiss her until she be wearied out.
Then wander o'er city and sea and land,
Touching all with thine opiate wand—
    Come, long-sought!

When I arose and saw the dawn,
    I sighed for thee;
When light rode high, and the dew was gone,
And noon lay heavy on land and tree,
And the weary Day turned to her rest,
Lingering like an unloved guest,
    I sigh'd for three.

Thy brother Death came, and cried,
    ' Wouldst thou me? '
Thy sweet child Sleep, the filmy-eyed,
Murmur'd like a noontide bee,
' Shall I nestle near thy side?
Wouldst thou me? '—And I replied,
    ' No, not thee ! "

Death will come when thou art dead,
      Soon, too soon—
Sleep will come when thou art fled.
Of neither would I ask the boon
I ask of thee, belovèd Night—
Swift be thine approaching flight,
      Come soon, soon!

Percy Bysshe Shelley

3 THE CLOUDS, RAIN AND RAINBOWS

CLOUDS

You do look, my son, in a moved sort,
As if you were dismay'd : be cheerful, sir.
Our revels now are ended. These our actors,
As I foretold you, were all spirits and
Are melted into air, into thin air :
And, like the baseless fabric of this vision,
The cloud-capp'd towers, the gorgeous palaces,
The solemn temples, the great globe itself,
Yea, all which it inherit, shall dissolve
And, like this insubstantial pageant faded,
Leave not a rack behind. We are such stuff
As dreams are made on, and our little life
Is rounded with a sleep. . . .

Shakespeare   The Tempest

CLOUDS

Down the blue night the unending columns press
   In noiseless tumult, break and wave and flow,
   Now tread the far South, or lift rounds of snow
Up to the white moon's hidden loveliness.

Some pause in their grave wandering comradeless,
  And turn with profound gesture vague and slow,
    As who would pray good for the world, but know
Their benediction empty as they bless.

They say that the Dead die not, but remain
  Near to the rich heirs of their grief and mirth.
    I think they ride the calm mid-heaven, as these,
In wise majestic melancholy train,
    And watch the moon, and the still-raging seas,
And men, coming and going on the earth.
                                        Rupert Brooke

THE VIEW FROM THE WINDOW

Like a painting it is set before one,
But less brittle, ageless; these colours
Are renewed daily with variations
Of light and distance that no painter
Achieves or suggests. Then there is movement,
Change, as slowly the cloud bruises
Are healed by sunlight, or snow caps
A black mood; but gold at evening
To cheer the heart. All through history
The great brush has not rested,
Nor the paint dried; yet what eye,
Looking coolly, or, as we now,
Through the tears' lenses, ever saw
This work and it was not finished?
                                        R. S. Thomas

THE RAIN

Rain, do not hurt my flowers, but quickly spread
Your honey drops: presse not to smell them here:
When they are ripe, their odour will ascend
And at your lodging with their thanks appear.
                                        George Herbert

RAIN

That is rain on dry ground. We heard it:
We saw the little tempest in the grass,
The panic of anticipation: heard
The uneasy leaves flutter, the air pass
In a wave, the fluster of the vegetation;

Heard the first spatter of drops, the outriders
Larruping on the road, hitting against
The gate of the drought, and shattering
On to the lances of the tottering meadow.
It is rain; it is rain on dry ground,

Rain riding suddenly out of the air,
Battering the bare walls of the sun.
It is falling on to the tongue of the blackbird,
Into the heart of the thrush; the dazed valley
Sings it down. Rain, rain on dry ground! . . .

  The rain stops.
  The air is sprung with green.
  The intercepted drops
  Fall at their leisure; and between
  The threading runnels on the slopes
  The snail drags his caution into the sun.
     Christopher Fry Rain on Dry Ground

TURN OF THE MOON

Never forget who brings the rain
In swarthy goatskin bags from a far sea:
It is the Moon as she turns, repairing
Damages of long drought and sunstroke.

Never count upon rain, never foretell it,
For no power can bring rain
Except the Moon as she turns; and who can rule her?

She is prone to delay the necessary floods,
Lest such a gift might become obligation,
A month, or two, or three; then suddenly
Not relenting but by way of whim
Will perhaps conjure from the cloudless west
A single rain-drop to surprise with hope
Each haggard, unturned face.

Were the Moon a Sun, we would count upon her
To bring rain seasonably as she turned;
Yet no-one thinks to thank the regular Sun
For shining fierce in summer, mild in winter—
Why should the Moon so drudge?

But if one night she brings us, as she turns,
Soft, steady, even, copious rain
That harms no leaf nor flower, but gently falls
Hour after hour, sinking to the tap roots,
And the sodden earth exhales at dawn
A long sigh scented with pure gratitude,
Such rain—the first rain of our lives, it seems,
Neither foretold, cajoled, nor counted on—
Is woman giving as she loves.

Robert Graves

THE RAINBOW

And God said . . . I do set my bow in the cloud, and it shall be for a token of a covenant between me and the earth. And it shall come to pass, when I bring a cloud over the earth, that the bow shall be seen in the cloud. . . . While the earth remaineth, seed time and harvest, and cold and heat, and summer and winter, and day and night shall not cease.

The Book of Genesis

Look upon the rainbow, and praise him that made it; very
beautiful it is in the brightness thereof. It compasseth the
heaven about with a glorious circle, and the hands of the most
High have bended it.

The Apocrypha   The Book of Ecclesiasticus

A MOON RAINBOW

But lo, what think you; suddenly
The rain and the wind ceased, and the sky
Received at once the full fruition
Of the moon's consummate apparition.
The black cloud barricade was riven,
Ruined beneath her feet, and driven
Deep in the West; while, bare and breathless,
North and South and East lay ready
For a glorious thing that, dauntless, deathless,
Sprang across them and stood steady.

'Twas a moon-rainbow, vast and perfect,
From heaven to heaven extending, perfect
As the mother-moon's self, full in face,
It rose, distinctly at the base
With its severe proper colours chorded
Which still in the rising, were compressed,
Until at last they coalesced,
And supreme the spectral creature lorded
In a triumph of whitest white,—
Above which intervened the night.
But above night too, like only the next,
The second of a wondrous sequence.
Reaching in rare and rarer frequence,
Till the heaven of heavens were circumflexed.

Another rainbow rose, a mightier,
Fainter, flushier, and flightier,—

Rapture dying along its verge.
Oh, whose foot shall I see emerge,
Whose, from the straining topmost dark,
On to the keystone of that arc?

Robert Browning

4 FOUNTAIN AND STREAM, ICE AND SNOW

THE RIVER GOD

I am this fountain's god. Below,
My waters to a river grow,
And 'twixt two banks with osiers set,
That only prosper in the wet,
Through the meadows do they glide,
Wheeling still on every side,
Sometimes winding round about,
To find the evenest channel out.
And if thou wilt go with me
Leaving mortal company,
In the cool streams shalt thou lie,
Free from harm as well as I:
I will give thee for thy food
No fish that useth in the mud;
But trout and pike, that love to swim
Where the gravel from the brim
Through the pure streams may be seen:
Orient pearl fit for a queen
Will I give thy love to win,
And a shell to keep them in;
Not a fish in all my brook,
That shall disobey thy look,
But when thou wilt come sliding by,
And from thy white hand take a fly
And to make thee understand
How I can my waves command,

They shall bubble whilst I sing,
Sweeter than the silver string.
Do not fear to put thy feet
Naked in the river sweet;
Think not leech, or newt, or toad,
Will bite thy foot when thou hast trod;
Nor let the water rising high
As thou wad'st in, make thee cry
And sob; but ever live with me,
And not a wave shall trouble thee.

John Fletcher

FOUNTAIN

Let it disturb no more at first
Than the hint of a pool predicted far in a forest,
Or a sea so far away that you have to open
Your window to hear it.
Think of it then as elemental, as being
Necessity.

Not for a cup to be taken to it and not
For lips to linger or eye to receive itself
Back in reflection, simply
As water the patient moon persuades and stirs.

And then step closer,
Imagine rivers you might indeed embark on,
Waterfalls where you could
Silence an afternoon by staring but never
See the same tumult twice.
Yes come out of the narrow street and enter
The full piazza. Come where the noise compels.
Statues are bowing down to the breaking air.

Observe it there——the fountain, too fast for shadows,
Too wild for the lights which illuminate it to hold,

Even a moment, an ounce of water back;
Stare at such prodigality and consider
It is the elegance here, it is the taming,
The keeping fast in a thousand flowering sprays,
That builds this energy up but lets the watchers
See in that stress an image of utter calm,
A stillness, there. It is how we must have felt
Once at the edge of some perpetual stream,
Fearful of touching, bringing no thirst at all,
Panicked by no perception of ourselves
But drawing the water down to the deepest wonder.

Elizabeth Jennings

BEYOND POSSESSION

Our images withdraw, the rose returns
To what it was before we looked at it.
We lift our look from where the water runs
And it's pure river once again, we write
No emblems on the trees. A way begins
Of living where we have no need to beat
The petals down to get the scent of rose
Or sign our features where the water goes.

All is itself. Each man himself entire,
Not even plucking out his thoughts, not even
Bringing a tutored wilfulness to bear
Upon the rose, the water. Each has given
Essence of water back to itself, essence of flower,
Till he is yoked to his own heart and driven
Inward to find a private kind of peace
And not a mind reflecting his own face.

Yet must go deeper still, must move to love
Where thought is free to let the water ride,
Is liberal to the rose giving it life
And setting even its own shadow aside

Till flower and water blend with freedom of
Passion that does not close them in and hide
Their deepest natures; but the heart is strong
To beat with rose and river in one song.
Elizabeth Jennings

SNOW

By his commandment he maketh the snow to fall apace, and
    sendeth swiftly the lightnings of his judgement.
Through this the treasures are opened: and clouds fly forth
    as fowls.
By his great power he maketh the clouds firm, and the hail-
    stones are broken small. . . .
The noise of the thunder maketh the earth to tremble: so doth
    the northern storm and the whirlwind: as birds flying
    he scattereth the snow, and the falling down thereof is
    as the lighting of grasshoppers.
The eye marvelleth at the beauty of the whiteness thereof,
    and the heart is astonished at the raining of it.
The hoarfrost also as salt he poureth on the earth, and being
    congealed, it lieth on the top of sharp stakes.
When the cold north wind bloweth, and the water is congealed
    into ice, it abideth upon every gathering together of
    water, and closeth the water as with a breastplate.
It devoureth the mountains, and burneth the wilderness, and
    consumeth the grass as fire.
A present remedy of all is a mist coming speedily: a dew
    coming after heat refresheth.
The Apocrypha   The Book of Ecclesiasticus

ON A GENTLEWOMAN
WALKING IN THE SNOWE

I saw faire Cloris walke alone
Where feather'd raine came softly downe,
And Jove descended from his tower
To court her in a silver shower;

The wanton snowe flewe to her breast
Like little birds into their nest,
And overcome with whiteness there
For greife it thaw'd into a teare,
Thence falling on her garment's hem
For greife it freez'd into a gem.

                                    William Strode

5 THE SEASONS

A SONG OF THE FOUR SEASONS

When Spring comes laughing
    By vale and hill,
By wind-flower walking
    and daffodil,—
Sing stars of morning,
    Sing morning skies,
Sing blue of speedwell,—
    And my Love's eyes.

When comes the Summer,
    Full-leaved and strong,
And gay birds gossip
    The orchard long,—
Sing bird, sweet honey
    That no bee sips;
Sing, red, red roses,—
    And my Love's lips.

When Autumn scatters
    The leaves again,
And piled sheaves bury
    The broad-wheeled wain,—
Sing flutes of harvest
    Where men rejoice;
Sing rounds of reapers,—
    And my Love's voice.

But when comes Winter
  With hail and storm,
And red fire roaring,
  And ingle warm,
Sing first sad going
  Of friends that part;
Then sing glad meeting,—
  And my Love's heart.

Austin Dobson

SPRING

When daisies pied and violets blue,
  And lady-smocks all silver-white,
And cuckoo-buds of yellow hue
  Do paint the meadows with delight,
The cuckoo then, on every tree,
Mocks married men for thus sings he,
          Cuckoo!
Cuckoo, cuckoo!—O word of fear,
Unpleasing to a married ear!

When shepherds pipe on oaten straws,
  And merry larks are ploughman's clocks,
When turtles tread, and rooks, and daws,
  And maidens bleach their summer smocks
The cuckoo then, on every tree,
Mocks married men; for thus sings he,
          Cuckoo!
Cuckoo, cuckoo!—O word of fear,
Unpleasing to a married ear!

William Shakespeare Love's Labour Lost

TO SPRING

O thou with dewy locks, who lookest down
Through the clear windows of the morning, turn
Thine angel eyes upon our western isle,
Which in full choir hails thy approach, O Spring!

The hills tell one another, and the listening
Valleys hear; all our longing eyes are turn'd
Up to thy bright pavilions : issue forth
And let thy holy feet visit our clime!

Come o'er the eastern hills, and let our winds
Kiss thy perfumèd garments; let us taste
Thy morn and evening breath; scatter thy pearls
Upon our lovesick land that mourns for thee.

O deck her forth with thy fair fingers; pour
Thy soft kisses on her bosom; and put
Thy golden crown upon her languish'd head,
Whose modest tresses are bound up for thee.

William Blake

THE PASTURE

I'm going out to clean the pasture spring;
I'll only stop to rake the leaves away
(And wait to watch the water clear, I may):
I sha'n't be gone long.—You come too.

I'm going out to fetch the little calf
That's standing by the mother. It's so young
It totters when she licks it with her tongue.
I sha'n't be gone long.—You come too.

Robert Frost

APRIL RISE

If ever I saw blessing in the air
I see it now in this still early day
Where lemon-green the vaporous morning drips
Wet sunlight on the powder of my eye.

Blown bubble-film of blue, the sky wraps round
Weeds of warm light whose every root and rod
Splutters with soapy green, and all the world
Sweats with the bead of summer in its bud.

If ever I heard blessing it is there
Where birds in trees that shoals and shadows are
Splash with their hidden wings and drops of sound
Break on my ears their crests of throbbing air.

Pure in the haze the emerald sun dilates
The lips of sparrows milk the mossy stones,
While white as water by the lake a girl
Swims her green hand among the gathered swans,

Now, as the almond burns its smoking wick,
Dropping small flames to light the candled grass;
Now, as my low blood scales its second chance,
If ever world were blessed, now it is.

Laurie Lee

THOUGHTS IN A SUMMER GARDEN

How vainly men themselves amaze
To win the palm, the oak, or bays,
And their uncessant labours see
Crown'd from some single herb or tree,
Whose short and narrow-vergèd shade
Does prudently their toils upbraid;

While all the flowers and trees do close
To weave the garlands of repose!

Fair Quiet, have I found thee here.
And Innocence thy sister dear?.
Mistaken long, I sought you then
In busy companies of men :
Your sacred plants, if here below,
Only among the plants will grow :
Society is all but rude
To this delicious solitude.

No white nor red was ever seen
So amorous as this lovely green.
Fond lovers, cruel as their flame,
Cut in these trees their mistress' name :
Little, alas! they know or heed
How far these beauties hers exceed!
Fair trees! wheres'e'er your barks I wound,
No name shall but your own be found.

When we have run our passions' heat,
Love hither makes his best retreat :
The gods, that mortal beauty chase,
Still in a tree did end their race;
Apollo haunted Daphne so
Only that she might laurel grow;
And Pan did after Syrinx speed
Not as a nymph, but for a reed.

What wondrous life in this I lead!
Ripe apples drop upon my head;
The luscious clusters of the vine
Upon my mouth do crush their wine;
The nectarine and curious peach
Into my hands themselves do reach;
Stumbling on melons, as I pass,
Ensnared with flowers, I fall on grass.

Meanwhile the mind from pleasure less
Withdraws into its happiness;
The mind, that ocean where each kind
Does straight its own resemblance find;
Yet it creates, transcending these,
Far other worlds, and other seas;
Annihilating all that's made
To a green thought in a green shade.

Here at the fountain's sliding foot,
Or at some fruit-tree's mossy root,
Casting the body's vest aside,
My soul into the boughs does glide;
There, like a bird, it sits and sings,
Then whets and combs its silver wings,
And, till prepared for longer flight,
Waves in its plumes the various light.

Such was that happy Garden-state
While man there walk'd without a mate:
After a place so pure and sweet,
What other help could yet be meet!
But 'twas beyond a mortal's share
To wander solitary there:
Two paradises 'twere in one,
To live in Paradise alone.

How well the skilful gard'ner drew
Of flowers and herbs this dial new!
Where, from above, the milder sun
Does through a fragrant zodiac run:
And, as it works, th'industrious bee
Computes its time as well as we.
How could such sweet and wholesome hours
Be reckon'd, but with herbs and flowers!

                                        Andrew Marvell

MAGNOLIA TREE IN SUMMER

'Up above those top leaves, what do you see,
High as our zenith, or our apogee?
I am holding the ladder foot, lest you fall;
Call down loud, and tell me all!'
I stood by the rungs quite still, to hear
And watched his scissors trim and shear:
His voice rings through the leaves so cool
Between these clippings thick as wool.
'I have all the blossoms near me
Where I stand now—Can you hear me?—
All the blossoms, all the flowers
I see as from a hundred towers:
Wisps of wool, or flakes of snow
Are but petals I let go.
This branch is like my window-ledge
High in the eaves where young birds fledge;
Perhaps I'll find the wind's soft nest,
Lined with feathers from her breast—
Or would you like a white flower best?'—
'Do not take her dappled egg:
Do not shake her nest, I beg:
Bring me down a flower instead,
Soft as milk, and white as bread.'
He climbs the tree-stem like a mast:
He shouts, 'Now hold my ladder fast!'
I held it while he clipped the stem
Pulling the leaves to cut at them—
Now he's climbing down it seems,
A stairway built of sun's bright beams
In timbers, straight and strong, of gold
Sloped like the ladder that I hold.
He says, 'Here is the flower I've cut'.
I take it, thank him, smell it, but,
Thinking why his path was lit,
I hear the sun explaining it.

'This man knows where the wind's nest lies
In thinnest branches near the skies :
He never shook it, never tried,
To steal the eggs that lay inside;
So she holds still the boughs, and I
Gild his ladder from on high;
The flower he gives into your hand
Is sweet as honey, gold as sand—
If either of you climb again,
No wind will blow, I'll send no rain;
She'll flash for you her feathers bright
And I will keep you in my sight,
Like golden stars you'll walk up here,
And shine among us, free from fear!'

Sacheverell Sitwell

TO AUTUMN

Season of mists and mellow fruitfulness!
　　Close bosom-friend of the maturing sun;
Conspiring with him how to load and bless
　　With fruit the vines that round the thatch-eaves run;
To bend with apples the moss'd cottage-trees,
　　And fill all fruit with ripeness to the core;
　　　To swell the gourd, and plump the hazel shells
　　With a sweet kernel; to set budding more,
And still more, later flowers for the bees,
Until they think warm days will never cease,
　　For Summer has o'er-brimm'd their clammy cells.

Who hath not seen thee oft amid thy store?
　　Sometimes whoever seeks abroad may find
Thee sitting careless on a granary floor,
　　Thy hair soft-lifted by the winnowing wind;
Or on a half-reap'd furrow sound asleep,
　　Drowsed with the fume of poppies, while thy hook
　　　Spares the next swath and all its twinèd flowers;

And sometimes like a gleaner thou dost keep
   Steady thy laden head across a brook;
  Or by a cider-press, with patient look,
    Thou watchest the last oozings hours by hours,

Where are the songs of Spring? Ay, where are they?
   Think not of them, thou hast thy music too,—
While barrèd clouds bloom the soft-dying day,
  And touch the stubble-plains with rosy hue;
Then in a wailful choir the small gnats mourn
   Among the river sallows, borne aloft
    Or sinking as the light wind lives or dies;
And full-grown lambs loud bleat from hilly bourn;
  Hedge-crickets sing; and now with treble soft
  The redbreast whistles from a garden-croft;
    And gathering swallows twitter in the skies.

John Keats

HURRAHING IN HARVEST

Summer ends now; now, barbarous in beauty, the stooks arise
   Around; up above, what wind-walks! what lovely behaviour
  Of silk-sack clouds! has wilder, wilful-wavier
Meal-drift moulded ever and melted across skies?

I walk, I lift up, I lift up heart, eyes,
   Down all that glory in the heavens to glean our Saviour;
  And, éyes, heárt, what looks, what lips yet gave you a
Rapturous love's greeting of realer, of rounder replies?

And the azurous hung hills are his world-wielding shoulder
   Majestic—as a stallion stalwart, very-violet-sweet!—
These things, these things were here and but the beholder
  Wanting; which two when they once meet,
The heart rears wings bold and bolder
   And hurls for him, O half hurls earth for him off under his
    feet.

Gerard Manley Hopkins

AUTUMN APPLES

Behold the apples' rounded worlds:
juice-green of July rain,
the black polestar of flower, the rind
mapped with its crimson stain.

The russet, crab and cottage red
burn to the sun's hot brass,
then drop like sweat from every branch
and bubble in the grass.

They lie as wanton as they fall,
and when they fall and break,
the stallion clamps his crunching jaws,
the starling stabs his beak.

In each plump gourd the cidery bite
of boys' teeth tears the skin;
the waltzing wasp consumes his share,
the bent worm enters in.

I, with an easy hunger, take
entire my season's dole;
welcome the ripe, the sweet, the sour,
the hollow and the whole.

Laurie Lee

POEM IN OCTOBER

It was my thirtieth year to heaven
Woke to my hearing from harbour and neighbour wood
And the mussel pooled and the heron
Priested shore
The morning beckon
With water praying and call of seagull and rock
And the knock of sailing boats on the net-webbed wall

Myself to set foot
That second
In the still sleeping town and set forth.

My birthday began with the water-
Birds and the birds of the winged trees flying my name
Above the farms and the white horses
And I rose
In rainy autumn
And walked abroad in a shower of all my days.
High tide and the heron dived when I took the road
Over the border
And the gates
Of the town closed as the town awoke

A springful of larks in a rolling
Cloud and the roadside bushes brimming with whistling
Blackbirds and the sun of October
Summery
On the hill's shoulder,
Here were fond climates and sweet singers suddenly
Come in the morning where I wandered and listened
To the rain wringing
Wind blow cold
In the wood faraway under me.

Pale rain over the dwindling harbour
And over the sea-wet church the size of a snail
With its horns through mist and the castle
Brown as owls,
But all the gardens
Of spring and summer were blooming in the tall tales
Beyond the border and under the lark-full cloud.
There could I marvel
My birthday
Away but the weather turned around.

It turned away from the blithe country,
And down the other air and the blue altered sky

Streamed again a wonder of summer
With apples
Pears and red-currants,
And I saw in the turning so clearly a child's
Forgotten mornings when he walked with his mother
Through the parables
Of sunlight
And the legends of the green chapels.

And the twice told fields of infancy
That his tears burned my cheeks and his heart moved in mine.
These were the woods the river and sea
Where a boy
In the listening
Summertime of the dead whispered the truth of his joy
To the trees and the stars and the fish in the tide.
And the mystery
Sang alive
Still in the water and singing birds.

And then could I marvel my birthday
Away but the weather turned around. And the true
Joy of the long-dead child sang burning
In the sun
It was my thirtieth
Year to heaven stood there then in the summer noon
Though the town below lay leaved with October blood.
O may my heart's truth
Still be sung
On this high hill in a year's turning.

Dylan Thomas

WINTER

When icicles hang by the wall,
And Dick the shepherd blows his nail,
And Tom bears logs into the hall,
And milk comes frozen home in pail,

When blood is nipp'd, and ways be foul,
Then nightly sings the staring owl,
        To-whit!
To-who!—a merry note,
While greasy Joan doth keel the pot.

When all aloud the wind doth blow,
    And coughing drowns the parson's saw,
And birds sit brooding in the snow,
    And Marian's nose looks red and raw,
When roasted crabs hiss in the bowl,
Then nightly sings the staring owl,
        To-whit!
To-who!—a merry note,
While greasy Joan doth keel the pot.
            William Shakespeare   Love's Labour's Lost

FROST AT MIDNIGHT

The Frost performs its secret ministry,
Unhelped by any wind. The owlet's cry
Came loud—and hark, again! loud as before.
The inmates of my cottage, all at rest,
Have left me to that solitude which suits
Abstruser musings : save that at my side
My cradled infant slumbers peacefully.
'Tis calm indeed! so calm, that it disturbs
And vexes meditation with its strange
And extreme silentness. Sea, hill, and wood,
This populous village! Sea, and hill, and wood,
With all the numberless goings-on of life,
Inaudible as dreams! the thin blue flame
Lies on my low-burnt fire, and quivers not;
Only that film which fluttered on the grate
Still flutters there, the sole unquiet thing.
Methinks, its motion in this hush of nature
Gives it dim sympathies with me who live,
Making it a companionable form,

Whose puny flaps and freaks the idling Spirit
By its own moods interprets, everywhere
Echo or mirror seeking of itself,
And makes a toy of Thought.

                          But O! how oft,
How oft, at school, with most believing mind,
Presageful, have I gazed upon the bars,
To watch that fluttering *stranger*! and as oft
With unclosed lids, already had I dreamt
Of my sweet birth-place, and the old church-tower,
Whose bells, the poor man's only music, rang
From morn to evening, all the hot Fair-day,
So sweetly, that they stirred and haunted me
With a wild pleasure, falling on mine ear
Most like articulate sounds of things to come!
So gazed I, till the soothing things, I dreamt,
Lulled me to sleep, and sleep prolonged my dreams!
And so I brooded all the following morn,
And by the stern preceptor's face mine eye
Fixed with mock study on my swimming book:
Save if the door half opened, and I snatched
A hasty glance, and still my heart leaped up,
For still I hoped to see the *stranger's* face,
Townsman, or aunt, or sister more beloved,
My playmate when we both were clothed alike!

  Dear Babe, that sleepest cradled by my side,
Whose gentle breathings, heard in this deep calm,
Fill up the interspersed vacancies
And momentary pauses of the thought!
My babe so beautiful! it thrills my heart
With tender gladness, thus to look at thee,
And think that thou shalt learn far other love,
And in far other scenes! For I was reared
In the great city, pent mid cloisters dim,
And saw naught lovely but the sky and stars.
But thou, my babe! shalt wander like a breeze
By lakes and sandy shores, beneath the crags

Of ancient mountain and beneath the clouds,
Which image in their bulk both lakes and shores
And mountain crags : so shalt thou see and hear
The lovely shapes and sounds intelligible
Of that eternal language, which thy God
Utters, Who from eternity doth teach,
Himself in all, and all things in Himself
Great universal Teacher! He shall mould
Thy spirit, and by giving make it ask.

Therefore all seasons shall be sweet to thee,
Whether the summer clothe the general earth
With greenness, or the redbreast sit and sing
Betwixt the tufts of snow on the bare branch
Of mossy apple-tree, while the high thatch
Smokes in the sun-thaw; whether the rain-drops fall,
Heard only in the trances of the blast,
Or if the secret ministry of frost
Shall hang them up in silent icicles,
Quietly shining to the quiet Moon.

Samuel Taylor Coleridge

SPATE IN WINTER MIDNIGHT

The streams fall down and through the darkness bear
Such wild and shaking hair,
Such looks beyond a cool surmise,
Such lamentable uproar from night skies
As turn the owl from honey of blood and make
Great stags stand still to hear the darkness shake.

Through Troys of bracken and Babel towers of rocks
Shrinks now the looting fox,
Fearful to touch the thudding ground
And flattened to it by the mastering sound.
And roebuck stilt and leap sideways; their skin
Twitches like water on the fear within.

Black hills are slashed white with this falling grace.
Whose violence buckles space
To a sheet-iron thunder. This
Is noise made universe, whose still centre is
Where the cold adder sleeps in his small bed.
Curled neatly round his neat and evil head.

Norman MacCaig

6 FLOWERS, BIRDS, AND WINGED CREATURES

SEEDS

In this brown husk a dale of hawthorn dreams,
A cedar in this narrow cell is thrust
That will drink deeply of a century's streams.
These lilies shall make summer on my dust.

Here in their safe and simple house of death,
Sealed in their shells, a million roses leap.
Here I can blow a garden with my breath,
And in my hand a forest lies asleep.

Muriel Stuart   from The Seed Shop

A CHANTED CALENDAR

First came the primrose,
On the bank high,
Like a maiden looking forth
From the window of a tower
When the battle rolls below,
So look'd she,
And saw the storms go by.

Then came the wind-flower
In the valley left behind.
As a wounded maiden, pale
With purple streaks of woe,
When the battle has roll'd by
Wanders to and fro,
So totter'd she,
Dishevell'd in the wind.

Then came the daisies,
On the first of May,
Like a banner'd show's advance
While the crowd runs by the way,
With ten thousand flowers about them they came trooping
through the fields.
As a happy people come,
So came they,
As a happy people come
When the war has roll'd away,
With dance and tabor, pipe and drum,
And all make holiday.

Then came the cowslip,
Like a dancer in the fair,
She spread her little mat of green,
And on it danced she.
With a fillet bound about her brow,
A fillet round her happy brow,
A golden fillet round her brow,
And rubies in her hair.

Sydney Dobell

I WALKED THE OTHER DAY

I walk'd the other day (to spend my hour)
    Into a field
Where I sometimes had seen the soil to yield
    A gallant flow'r,

But winter now had ruffled all the bow'r
    And curious store
  I knew there heretofore.

Yet I whose search lov'd not to peep and peer
    I'th'face of things
Thought with my self, there might be other springs
    Beside this here
Which, like cold friends, sees us but once a year,
    And so the flow'r
  Might have some other bow'r.

Then taking up what I could nearest spy
    I digg'd about
That place where I had seen him to grow out,
    And by and by
I saw the warm recluse alone to lie
    Where fresh and green
  He lived of us unseen.

Many a question intricate and rare
    Did I there strow,
But all I could extort was, that he now
    Did there repair
Such losses as befel him in this air
    And would e'er long
  Come forth most fair and young.

This past, I threw the clothes quite o'er his head,
    And stung with fear
Of my own frailty dropped down many a tear
    Upon his bed,
Then sighing whisper'd, Happy are the dead!
    What peace doth now
  Rock him asleep below?

And yet, how few believe such doctrine springs
    From a poor root
Which all the winter sleeps here under foot
    And hath no wings

To raise it to the truth and light of things,
    But is still trod
  By ev'ry wand'ring clod.

O thou! whose spirit did at first inflame
    And warm the dead,
And by a sacred incubation fed
    With life this frame
Which once had neither being, form, nor name,
    Grant I may so
  Thy steps track here below,

That in these masques and shadows I may see
    Thy sacred way,
And by those hid ascents climb to that day
    Which breaks from thee
Who art in all things, though invisibly;
    Show me thy peace,
  Thy mercy, love, and ease,

And from this care, where dreams and sorrows reign
    Lead me above
Where light, joy, leisure, and true comforts move
    Without all pain,
There, hid in thee, show me his life again
    At whose dumb urn
  Thus all the year I mourn.

                                        Henry Vaughan

  I've heard, I've heard,
  The long low note of a bird,
  The nightingale fluting his heart's one word.

  I know, I know,
  Pink carnations heaped with snow,
  In summer and winter alike they blow.

  I've lain, I've lain, Under roses' delicate rain,
  That fall and whisper and fall again.

Come woe, come white
Shroud o'the world, black night,
I have had love and the sun's light.

Margaret Woods

SOCRATES SPEAKS

And, as it seems, I appear to you to be inferior to swans with
respect to divination, who, when they perceive that they must
needs die, though they have been used to sing before, sing
then more than ever, rejoicing that they are about to depart to
that deity whose servants they are. But men, through their
own fear of death, belie the swans too, and say that they,
lamenting their death, sing their last song through grief,
and they do not consider that no bird sings when it is hungry
or cold, or is afflicted with any other pain, not even the nightingale, or swallow, or the hoopoes, which they say sing lamenting through grief. But neither do these birds appear to me to
sing through sorrow, nor yet do swans; but in my opinion,
belonging to Apollo, they are prophetic, and foreseeing the
blessings of Hades, they sing and rejoice on that day more
excellently than at any preceding time. But I too consider
myself to be a fellow-servant of the swans, and sacred to the
same god, and that I have received the power of divination
from our common master no less than they, and that I do not
depart from this life with less spirits than they.

Phaedo Five Dialogues of Plato On Poetic Inspiration

FROM PROTHALAMION

With that I saw two Swannes of goodly hewe
Come softly swimming downe along the Lee;
Two fairer Birds I yet did never see;
The snow, which doth the top of Pindus strew,
Did never whiter shew;
Nor Jove himselfe, when he a Swan would be,
For love of Leda, whiter did appeare;

Yet Leda was (they say) as white as he,
Yet not so white as these, nor nothing neare;
So purely white they were,
That even the gentle streame, the which them bare,
Seem'd foule to them, and bad his billowes spare
To wet their silken feathers, least they might
Soyle their fayre plumes with water not so fayre,
And marre their beauties bright,
That shone as heavens light,
Against their Brydale day, which was not long:
   Sweet Themmes! runne softly, till I end my Song.
Edmund Spenser

AFTER THE STORM

Hither thou com'st: the busy wind all night
Blew through thy lodging, where thine own warm wing
Thy pillow was. Many a sullen storm,
For which coarse man seems much the fitter born,
     Rain'd on the bed
     And harmless head.

And now as fresh and cheerful as the light
Thy little heart in early hymns doth sing
Unto that Providence, Whose unseen arm
Curb'd them, and cloth'd thee well and warm.
     All things that be praise Him; and had
     Their lesson taught them when first made.

So hills and valleys into singing break;
And though poor stones have neither speech nor tongue,
While active winds and streams both run and speak,
Yet stones are deep in admiration.
Thus praise and prayer here beneath the sun
Make lesser mornings, when the great are done.
Henry Vaughan   From Olor Iscamus

STORMCOCK IN ELDER

In my dark hermitage, aloof
From the world's sight and the world's sound,
By the small door where the old roof
Hangs but five feet above the ground,
I groped along the shelf for bread
But found celestial food instead:

For suddenly close at my ear,
Loud, loud and wild, with wintry glee,
The old unfailing chorister
Burst out in pride of poetry;
And through the broken roof I spied
Him by his singing glorified.

Scarcely at arm's-length from the eye,
Myself unseen, I saw him there;
The throbbing throat that made the cry,
The breast dewed from the misty air,
The polished bill that opened wide
And showed the pointed tongue inside:

The large eye, ringed with many a ray
Of minion feathers, finely laid,
The feet that grasped the elder-spray:
How strongly used, how subtly made
The scale, the sinew, and the claw,
Plain through the broken roof I saw;

The flight-feathers in tail and wing,
The shorter coverts, and the white
Merged into russet, marrying
The bright breast to the pinions bright,
Gold sequins, spots of chestnut, shower
Of silver, like a brindled flower.

Soldier of fortune, northwest Jack,
Old hard-times' braggart, there you blow!
But tell me ere your bagpipes crack
How you can make so brave a show,
Full-fed in February, and dressed
Like a rich merchant at a feast.

One-half the world, or so they say,
Knows not how half the world may live;
So sing your song and go your way,
And still in February contrive
As bright as Gabriel to smile
On elder-spray by broken tile.

Ruth Pitter

VESPER

O Blackbird, what a boy you are!
How you do go it!
Blowing your bugle to the one sweet star—
How you do blow it!

And can she hear you, blackbird boy, so far?
Or is it wasted breath?
'Good Lord! She is so bright
To-night!'
The blackbird saith.

Thomas Edward Brown

A BLACKBIRD SINGING

It seems wrong that out of this bird,
Black, bold, a suggestion of dark
Places about it, there yet should come
Such rich music, as though the notes'
Ore were changed to a rare metal
At one touch of that bright bill.

You have heard it often, alone at your desk
In a green April, your mind drawn
Away from its work by sweet disturbance
Of the mild evening outside your room.

A slow singer, but loading each phrase
With history's overtones, love, joy
And grief learned by his dark tribe
In other orchards and passed on
Instinctively as they are now,
But fresh always with new tears.

                                        R. S. Thomas

SAINT FRANCIS AND THE BIRDS

And as he went on his way, with great fervour, St. Francis lifted up his eyes, and saw on some trees by the wayside a great multitude of birds; and being much surprised, he said to his companions, 'Wait for me here by the way, whilst I go and preach to my little sisters the birds'; and entering into the field, he began to preach to the birds which were on the ground, and suddenly all those also on the trees came round him, and all listened while St. Francis preached to them, and did not fly away until he had given them his blessing. And Brother Masseo related afterwards to Brother James of Massa how St. Francis went among them and even touched them with his garments, and how none of them moved. Now the substance of the sermon was this: 'My little sisters the birds, ye owe much to God, your Creator, and ye ought to sing His praise at all times and in all places, because He has given you liberty to fly about into all places; and though ye neither spin nor sew, He has given you a twofold and a threefold clothing for yourselves and for your offspring. Two of all your species He sent into the Ark with Noe that you might not be lost to the world; besides which, He feeds you, though ye neither sow nor reap. He has given you fountains and rivers to quench your thirst, mountains and valleys in which to take refuge, and trees in which to build your nests! so

that your Creator loves you much, having thus favoured you
with such bounties. Beware, my little sisters, of the sin of
ingratitude, and study always to give praise to God.' As he
said these words, all the birds began to open their beaks, to
stretch their necks, to spread their wings, and reverently to
bow their heads to the ground, endeavouring by their motions
and by their songs to manifest their joy to St. Francis. And
the saint rejoiced with them. He wondered to see such a
multitude of birds, and was charmed with their beautiful
variety, with their attention and familiarity, for all of which
he devoutly gave thanks to the Creator. Having finished his
sermon, St. Francis made the sign of the cross, and gave them
leave to fly away. Then all those birds rose up into the air,
singing most sweetly; and, following the sign of the cross,
which St. Francis had made, they divided themselves into four
companies. One company flew towards the east, another towards
the west, one towards the south, and one towards the north;
each company as it went singing most wonderfully; signifying
thereby, that as St. Francis, the bearer of the cross of Christ,
had preached to them and made upon them the sign of the
cross, after which they had divided among themselves for four
parts of the world, so the preaching of the cross of Christ,
renewed by St. Francis, would be carried by him and his
brethren over all the world, and that the humble friars, like
little birds, should possess nothing in this world, but should
cast all the care of their lives on the providence of God.

Little Flowers of St. Francis

At St. Mary of the Angels, a grasshopper was continually
chirping, which, by its song, excited the servant of God to
praise the Lord; for he had learnt, even in the most insignifi-
cant creatures, to admire the wonderful works of the Creator.
One day he called the grasshopper to him, which, as if it had
been divinely admonished to obey, perched at once upon his
hand. And he said to it, ' Sing, my sister grasshopper; rejoice
and praise the Lord thy Creator '. And the creature began at
once to chirp, and ceased not until, at the command of the
Father, it sprang back again to its own place. Thus for eight

days together it remained on that same branch, daily coming to the holy man at his command, and departing again when he sent it away. At length the man of God said to his companions: 'Let us give leave to our sister grasshopper to depart, for she hath now sufficiently cheered us by her song, and for these eight days past hath exalted us to praise our God.' And immediately it departed, nor did it ever appear there again, as if it dared not in any wise transgress his command.

St. Bonaventure   Life of St. Francis of Assisi

ON THE GRASSHOPPER AND CRICKET

The poetry of earth is never dead:
   When all the birds are faint with the hot sun,
That is the Grasshopper's—he takes the lead
   In summer luxury,—he has never done
   With his delights; for when tired out with fun
He rests at ease beneath some pleasant weed.
The poetry of earth is ceasing never:
   On a lone winter evening, when the frost
     Has wrought a silence, from the stove there shrills
The Cricket's song, in warmth increasing ever,
   And seems to one in drowsiness half lost,
    The Grasshopper's among some grassy hills.

John Keats

THE MOWER TO THE GLOW-WORMS

   Ye living Lamps, by whose dear light
   The Nightingale does sit so late,
   And studying all the Summer-night,
   Her matchless Songs does meditate;

   Ye Country Comets, that portend
   No War, nor Princes funeral,
   Shining unto no higher end
   Than to presage the Grasses fall;

Ye Glow-worms, whose officious Flame
To wandring Mowers shows the way,
That in the Night have lost their aim,
And after foolish Fires do stray;

Your courteous Lights in vain you waste,
Since *Juliana* here is come
For She my Mind hath so displac'd
That I shall never find my home.

Andrew Marvell

THE BUTTERFLY

Of all the race of silver-wingèd Flies
Which doo possess the Empire of the aire,
Betwixt the centred earth, and azure skies,
Was none more favorable nor more faire,
Whilst heaven did favour his felicities.
Lastly his shinie wings as silver bright,
Painted with thousand colours, passing faire
All Painter's skill, he did about him dight:
Not halfe so manie sundrie colours are
In Iris brave, ne heaven doth shine so bright,
Distinguised with manie a twinckling starre,
Nor Junoe's Bird in her ey-spotted traine
So manie goodly colours doth containe.

To the gay gardens his unstaid desire
Him wholly carried, to refresh his sprights:
There lavish Nature in her best attire,
Pours foorth sweet odors, and alluring sights;
And Arte with her contending, doth aspire
T'excell the naturall, with made delights.
And all that faire or pleasant may be found,
In riotesse excesse doth there abound.

There he arriving, round about doth flie,
From bed to bed, from one to other border,

And takes survey with curious busie eye
Of everie flowre and herbe there set in order,
Now this, now that he tasteth tenderly,
Yet none of them he rudely doth disorder,
Ne with his feete their silken leaves deface;
But pastures on the pleasures of each place.

And evermore with most varietie,
And change of sweetresse (for all change is sweet)
He casts his glutton sense to satisfie,
Now sucking of the sap of herbe most meete,
Or of the deaw, which yet on them doth lie,
Now in the same bathing his tender feete:
And then he pearcheth on some branch thereby
To weather him, and his moist wings to dry.

Edmund Spenser

BUTTERFLIES

Here, by this crumbling wall
We'll spread the feast, then watch what guests it brings.
Earth-rooted flowers to flowers of heaven shall call,
And all the gorgeous air shall wink with wings.

We'll choose what they love most
As all men must, whose guests are of the sky:
Not lavender, of lost gardens the sweet ghost;
But heliotrope, young Psyche's cherry-pie.

Be sure she does not pine
For any phantom feast, that heavenly Maid!
'Tis we that make a wraith of things divine,
And think the very soul into a shade.

The Chilian orange ball
First of the shrubs that Tortoise-shells prefer,
Must hang its honeyed clusters over all
And tempt the freckled Blues to flutter near.

With globes of fragrant gold
Luring the green-veined White from near and far,
While faultless Painted Ladies here unfold
Their pearly fans, inlaid with moon and star;

Till later Buddleias trail
Their long racemes of violet and of rose,
Round which the glorious Admirals dip and sail,
And swarthy Peacocks flit and sip and doze.

Hedging them closely round
Veronica must spread her spikes of blue,
That sun and flowers may in one sleep be drowned
Yet keep her own Fritillaries fluttering, too.

Blue is their heart's delight.
Therefore, though crimson petals also please,
And soft white wings will sail to bridal white
Like yachts with orange tips on blossoming seas;

We'll make them doubly blest
With this, the deepening blue of children's eyes;
For wingèd creatures love that colour best,
Which smiled upon them, once, in Paradise.

Alfred Noyes   The Butterfly Garden

MELAMPUS

With love exceeding a simple love of the things
That glide in grasses and rubble of woody wreck;
Or change their perch on a beat of quivering wings
From branch to branch, only restful to pipe and peck;
Or, bristled, curl at a touch their snouts in a ball;
Or cast their web between bramble and thorny hook;
The good physician Melampus, loving them all,
Among them walk'd, as a scholar who reads a book.

For him the woods were a home and gave him the key
Of knowledge, thirst for their treasures in herbs and flowers.
The secrets held by the creatures nearer than we
To earth he sought, and the link of their life with ours:
And where alike we are, unlike where, and the vein'd
Division, vein'd parallel, of a blood that flows
In them, in us, from the source by man unattain'd
Save marks he well what the mystical woods disclose. . . .

George Meredith

7 ANIMALS

I think I could turn and live with animals, they are so placid
    and self-contained,
I stand and look at them sometimes an hour at a stretch.
They do not sweat and whine about their condition,
They do not lie awake in the dark and weep for their sins,
They do not make me sick discussing their duty to God,
No one is dissatisfied—not one is demented with the mania of
    owning things,
Not one kneels to another, nor to his kind that lived thousands
    of years ago,
Not one is respectable or industrious over the whole earth.

Walt Whitman

THE TIGER

Tiger, tiger, burning bright
In the forests of the night,
What immortal hand or eye
Could frame thy fearful symmetry?

In what distant deeps or skies
Burnt the fire of thine eyes?
On what wings dare he aspire?
What the hand dare seize the fire?

And what shoulder and what art
Could twist the sinews of thy heart?
And, when thy heart began to beat,
What dread hand and what dread feet?

What the hammer? What the chain?
In what furnace was thy brain?
What the anvil? What dread grasp
Dare its deadly terrors clasp?

When the stars threw down their spears,
And water'd heaven with their tears,
Did he smile His work to see?
Did He who made the lamb make thee?

Tiger, tiger, burning bright
In the forests of the night,
What immortal hand or eye
Dare frame thy fearful symmetry?

William Blake

THE DONKEY

When fishes flew and forests walked
And figs grew upon thorn,
Some moment when the moon was blood
Then surely I was born:

With monstrous head and sickening cry
And ears like errant wings,
The devil's walking parody
On all four-footed things;

The tattered outlaw of the earth
Of ancient crooked will:
Starve, scourge, deride me: I am dumb,
I keep my secret still.

Fools! For I also had my hour;
One far fierce hour and sweet:
There was a shout about my ears,
And palms before my feet.

G. K. Chesterton

IN THE WILDERNESS

Christ of his gentleness
Thirsting and hungering
Walked in the wilderness;
Soft words of grace He spoke
Unto lost desert-folk
That listened wondering.
He heard the bitterns call
From ruined palace-wall,
Answered them brotherly.
He held communion
With the she-pelican
Of lonely piety.
Basilisk, cockatrice,
Flocked to His homilies,
With mail of dread device,
With monstrous barbèd stings,
With eager dragon-eyes;
Great rats on leather wings
And poor blind broken things,
Foul in their miseries.
And ever with Him went,
Of all His wanderings
Comrade, with ragged coat,
Gaunt ribs—poor innocent—
Bleeding foot, burning throat,
The guileless old scape-goat;
For forty nights and days
Followed in Jesus' ways,
Sure guard behind Him kept,
Tears like a lover wept.

Robert Graves

HORSES ON THE CAMARGUE

In the grey wastes of dread,
The haunt of shattered gulls where nothing moves
But in a shroud of silence like the dead,
I heard a sudden harmony of hooves,
And, turning, saw afar
A hundred snowy horses unconfined,
The silver runaways of Neptune's car
Racing, spray-curled, like waves before the wind.
Sons of the Mistral, fleet
As him with whose strong gusts they love to flee,
Who shod the flying thunders on their feet
And plumed them with the snortings of the sea;
Theirs is no earthly breed
Who only haunt the verges of the earth
And only on the sea's salt herbage feed—
Surely the great white breakers gave them birth.
For when for years a slave,
A horse of the Camargue, in alien lands,
Should catch some far-off fragrance of the wave
Carried far inland from his native sands,
Many have told the tale
Of how in fury, foaming at the rein,
He hurls his rider; and with lifted tail,
With coal-red eyes and cataracting mane,
Heading his course for home,
Though sixty foreign leagues before him sweep,
Will never rest until he breathes the foam
And hears the native thunder of the deep.
But when the great gusts rise
And lash their anger on these arid coasts,
When the scared gulls career with mournful cries
And whirl across the waste like driven ghosts:
When hail and fire converge,
The only souls to which they strike no pain
Are the white-crested fillies of the surge
And the white horses of the windy plain.

Then in their strength and pride
The stallions of the wilderness rejoice;
They feel their Master's trident in their side,
And high and shrill they answer to his voice.
With white tails smoking free,
Long streaming manes, and aching necks, they show
Their kinship to their sisters of the sea—
And forward hurl their thunderbolts of snow.
Still out of hardship bred,
Spirits of power and beauty and delight
Have ever on such frugal pastures fed
And loved to course with tempests through the night.

Roy Campbell

AN OTTER

Underwater eyes, an eel's
Oil of water body, neither fish nor beast is the otter:
Four-legged yet water-gifted, to outfish fish;
With webbed feet and long ruddering tail
And a round head like an old tomcat.

Brings the legend of himself
From before wars or burials, in spite of hounds and
vermin-poles;
Does not take root like the badger. Wanders, cries;
Gallops along land he no longer belongs to;
Re-enters the water by melting.

Of neither water nor land. Seeking
Some world lost when first he dived, that he cannot come
at since,
Takes his changed body into the holes of lakes;
As if blind, cleaves the stream's push till he licks
The pebbles of the source; from sea.

    To sea crosses in three nights
Like a king in hiding. Crying to the old shape of the
      starlit land,
  Over sunken farms where the bats go round,
    Without answer. Till light and birdsong come
    Walloping up roads with the milk wagon.

                              Ted Hughes

FLUSH OR FAUNUS

You see this dog. It was but yesterday
I mused forgetful of his presence here
Till thought on thought drew downward tear on tear;
When from the pillow, where wet-cheeked I lay,
A head as hairy as Faunus, thrust its way
Right sudden against my face,—two golden-clear
Great eyes astonished mine,—a drooping ear
Did flap me on either cheek to dry the spray!
I started first, as some Arcadian,
Amazed by goatly god in twilight grove;
But, as the bearded vision closelier ran
My tears off, I knew Flush, and rose above
Surprise and sadness,—thanking the true Pan,
Who, by low creatures, leads to heights of love.

                        Elizabeth B. Browning

TIM, AN IRISH TERRIER

It's wonderful dogs they're breeding now :
Small as a flea or large as a cow;
But my old lad Tim he'll never be bet
By any dog that ever he met.
' Come on,' says he, ' for I'm not kilt yet.'

No matter the size of the dog he'll meet,
Tim trails his coat the length o' the street.

D'ye mind his scar an' his ragged ear,
The like of a Dublin Fusilier?
He's a massacree dog that knows no fear.

But he'd stick to me till his latest breath;
An' he'd go with me to the gates of death.
He'd wait for a thousand years, maybe,
Scratching the door an' whining for me
If myself were inside in Purgatory.

So I laugh when I hear them make it plain
That dogs and men never meet again.
For all their talk who'd listen to thim,
With the soul in the shining eyes of him?
Would God be wasting a dog like Tim?

                                        W. M. Letts

THE SINGING CAT

It was a little captive cat
        Upon a crowded train
His mistress takes him from his box
        To ease his fret and pain

She holds him tight upon her knee
        The graceful animal
And all the people look at him
        He is so beautiful.

But oh he pricks and oh he prods
        And turns upon her knee
Then lifteth up his innocent voice
        In plaintive melody.

He lifteth up his innocent voice
        He lifteth up, he singeth
And to each human countenance
        A smile of grace he bringeth.

He lifteth up his innocent paw
        Upon her breast he clingeth
And everybody cries, Behold
        The cat, the cat that singeth.

He lifteth up, he singeth
        He lifteth up, he singeth
And all the people warm themselves
        In the love his beauty bringeth.

Stevie Smith

TO A CAT

Cat! who hast pass'd thy grand climacteric,
How many mice and rats hast in thy days
Destroy'd?—How many tit bits stolen? Gaze
With those bright languid segments green, and prick
Those velvet ears—but pr'ythee do not stick
Thy latent talons in me—and upraise
Thy gentle mew—and tell me all thy frays
Of fish and mice, and rats and tender chick.
Nay, look not down, nor lick thy dainty wrists—
For all the wheezy asthma—and for all
Thy tail's tip is nick'd off—and though the fists
Of many a maid have given thee many a maul,
Still is that fur as soft as when the lists
In youth thou enter'dst on glass-bottled wall.

John Keats

THE RESURRECTION OF THE ANIMALS

The writer speaks first of Paradisal man with the creatures

Wholly commanding himself, he commanded all lower lives
with which he came into contact. Even now we meet rare
individuals who have a mysterious power of taming beasts.
This power the Paradisal man enjoyed in eminence. The old
picture of the brutes sporting before Adam and fawning upon
him may not be wholly symbolical. Even now more animals

than you might expect are ready to adore man if they are given a reasonable opportunity : for man was made to be the priest and even, in one sense, the Christ, of the animals—the mediator through whom they apprehend so much of the Divine splendour as their irrational nature allows. . . .

Atheists naturally regard the co-existence of man and the other animals as a mere contingent result of interacting biological facts; and the taming of an animal by a man as a purely arbitrary interference of one species with another. The ' real ' or ' natural ' animal to them is the wild one, and the tame animal is an artificial or unnatural thing. But a Christian must not think so. Man was appointed by God to have dominion over the beasts, and everything a man does to an animal is either a lawful exercise, or a sacrilegious abuse, of an authority by divine right. The tame animal is therefore, in the deepest sense, the only ' natural ' animal—the only one we see occupying the place it was made to occupy, and it is on the tame animal that we must base all our doctrine of beasts. Now it will be seen that, in so far as the tame animal has a real self or personality, it owes this almost entirely to its master. If a good sheepdog seems ' almost human ' that is because a good shepherd has made it so. . . .

You must not think of a beast by itself, and call that a personality and then inquire whether God will raise and bless *that*. You must take the whole context *in* which the beast acquires its selfhood—namely ' The-goodman-and-the-good-wife - ruling - their - children - and - their - beasts - in - the - good - home-stead '. That whole context may be regarded as a ' body ' in the Pauline (or a closely sub-Pauline) sense; and how much of that ' body ' may be raised along with the goodman and his goodwife, who can predict? So much, presumably, as is necessary not only for the glory of God and the beatitude of the human pair, but for that particular glory and that particular beatitude which is eternally coloured by that particular terrestrial experience. And in this way it seems to me possible that certain animals may have an immortality, not in themselves, but in the immortality of their masters. And the difficulty about personal identity in a creature barely personal disappears when the creature is thus kept in its proper context. If you ask, concerning an animal thus raised as a member of the whole Body of the homestead, where its personal identity resides, I answer 'Where its identity always did reside even in the earth life—in its relation to the Body and, specially, to the master who is the head of that Body '. In other words, the man will know his dog : the dog will know its master and, in knowing him, will *be* itself. To ask that it should, in any other way, *know* itself, is probably to ask for what has no meaning. Animals aren't like that, and don't want to be.

When we are speaking of creatures so remote from us as wild beasts, and prehistoric beasts, we hardly know what we are talking about. It may well be that they have no selves and no sufferings. It may even be that each species has a corporate self—that Lionhood, not lions, has shared in the travail of creation and will enter into the restoration of all things. And if we cannot imagine even our own eternal life, much less can we imagine the life the beasts may have as our 'members '. If the earthly lion could read the prophecy of that day when he shall eat hay like the ox, he would regard it as a description not of heaven, but of hell. And if there is nothing in the lion but carnivorous sentience, then he is unconscious and his ' survival ' would have no meaning. But if there is a rudimentary Leonine self, to that also God can give a ' body ' as it pleases Him—a body no longer living by the destruction of the lamb, yet richly Leonine in the sense that it also expresses whatever energy and splendour and exulting power dwelled within the visible lion on this earth. I think, under correction, that the prophet used an eastern hyperbole when he spoke of the lion and the lamb *lying down* together. That would be rather impertinent of the lamb. To have lions and lambs that so consorted (except on some rare celestial Saturnalia of topsy-turvydom) would be the same as having neither lambs nor lions. I think the lion, when he has ceased to be dangerous, will still be awful : indeed, that we shall then first see that of which the present fangs and claws are a clumsy, and satanically perverted, imitation. There will still be something like the shaking of a golden mane : and often the good Duke will say, ' Let him roar again '.

C. S. Lewis   *The Problem of Pain*

NATURE

God's creative freedom is to be conceived as the freedom of a poet : the freedom to create a consistent, positive thing with its own inimitable flavour. Shakespeare need not create Falstaff : but if he does, Falstaff *must* be fat. God need not create this Nature. He might have created others. But granted *this* Nature, then doubtless no smallest part of her is there except because it expresses the character He chose to give her. It would be a miserable error to suppose that the dimensions of space and time, the death and re-birth of vegetation, the unity in multiplicity of organisms, the union in opposition of sexes, and the colour of each particular apple in Herefordshire this autumn, were merely a collection of useful devices forcibly welded together. They are the very idiom, almost the facial expression, the smell or taste, of an individual thing. The *quality* of Nature is present in them all just as the Latinity of Latin is present in every inflection or the ' Correggiosity ' of Correggio in every stroke of the brush.

Nature is by human (and probably by Divine) standards partly good and partly evil. We Christians believe that she has been corrupted. But the same tang or flavour runs through both her corruptions and her excellences. Everything is in character. Falstaff does not sin in the same way as Othello. Othello's fall bears a close relation to his virtues. If Perdita had fallen she would not have been bad in the same way as Lady Macbeth; if Lady Macbeth had remained good her goodness would have been quite different from that of Perdita. The evils we see in Nature are, so to speak, the evils proper to *this* Nature. Her very character decreed that if she were corrupted the corruption would take this form and not another. The horrors of parasitism and the glories of motherhood are good and evil worked out of the same basic theme or idea.

I spoke just now about the Latinity of Latin. It is more evident to us than it can have been to the Romans. The Englishness of English is audible only to those who know some other language as well. In the same way and for the same reason, only Supernaturalists really see Nature. You must go a little away from her, and then turn round, and look back. Then at least the true landscape will become visible. You must have tasted, however briefly, the pure water from beyond the world before you can be distinctly conscious of the hot, salty tang of Nature's current. To treat her as God, or as Everything, is to lose the whole pith and pleasure of her. Come out, look back, and then you will see . . . this astonishing cataract of bears, babies, and bananas : this immoderate deluge of atoms, orchids, oranges, cancers, canaries, fleas, gases, tornadoes and toads. How could you ever have thought this was the ultimate reality? How could you ever have thought that it was merely a stage—set for the moral drama of men and women? She is herself. Offer her neither worship nor contempt. Meet her and know her. If we are immortal, and she is doomed (as the scientists tell us) to run down and die, we shall miss this half-shy and half-flamboyant creature, this ogress, this hoyden, this incorrigible fairy, this dumb witch. But the theologians tell us that she, like ourselves, is to be redeemed. The ' vanity ' to which she was subjected was her disease, not her essence. She will be cured, but cured in character : not tamed (Heaven forbid) nor sterilised. We shall still be able to recognise our old enemy, friend, playfellow and foster-mother, so perfected as to be not less, but more, herself. And that will be a merry meeting.

C. S. Lewis   Miracles

Thy whole creation speaks Thy praise . . . that so our soul rises out of its mortal weariness unto Thee, helped upward by the things Thou hast made and passing beyond them unto Thee who hast wonderfully made them : and there refreshment is and strength unfailing.

St. Augustine   Confessions   Translated by E. J. Sheed

Also in this He shewed me a little thing, the quantity of an hazel-nut, in the palm of my hand; and it was as round as a ball. I looked thereupon with eye of my understanding, and thought : *What may this be?* And it was answered generally thus : *It is all that is made.* I marvelled how it might last, for methought it might suddenly have fallen to naught for littleness. And I was answered in my understanding : *It lasteth, and ever shall last for that God loveth it.* And so All-thing hath the Being in the love of God.

In this Little Thing I saw three properties. The first is that God made it, the second is that God loveth it, the third, that God keepeth it. But what is to me verily the Maker, the Keeper, and the Lover,—I cannot tell; for till I am Substantially oned to Him, I may never have full rest nor very bliss : that is to say, till I be so fastened to Him, that there is right nought that is made betwixt my God and me.

    Dame Julian of Norwich   Revelations of Divine Love

II. THE COMFORT WE HAVE IN DELIGHTING IN EACH OTHER

1 CHILDREN OF YESTERDAY

And when he was twelve years old, they went up after the custom of the feast;

And when they had fulfilled the days, as they were returning, the boy Jesus tarried behind in Jerusalem; and his parents knew it not;

But supposing him to be in the company, they went a day's journey; and they sought for him among their kinsfolk and acquaintance;

And when they found him not, they returned to Jerusalem, seeking for him.

And it came to pass, after three days they found him in the temple, sitting in the midst of the doctors, both hearing them, and asking them questions:

And all that heard him were amazed at his understanding and his answers.

And when they saw him they were astonished: and his mother said unto him, Son, why hast thou thus dealt with us? behold thy father and I sought thee sorrowing.

And he said unto them, How is it that ye sought me? wist ye not that I must be in my Father's house?

And they understood not the saying which he spake unto them.

And he went down with them, and came to Nazareth; and he was subject unto them: and his mother kept all these sayings in her heart.

And Jesus advanced in wisdom and stature, and in favour with God and men.

The Gospel according to St. Luke

THE LITTLE BLACK BOY

My mother bore me in the southern wild,
And I am black, but O ! my soul is white;
White as an angel is the English child,
But I am black, as if bereav'd of light.

My mother taught me underneath a tree,
And, sitting down before the heat of day,
She took me on her lap and kissèd me,
And, pointing to the east, began to say :

' Look on the rising sun,—there God does live,
And gives His light, and gives His heat away;
And flowers and trees and beasts and men receive
Comfort in morning, joy in the noonday.

' And we are put on earth a little space,
That we may learn to bear the beams of love;
And these black bodies and this sunburnt face
Is but a cloud, and like a shady grove.

' For when our souls have learn'd the heat to bear,
The cloud will vanish; we shall hear His voice,
Saying: " Come out from the grove, My love and care,
And round My golden tent like lambs rejoice".'

Thus did my mother say, and kissèd me;
And thus I say to little English boy.
When I from black and he from white cloud free,
And round the tent of God like lambs we joy,

I'll shade him from the heat, till he can bear
To lean in joy upon our Father's knee;
And then I'll stand and stroke his silver hair,
And be like him, and he will then love me.

William Blake

CHILDHOOD

All appeared new and strange at first, inexpressibly rare and delightful and beautiful. I was a little stranger which at my entrance into the world was saluted and surrounded with innumerable joys. My knowledge was Divine; I knew by intuition those things which since my apostasy I collected again by the highest reason. My very ignorance was advantageous. I seemed as one brought into the estate of innocence. All things were spotless and pure and glorious; and infinitely mine and joyful and precious. . . . I was entertained like an angel with the works of God in their splendour and glory; I saw all in the peace of Eden; heaven and earth did sing my Creator's praises, and could not make more melody to Adam than to me. All Time was Eternity, and a perpetual Sabbath. Is it not strange that an enfant should be heir of the whole world, and see those mysteries which the books of the learned never unfold?

The corn was orient and immortal wheat which never should be reaped nor was ever sown. I thought it had stood from everlasting to everlasting. The dust and stones of the street were as precious as gold: the gates were at first the end of the world. The green trees when I saw them first through one of the gates transported and ravished me; their sweetness and unusual beauty made my heart to leap, and almost mad with ecstasy, they were such strange and wonderful things. The Men! O what venerable and reverend creatures did the aged seem! Immortal Cherabims! And young men glittering and sparkling angels, and maids strange seraphic pieces of life and beauty! Boys and girls tumbling in the streets were moving jewels: I knew not that they were born or should die. But all things abided eternally as they were in their proper places. Eternity was manifest in the delight of the Day, and something infinite behind everything appeared, which talked with my expectation and moved my desire. The City seemed to stand in Eden or to be built in Heaven. The streets were mine, the temple was mine, the people were

mine, their clothes and gold and silver were mine, as much as
their sparkling eyes, fair skins, and ruddy faces. The skies
were mine, and so were the sun and moon and stars, and all the
world was mine; and I the only spectator and enjoyer of it.
I knew no churlish proprieties, nor bounds nor divisions; but
all proprieties and divisions were mine, all treasures and the
possessors of them.

Thomas Traherne   Centuries of Meditation

THE RETREAT

Happy those early days, when I
Shin'd in my Angel-infancy!
Before I understood this place
Appointed for my second race,

Or taught my soul to fancy aught
But a white celestial thought:
When yet I had not walk'd above
A mile or two from my first Love,
And looking back—at that short space—
Could see a glimpse of His bright face:
When on some gilded cloud, or flow'r,
My gazing soul would dwell an hour,
And in those weaker glories spy
Some shadows of eternity:
Before I taught my tongue to wound
My Conscience with a sinful sound,
Or had the black art to dispense
A several sin to ev'ry sense,
But felt through all this fleshly dress
Bright shoots of everlastingness.

 O how I long to travel back,
And tread again that ancient track!
That I might once more reach that plain
Where first I left my glorious train;

From whence th'enlighten'd spirit sees
That shady City of Palm-trees.
But ah! my soul with too much stay
Is drunk, and staggers in the way!
Some men a forward motion love,
But I by backward steps would move;
And when this dust falls to the urn,
In that state I came, return.

Henry Vaughan

From the Ode

INTIMATIONS OF IMMORTALITY FROM RECOLLECTIONS OF EARLY CHILDHOOD

There was a time when meadow, grove, and stream
The earth, and every common sight,
To me did seem
Apparell'd in celestial light,
The glory and the freshness of a dream.
It is not now as it hath been of yore;—
Turn whereso'er I may,
By night or day,
The things which I have seen I now can see no more.
The rainbow comes and goes,
And lovely is the rose;
The moon doth with delight
Look round her when the heavens are bare;
Waters on a starry night
Are beautiful and fair;
The sunshine is a glorious birth;
But yet I know, where'er I go,
That there has pass'd away a glory from the earth.

Our birth is but a sleep and a forgetting:
The Soul that rises with us, our life's Star,
Hath had elsewhere its setting,
And cometh from afar:

Not in entire forgetfulness,
And not in utter nakedness,
But trailing clouds of glory do we come
From God, who is our home:
Heaven lies about us in our infancy!
Shades of the prison-house begin to close
Upon the growing Boy,
But he beholds the light, and whence it flows,
He sees it in his joy;
The Youth, who daily farther from the east
Must travel, still is Nature's priest,
And by the vision splendid
Is on his way attended;
At length the Man perceives it die away,
And fade into the light of common day.

O joy! that in our embers
Is something that doth live,
That nature yet remembers
What was so fugitive!

The thought of our past years in me doth breed
Perpetual benediction: not indeed
For that which is most worthy to be blest—
Delight and liberty, the simple creed
Of childhood, whether busy or at rest,
With new-fledg'd hope still fluttering in his breast:—
Not for these I raise
The songs of thanks and praise;
But for those obstinate questionings
Of sense and outward things,
Fallings from us, vanishings;
Blank misgivings of a Creature
Moving about in worlds not realised,
High instincts before which our mortal Nature
Did tremble like a guilty thing surprised:
But for those first affections,
Those shadowy recollections,

Which, be they what they may,
Are yet the fountain-light of all our day,
Are yet a master-light of all our seeing;
Uphold us, cherish, and have power to make
Our noisy years seem moments in the being
Of the eternal Silence: truths that wake,
          To perish never:
Which neither listlessness, nor mad endeavour,
          Nor Man nor Boy,
Nor all that is at enmity with joy,
Can utterly abolish or destroy!
  Hence in a season of calm weather
          Though inland far we be,
Our souls have sight of that immortal sea
          Which brought us hither,
      Can in a moment travel thither,
And see the children sport upon the shore,
And hear the mighty waters rolling evermore.

William Wordsworth

TO HIS SON, VINCENT CORBET, ON HIS BIRTH-DAY, NOVEMBER 10, 1630, BEING THEN THREE YEARS OLD

What I shall leave thee none can tell,
But all shall say I wish thee well;
I wish thee, Vin, before all wealth,
Both bodily and ghostly health:
Not too much wealth, nor wit, come to thee,
So much of either may undoe thee.
I wish thee learning, not for show,
Enough for to instruct, and know;
Not such as Gentlemen require,
To prate at Table, or at Fire.
I wish thee all thy mother's graces,
Thy father's fortunes, and his places,
I wish thee friends, and one at Court,
Not to build on, but support;

To keep thee, not in doing many
Oppressions, but from suffering any.
I wish thee peace in all thy ways,
Nor lazy nor contentious days;
And when thy soul and body part,
As innocent as now thou art.

Richard Corbet

THE TOYS

My little son, who look'd from thoughtful eyes
And moved and spoke in quite grown-up wise,
Having my law the seventh time disobey'd,
I struck him, and dismiss'd
With hard words and unkiss'd,
His mother, who was patient, being dead.
Then, fearing lest his grief should hinder sleep,
I visited his bed,
But found him slumbering deep,
With darken'd eyelids, and thin lashes yet
From his late sobbing wet.
And I, with moan,
Kissing away his tears, left others of my own;
For on a table drawn beside his head,
He had put, within his reach,
A box of counters and a red-veined stone,
A piece of glass abraided from the beach
And six or seven shells,
A bottle with bluebells
And two French copper coins, ranged there with careful
        art,
To comfort his sad heart.
So when that night I pray'd
To God, I wept, and said :
Ah, when we lie at last with trancèd breath,
Not vexing Thee in death,
And Thou rememberest of what toys
We made our joys,

How weakly understood
Thy great commanded good,
Then, fatherly not less
Than I whom Thou hast moulded from the clay,
Thou'lt leave Thy wrath, and say,
' I will be sorry for their childishness '.

Coventry Patmore

THE QUARTETTE

Tom sang for joy, and Ned sang for joy, and old Sam sang
    for joy;
All we four boys piped up loud, just like one boy;
And the ladies that sate with the Squire—their cheeks were
    all wet,
For the noise of the voice of us boys, when we sang our
    Quartette.

Tom he piped low and Ned he piped low and old Sam he
    piped low;
Into a sorrowful fall did our music flow;
And the ladies that sate with the Squire vowed they'd never
    forget,
How the eyes of them cried for delight, when we sang our
    Quartette.

Walter de la Mare

HOLY THURSDAY

'Twas on a Holy Thursday, their innocent faces clean,
The children walking two and two, in red and blue and green,
Grey-headed beadles walk'd before, with wands as white as
    snow,
Till into the high dome of Paul's they like Thames' waters
    flow.

O what a multitude they seem'd, these flowers of London
    town!
Seated in companies they sit with radiance all their own.
The hum of multitudes was there, but multitudes of lambs,
Thousands of little boys and girls raising their innocent hands.

Now like a mighty wind they raise to Heaven the voice of
    song,
Or like harmonious thunderings the seat of Heaven among.
Beneath them sit the aged men, wise guardians of the poor;
Then cherish pity, lest you drive an angel from your door.
                               William Blake

TO LORD CHIEF JUSTICE NORTH
AT HIS HOUSE IN CHANCERY LANE,
FROM HIS MOTHER, LADY NORTH
                        Tostock. 10 October, 1697.

Dear Son,
    You cannot believe the great concern that was in the whole
family here last Wednesday, it being the day that the tailor
was to help dress little Frank in his breeches in order to the
making an everyday suit by it. Never had any bride that was
to be dressed upon her wedding night more hands about her,
some the legs and some the arms, the tailor buttoning and
others putting on the sword, and so many lookers on that had
I not had a finger amongst them I could not have seen him.
When he was quite dressed he acted his part as well as any of
them, for he desired he might go down to enquire for the
little gentleman that was there the day before in a black coat,
and speak to the men to tell the gentleman when he came
back from school that here was a gallant with very fine clothes
and a sword to have waited upon him and would come again
upon Sunday next. But this was not all, for there was great
contrivings while he was dressing who should have the first
salute, but he said if old Lane had been here she should, but
he gave it to me to quiet them all.
    They are very fit, everything, and he looks taller and prettier

than in his coats. Little Charles rejoiced as much as he did, for he jumped all the while about him and took notice of everything. I went to Bury and bought everything for another suit, which will be finished upon Saturday, so the coats are to be quite left off upon Sunday. I consider it is not yet term time and since you could not have the pleasure of the first sight I have resolved you should have a full relation from

Your most affectionate Mother, A. North.

When he was dressed he asked Buckle whether muffs were out of fashion because they had not sent him one.

Postman's Horn

THE POET'S WELCOME
TO HIS ILLEGITIMATE CHILD

Thou's welcome, wean! mishanter fa' me,
If ought of thee, or of thy mammy,
Shall ever danton me, or awe me,
　　My sweet wee lady,
Or if I blush when thou shalt ca' me
　　Tit-ta or daddy.

Wee image of my bonny Betty,
I fatherly will kiss and daut thee,
As dear and near my heart I set thee
　　Wi' as guid will,
As a' the priests had seen me get thee
　　That's out o' hell.

What though they ca' me fornicator,
And tease my name in kintra clatter:
The mair they talk I'm kenn'd the better,
　　E'en let them clash!
An auld wife's tongue's feckless matter
　　To gie ane fash.

Sweet fruit o' mony a merry dint,
My funny toil is now a' tint,
Sin' thou came to the world asklent,
               Which fools may scoff at;
In my last plack thy part's be in't—
               The better half o't.

And if thou be what I wad hae thee,
And tak the counsel I shall gie thee,
A lovin' father I'll be to thee,
               If thou be spared :
Through a' thy childish years I'll ee thee,
               And think't weel wared.

Guid grant that thou may aye inherit
Thy mither's person, grace, and merit,
And thy poor worthless daddy's spirit,
               Without his failin's,
'Twill please me mair to hear and see't
               Than stockit mailins.

                                        Robert Burns

2 CHILDREN OF TODAY

CHILDREN'S SONG

We live in our own world,
A world that is too small
For you to stoop and enter
Even on hands and knees,
The adult subterfuge.
And though you probe and pry
With analytic eye,
And eavesdrop all our talk
With an amused look,

You cannot find the centre
Where we dance, where we play,
Where life is still asleep
Under the closed flower,
Under the smooth shell
Of eggs in the cupped nest
That mock the faded blue
Of your remoter heaven.

                                    R. S. Thomas

FÉRI'S DREAM

I had a little dog, and my dog was very small;
He licked me in the face, and he answered to my call;
Of all the treasures that were mine, I loved him best of all.

His nose was fresh as morning dew and blacker than the night;
I thought that it could even snuff the shadows and the light;
And his tail he held bravely, like a banner in a fight.

His body covered thick with hair was very good to smell;
His little stomach underneath was pink as any shell;
And I loved him and honoured him, more than words can tell.

We ran out in the morning, both of us, to play,
Up and down across the fields for all the sunny day;
But he ran so swiftly—he ran right away.

I looked for him, I called for him, intreatingly. Alas,
The dandelions could not speak, though they had seen him pass,
And nowhere was his waving tail among the waving grass.

The sun sank low. I ran; I prayed: ' If God has not the power
To find him, let me die. I cannot live another hour.'
When suddenly I came upon a great yellow flower.

And all among its petals, such was Heaven's grace,
In that golden hour, in that golden place,
All among its petals, was his hairy face.

                              Frances Cornford Féri Bekassy

EARLY MORNING FEED

The father darts out on the stairs
To listen to the keening
In the upper room, for a change of note
That signifies distress, to scotch disaster,
The kettle humming in the room behind.

He thinks, on tiptoe, ears a-strain,
The cool dawn rising like the moon:
'Must not appear and pick him up;
He mustn't think he has me springing
To his beck and call ',
The kettle rattling behind the kitchen door.

He has him springing
A-quiver on the landing—
For a distress-note, a change of key,
To gallop up the stairs to him
To take him up, light as a violin,
And stroke his back until he smiles.
He sidles in the kitchen
And pours his tea . . .

And again stands hearkening
For milk cracking the lungs.
There's a little panting,
A cough: the thumb's in: he'll sleep,
The cup of tea cooling on the kitchen table.
Can he go in now to his chair and think
Of the miracle of breath, pick up a book,
Ready at all times to take it at a run
And intervene between him and disaster,
Sipping his cold tea as the sun comes up?

He returns to bed
And feels like something, with the door ajar,
Crouched in the bracken, alert, with big eyes
For the hunter, death, disaster.

Peter Redgrove

SCHOOL'S OUT

Girls scream,
   Boys shout;
Dogs bark,
   School's out.

Cats run,
   Horses shy;
Into trees
   Birds fly.

Babes wake
   Open-eyed.
If they can,
   Tramps hide.

Old man,
   Hobble home;
Merry mites,
   Welcome.

William Henry Davies

HAPPINESS

John had
Great big
Waterproof
Boots on;
John had a
Great big
Waterproof
Hat;

John had a
Great big
Waterproof
Mackintosh—
And that
(Said John)
Is
That.

A. A. Milne

TIMOTHY WINTERS

Timothy Winters comes to school
With eyes as wide as a football-pool,
Ears like bombs and teeth like splinters:
A blitz of a boy is Timothy Winters.

His belly is white, his neck is dark,
And his hair is an exclamation mark,
His clothes are enough to scare a crow
And through his britches the blue winds blow.

When teacher talks he won't hear a word
And he shoots down dead the arithmetic-bird,
He licks the patterns off his plate
And he's not even heard of the Welfare State.

Timothy Winters has bloody feet
And he lives in a house on Suez Street,
He sleeps in a sack on the kitchen floor
And they say there aren't boys like him any more.

Old Man Winters likes his beer
And his missus ran off with a bombardier,
Grandma sits in the grate with a gin
And Timothy's dosed with an aspirin.

The Welfare Worker lies awake
But the law's as tricky as a ten-foot snake,
So Timothy Winters drinks his cup
And slowly goes on growing up.

At Morning Prayers the Master helves
For children less fortunate than ourselves,
And the loudest response in the room is when
Timothy Winters roars ' Amen!'

So come one angel, come on ten:
Timothy Winters says ' Amen
Amen amen amen amen '.
Timothy Winters, Lord.
                        Amen.

                                    Charles Causley

UNDER THE APPLE BOUGHS

Now as I was young and easy under the apple boughs
About the lilting house and happy as the grass was green,
        The night above the dingle starry,
            Time let me hail and climb
        Golden in the heydays of his eyes,
And honoured among wagons I was prince of the apple towns
And once below a time I lordly had the trees and leaves
            Trail with daisies and barley
        Down the rivers of the windfall light.

And as I was green and carefree, famous among the barns
About the happy yard and singing as the farm was home,
        In the sun that is young once only,
            Time let me play and be
        Golden in the mercy of his means.
And green and golden I was huntsman and herdsman, the calves
Sang to my horn, the foxes on the hills barked clear and cold,
            And the sabbath rang slowly
        In the pebbles of the holy streams.

All the sun long it was running, it was lovely, the hay
Fields high as the house, the tunes from the chimneys, it was air
    And playing, lovely and watery
      And fire green as grass.
    And nightly under the simple stars
As I rode to sleep the owls were bearing the farm away,
All the moon long I heard, blessed among stables, the nightjars
    Flying with the ricks, and the horses
      Flashing into the dark.

And then to awake, and the farm, like a wanderer white
With the dew, come back, the cock on his shoulder : it was all
    Shining, it was Adam and maiden,
      The sky gathered again
    And the sun grew round that very day.
So it must have been after the birth of the simple light
In the first, spinning place, the spellbound horses walking warm
    Out of the whinnying green stable
      On to the fields of praise.

And honoured among foxes and pheasants by the gay house
Under the new made clouds and happy as the heart was long,
    In the sun born over and over,
      I ran my heedless ways,
     My wishes raced through the house high hay
And nothing I cared, at my sky blue trades, that time allows
In all his tunefull turning so few and such morning songs
    Before the children green and golden
      Follow him out of grace.

Nothing I cared, in the lamb white days, that time would take me
Up to the swallow thronged loft by the shadows of my hand,
    In the moon that is always rising,
      Nor that riding to sleep
     I should hear him fly with the high fields
And wake to the farm forever fled from the childless land.
Oh as I was young and easy in the mercy of his means,
      Time held me green and dying
     Though I sang in my chains like the sea.
                   Dylan Thomas   Fern Hill

THE FISHERS

The embattled towers, the level lilied moat,
Between the lily-leaves the inverted sky,
The impending alders and the quivering float
Charmed the vexed spirit, and it was not I,
But contemplating essence that surveyed
The brightness, and the water, and the shade.

There stole two silent children to my side,
And sat down with a still attentive air;
The elder thin, and dark, and dignified,
The younger smiling, five years old, and fair:
Quietly as the ousel and the wren
They bore themselves, for they were fishermen.

Despite their wounded trousers and their knees
Calloused with wear, I could not think them boys,
(Creatures who shatter all the summer's ease,
Whooping like furies, born to rhyme with noise);
Composed and courteous beings, full of grace,
They seemed the quiet spirits of the place.

The elder fixed his quick black wild-duck eye
Far in the depths, to watch for the great pike:
The younger looked and murmured blissfully
At waterfowl and cranefly and the like,
Naming the dabchick, and with eye intent
Pointing with snail-horn finger where she went.

And turning to the meadow in the sun
Smiled at three mares in the dim whitethorn shade;
Blessed them like Adam in the new-begun
World, when the immemorial names were made:
Like Adam innocent, like Adam fond,
He whispered, *Blossom, Sweetheart, Diamond.*

His fellow brooded like a child of stone,
Yet not unhappy : he was touched by care,
And care accepted; that grave union
Of virtue that the travelling soul must wear,
Decent compunction, strong philosophy,
Showed like the sign of a brave man to be.

Such were these fishers; one in love with all
That fell beneath his soft enamoured look,
And one in search of the old magical
Surcease and silver healing of the brook,
Friends, though asunder; and (I saw them then
With Izaak's eye), Anglers, and honest men.

And the tall flower was peace made visible,
The air was ambient love; the flashing fly
Was the soul's dear mysterious parable,
Proclaiming the immortal silently;
And sweetest kindness sat beneath the trees
In two unasked, affectionate presences.

Good children, I am glad we made no kill;
That would have tarnished what I felt for you.
Two gentle souls, in whom was nothing ill,
Looked from the dark eye and the dreaming blue,
Where by the water and the tower of might
The hurt healed, and the mind was filled with light.

Ruth Pitter

TO MY DAUGHTER

Bright clasp of her whole hand around my finger,
My daughter, as we walk together now,
All my life I'll feel a ring invisibly
Circles this bone with shining : when she is grown
Far from today as her eyes are far already.

Stephen Spender

MISSING MY DAUGHTER

This wallpaper has lines that rise
Upright like bars, and overhead,
The ceiling's patterned with red roses.
On the wall opposite the bed
The staring looking-glass encloses
Six roses in its white of eyes.

Here at my desk, with note-book open
Missing my daughter, makes those bars
Draw their lines upward through my mind.
This blank page stares at me like glass
Where stared-at roses wish to pass
Through petalling of my pen.

An hour ago, there came an image
Of a beast that pressed its muzzle
Between bars. Next, through tick and tock
Of the reiterating clock
A second glared with the white dazzle
Of deserts. The door, in a green mirage,

Opened. In my daughter came.
Her eyes were wide as those she has,
The round gaze of her childhood was
White as the distance in the glass
Or on a white page, a white poem.
The roses raced around her name.

Stephen Spender

THROUGH THE BLOWING LEAVES

Little girls, through the blowing leaves
Scattered all around on the grass,
More like the very light that weaves
Patterns when they pass.

Swift gold and blue, fleet brown and red,
Their dresses blow, with a scarf of birds
Blowing over the hill ahead—
And their light laughter and words
Drift back to us like a song, like wings
That circle and catch the sun and glisten. . .
And thinking, perhaps, of other things
We pause to watch—and listen,
And call them back at last, with a sigh,
Hearing the sound of wind and the blowing
Leaves—and the little girls run by
With flower-like faces glowing.

Glenn Ward Dresbach

IN THE SHELTER

In a shelter one night, when death was taking the air
Outside, I saw her, seated apart—a child
Nursing her doll, to one man's vision enisled
With radiance which might have shamed even death to its lair.

Then I thought of our Christmas roses at home—the dark
Lanterns comforting us a winter through
With the same dusky flush, the same bold spark
Of confidence, O sheltering child, as you.

Genius could never paint the maternal pose
More deftly than accident had roughed it there,
Setting amidst our terrors, against the glare
Of unshaded bulbs and whitewashed brick, that rose.

Instinct was hers, and an earthquake hour revealed it
In flesh—the meek-laid lashes, the glint in the eye
Defying wrath and reason, the arms that shielded
A plaster doll from an erupting sky.

No argument for living could long sustain
These ills : it needs a faithful eye, to have seen all
Love in the droop of a lash and tell it eternal
By one pure bead of its dew-dissolving chain.

Dear sheltering child, if again misgivings grieve me
That love is only a respite, an opal bloom
Upon our snow-set fields, come back to revive me
Cradling your spark through blizzard, drift and tomb.

C. Day Lewis

Children look down upon the morning-grey
Tissue of mist that veils a valley's lap :
Their fingers itch to tear it and unwrap
The flags, the roundabouts, the gala day.
They watch the spring rise inexhaustibly—
A breathing thread out of the eddied sand,
Sufficient to their day : but half their mind
Is on the sailed and glittering estuary.
Fondly we wish their mist might never break,
Knowing it hides so much that best were hidden :
We'd chain them by the spring, lest it should broaden
For them into a quicksand and a wreck.
But they must slip through our fingers like the source,
Like mist, like time that has flagged out their course.

C. Day Lewis   O Dreams, O Destinations

3 LOVERS

NO THYNG YS TO MAN SO DERE

No thyng ys to man so dere
As wommanys love in gode manère.
A gode womman is mannys blys,
There her love right and stedfast ys.

There ys no solas onder hevene
Of all that a man may nevene[1]
That shulde a man so moche glew[2]
As a gode womman that loveth true.
Ne derer is none in Goddis hurde[3]
Than a chaste womman with lovely worde.

Robert Mannying of Brunne

[1]name   [2]gladden   [3]flock

DANTE AND BEATRICE
IN THE EARTHLY PARADISE

Dante finds the lovely lady sent to guide him to Beatrice

' Eager to search, in and throughout its ways
    The sacred wood, whose thick and leafy tent,
    Spread in my sight, tempered the new sun's rays,

' I made no pause, but left the cliff and went
    With lingering steps across the level leas
    Where all the soil breathed out a fragrant scent.

' A delicate air, that no inconstancies
    Knows in its motion, on my forehead played,
    With force no greater than a gentle breeze,

' And quivering at its touch the branches swayed,
    All toward that quarter where the holy hill
    With the first daylight stretches out its shade;

' Yet ne'er swayed from the upright so, but still
    The little birds the topmost twigs among
    Spared not to practise all their tiny skill;

' Rather they welcomed with rejoicing song
    The dawn-wind to the leaves, which constantly
    To their sweet chant the burden bore along.

' So, in Chiassi's pinewood by the sea,
    From bough to bough the gathering murmurs swell
    When Aeolus has set Scirocco free.

' Now, when my footsteps, slowly as they fell,
    So far within the ancient wood were set
    That where I'd first come in I could not tell,

' Lo! they were halted by a rivulet
    Which ran from right to left, its ripples small
    Bending the grasses on the edge of it;

' And whatso waters over here we call
    Clearest, were cloudy by comparison
    With this, which hides not anything at all.

' Though darkly, darkly it goes flowing on
    Beneath the everlasting shade, which never
    Lets any ray strike there of sun or moon.

' I stayed my feet, but let my eyes pass over
    To see the fresh and various profusion
    Of flowery branches on yon side the river;

' And there appeared to me—as when the intrusion
    Of some new wonder takes one unaware
    And throws all one's ideas into confusion—

' A lady all alone, who wandered there
    Singing and plucking flower on floweret gay,
    With which her path was painted everywhere.

' " Prithee, fair lady, that in love's warm ray
    Dost sun thyself—if looks, that wont to be
    The index of the heart, mean what they say—

' " Advance," said I, " if it seem good to thee,
    So near the river that, when thou dost sing,
    The words thou singest may be clear to me.

' " O thou dost put me to remembering
  Of who and what were lost, that day her mother
  Lost Proserpine, and she the flowers of spring."

' As a dancing lady turns with her toes together,
  Foot by foot set close and close to the ground,
  And scarcely putting the one before the other,

' So she to me, as moves a maiden bound
  By sweet decorum, modest eyes downbent,
  Among the red and yellow flowers turned round;

' And of my prayer she gave me full content
  Coming so close that I could well divine
  Not only the sweet sounds but what they meant.

' So when she'd come to where the crystalline
  Clear water bathes the grasses, she at once
  Did me the grace to lift her eyes to mine.

' Never, for sure, did such bright radiance glance
  From Venus' eyelids, when her wayward child
  Had pierced her with his dart by strange mischance.

' So, upright on the other bank, she smiled,
  Still twining in her hands the blossoms pied,
  Which without seed on that high land grow wild.'

*Beatrice comes to meet Dante, drawn upon a triumph-car, the
angels strewing her with flowers.*

' Oft have I seen, when break of day was nigh,
  The orient flushing with a rose-red gleam,
  The rest of heaven adorned with calm blue sky,

' Seen the sun's face rise shadowy and dim
  Through veils of mist, so tempering his powers,
  The eye might long endure to look on him;

'So, even so, through cloud on cloud of flowers
    Flung from angelic hands and falling down
    Over the car and all around in showers,

'In a white veil beneath an olive-crown
    Appeared to me a lady cloaked in green,
    And living flame the colour of her gown;

'And instantly, for all the years between
    Since her mere presence with a kind of fright
    Could awe me and make my spirit faint within,

'There came on me, needing no further sight,
    Just by that strange, outflowing power of hers,
    The old, old love in all its mastering might.

'And, smitten through the eyesight unawares
    By that high power which pierced me, heart and reins,
    Long since, when I was but a child in years,

'I turned to leftward—full of confidence
    As any little boy who ever came
    Running to mother with his fears and pains—. . .

'And not for all that our first mother lost
    Could I forbid the smutching tears to steep
    My cheeks, once washed with dew from all their dust.'

IN HEAVEN

*As they mount through the circles of heaven Dante gazes upon
the face of Beatrice*

'Were everything I've ever said of her
    Rolled up into a single jubilee,
    Too slight a hymn for this new task were there.

'Beauty past knowledge was displayed to me—
    Not only ours : the joy of it complete
    Her Maker knows, I think, and only He.

'From this point on I must admit defeat
    Sounder than poet wrestling with his theme,
    Comic or tragic, e'er was doomed to meet;

'For her sweet smile remembered, as the beam
    Of sunlight blinds the weakest eyes that gaze
    Bewilders all my wits and scatters them.

'From the first hour I looked upon her face
    In this life, till that vision, I could trust
    The poet in me to pursue her praise;

'Now in her beauty's wake my song can thrust
    Its following flight no farther; I give o'er
    As, at his art's end, every artist must.'

*Dante beholds Beatrice enthroned in the Celestial Rose, and
bids her farewell*

'"Lift up thine eyes, yonder thy Lady see
    In the third circle from the highest place,
    Enthroned where merit destined her to be."

'Without a word I lifted up my gaze,
    And there I saw her in her glory crowned,
    Reflecting from herself the eternal rays.

'The greatest height whence thunderings resound
    Less distant is from mortal vision, though
    Plunged in the deepest ocean it were found,

'Than was my sight from Beatrice, and lo!
    By no material means made visible,
    Distinct her image came to me below.

' " O thou in whom my hopes securely dwell,
  And who, to bring my soul to Paradise,
  Didst leave the imprint of thy steps in Hell,

' " Of all that I have looked on with these eyes
  Thy goodness and thy power have fitted me
  The holiness and grace to recognize.

' " Thou has led me, a slave, to liberty,
  By every path, and using every means
  Which to fulfil this task were granted thee.

' " Keep turned towards me thy munificence
  So that my soul which thou hast remedied
  May please thee when it quits the bonds of sense."

' Such was my prayer and she, so distant fled,
  It seemed, did smile and look on me once more,
  Then to the eternal fountain turned her head.'
              Dante   The Divine Comedy   Paradise
    Translated by Dorothy L. Sayers and Barbara Reynolds

From you I have been absent in the spring,
When proud-pied April, dress'd in all his trim,
Hath put a spirit of youth in everything,
That heavy Saturn laugh'd and leap'd with him.
Yet nor the lays of birds, nor the sweet smell
Of different flowers in odour and in hue,
Could make me any summer's story tell,
Or from their proud lap pluck them where they grew;
Nor did I wonder at the Lily's white,
Nor praise the deep vermilion in the Rose;
They were but sweet, but figures of delight,
Drawn after you, you pattern of all those.
    Yet seem'd it winter still, and, you away,
    As with your shadow I with these did play.
                        Shakespeare   Sonnets

ROMEO AND JULIET

Romeo   He jests at scars that never felt a wound.
          (*Juliet appears above at a window.*)
But, soft! what light through yonder window breaks?
It is the east, and Juliet is the sun.
Arise, fair sun, and kill the envious moon,
Who is already sick and pale with grief,
That thou her maid art far more fair than she:
Be not her maid, since she is envious;
Her vestal livery is but sick and green
And none but fools do wear it; cast it off.
It is my lady, O, it is my love!
O, that she knew she were!
She speaks, yet she says nothing: what of that?
Her eye discourses; I will answer it.
I am too bold, 'tis not to me she speaks:
Two of the fairest stars in all the heaven,
Having some business, do entreat her eyes
To twinkle in their spheres till they return.
What if her eyes were there, they in her head?
The brightness of her cheek would shame those stars,
As daylight doth a lamp; her eyes in heaven
Would through the airy region stream so bright
That birds would sing and think it were not night.
See, how she leans her cheek upon her hand!
O, that I were a glove upon that hand,
That I might touch that cheek!
Juliet   Ay me!
Romeo   She speaks:
O, speak again, bright angel! for thou art
As glorious to this night, being o'er my head,
As is a wingèd messenger of heaven
Unto the white-upturnèd wondering eyes
Of mortals that fall back to gaze on him
When he bestrides the lazy-pacing clouds
And sails upon the bosom of the air.

                                    Shakespeare

OTHELLO AND DESDEMONA

Othello   Her father loved me : oft invited me :
Still question'd me the story of my life,
From year to year, the battles, sieges, fortunes,
That I have pass'd.
I ran it through, even from my boyish days,
To the very moment that he bade me tell it :
Wherein I spake of most disastrous chances,
Of moving accidents by flood and field,
Of hair-breadth scapes i' the imminent deadly breach,
Of being taken by the insolent foe
And sold to slavery, of my redemption thence
And portance in my travels' history :
Wherein of antres vast and deserts idle,
Rough quarries, rocks and hills whose heads touch heaven,
It was my hint to speak,—such was the process;
And of the Cannibals that each other eat,
The Anthropophagi and men whose heads
Do grow beneath their shoulders. This to hear
Would Desdemona seriously incline :
But still the house-affairs would draw her thence :
Which ever as she could with haste dispatch
She'ld come again, and with a greedy ear
Devour up my discourse : which I observing
Took once a pliant hour, and found good means
To draw from her a prayer of earnest heart
That I would all my pilgrimage dilate,
Whereof by parcels she had something heard,
But not intentively : I did consent
And often did beguile her of her tears,
When I did speak of some distressful stroke
That my youth suffer'd. My story being done,
She gave me for my pains a world of sighs :
She swore, in faith, 'twas strange, 'twas passing strange,
'Twas pitiful, 'twas wondrous pitiful :
She wish'd she had not heard it, yet she wish'd
That heaven had made her such a man : she thank'd me,

And bade me, if I had a friend that loved her,
I should but teach him how to tell my story,
And that would woo her. Upon this hint I spake:
She loved me for the dangers I had pass'd,
And I loved her that she did pity them.
This only is the witchcraft I have used:
Here comes the lady; let her witness it.

Shakespeare

TO ANTHEA,
WHO MAY COMMAND HIM ANYTHING

Bid me to live, and I will live
   Thy Protestant to be;
Or bid me love, and I will give
   A loving heart to thee.

A heart as soft, a heart as kind,
   A heart as sound and free
As in the whole world thou canst find,
   That heart I'll give to thee.

Bid that heart stay, and it will stay
   To honour thy decree:
Or bid it languish quite away,
   And't shall do so for thee.

Bid me to weep, and I will weep
   While I have eyes to see:
And, having none, yet will I keep
   A heart to weep for thee.

Bid me despair, and I'll despair
   Under that cypress-tree:
Or bid me die, and I will dare
   E'en death to die for thee.

Thou art my life, my love, my heart,
  The very eyes of me:
And hast command of every part
  To live and die for thee.

Robert Herrick

A WIFE TO A HUSBAND

How do I love thee? Let me count the ways.
I love thee to the depth and breadth and height
My soul can reach, when feeling out of sight
For the end of Being and ideal Grace.
I love thee to the level of everyday's
Most quiet need, by sun and candlelight.
I love thee freely, as men strive for Right;
I love thee purely, as they turn from Praise.
I love thee with the passion put to use
In my old griefs, and with my childhood's faith.
I love thee with a love I seemed to lose
With my lost saints,—I love thee with the breath,
Smiles, tears, of all my life!—and, if God choose,
I shall but love thee better after death.

Elizabeth Barrett Browning   Sonnets from the Portuguese

A HUSBAND TO A WIFE

Trusty, dusky, vivid, true,
With eyes of gold and bramble-dew,
Steel true and blade-straight,
The great artificer
Made my mate.

Honour, anger, valour, fire;
A love that life could never tire,
Death quench or evil stir,
The mighty master
Gave to her.

Teacher, tender, comrade, wife,
 A fellow-farer true through life,
 Heart-whole and soul-free,
 The august father
 Gave to me.

        Robert Louis Stevenson

JANE'S MARRIAGE

Jane went to Paradise:
That was only fair.
Good Sir Walter met her first,
And led her up the stair.
Henry and Tobias,
And Miguel of Spain,
Stood with Shakespeare at the top,
To welcome Jane.

Then the three archangels
Offered out of hand,
Anything in Heaven's gift
That she might command.
Azrael's eyes upon her,
Raphael's wings above,
Michael's sword against her heart,
Jane said: 'Love.'

Instantly the under-
Standing Seraphim
Laid their fingers on their lips
And went to look for him.
Stole across the Zodiac,
Harnessed Charles's Wain,
And whispered round the nebulae
'Who loved Jane?'

In a private limbo
Where none had thought to look,

Sat a Hampshire gentleman
Reading of a book.
It was called 'Persuasion',
And it told the plain
Story of the love between
Him and Jane.

He heard the question
Circle Heaven through—
Closed the book and answered:
'I did—and do!'
Quietly but speedily
(As Captain Wentworth moved)
Entered into Paradise
The man Jane loved!

Rudyard Kipling

O hurry where by water among trees
The delicate-stepping stag and his lady sigh,
When they have but looked upon their images,—
O that none ever loved but you and I!

Or have you heard that sliding silver-shoed
Pale silver-proud queen-woman of the sky,
When the sun looked out of his golden hood,—
O that none ever loved but you and I!

O hurry to the ragged wood, for there
I'll hollo all those lovers out and cry—
O my share of the world, O yellow hair!
No one has ever loved but you and I.

William B. Yeats The Ragged Wood

IN A BATH TEASHOP

'Let us not speak, for the love we bear one another—
    Let us hold hands and look.'
She, such a very ordinary little woman;
    He, such a thumping crook;
But both, for a moment, little lower than the angels
    In the teashop's ingle-nook.

John Betjeman

4 SAINTS AND HEROES

He was as the morning star in the midst of a cloud, and as
    the moon at the full:
As the sun shining upon the temple of the most High, and
    as the rainbow giving light in the bright clouds:
And as the flower of roses in the spring of the year, as lilies
    by the rivers of water, and as the branches of the frankin-
    cense tree in the time of summer:
As fire and incense in the censer, and as a vessel of beaten
    gold set with all manner of precious stones:
And as a fair olive tree budding forth fruit, and as a cypress
    tree which groweth up to the clouds.
When he put on a robe of honour, and was clothed with the
    perfection of glory, when he went up to the holy altar,
    he made the garment of holiness honourable.

The Apocrypha   The Book of Ecclesiasticus

Lastly there is a sort of God's dear servants, who walk in per-
fectness . . . and they have a degree of charity and divine
knowledge, more than we can discourse of, and more certain
than the demonstrations of geometry, and indeficient as the
light of heaven. . . . But I shall say no more of this at this
time, for this is to be felt, not talked of; and they that never

touched it with their finger may, secretly perhaps, laugh at it
in their heart and be never the wiser. All that I shall now say
of it is that a good man is united to God as a flame touches
flame.

Jeremy Taylor　from a sermon preached at Dublin

JOY OF MY LIFE !

Joy of my life ! while left me here,
　　And still my Love !
How in thy absence thou dost steere
　　Me from above !
　　A life well led
　　This truth commends,
　　With quick, or dead
　　It never ends.

Stars are of mighty use : the night
　　Is dark, and long ;
The Road foul, and where one goes right,
　　Six may go wrong.
　　One twinkling ray
　　Shot o'er some cloud,
　　May clear much way
　　And guide a crowd.

Gods Saints are shining lights : who stays
　　Here long must passe
O'er dark hills, swift streames, and steep ways
　　As smooth as glasse ;
　　But these all night
　　Like Candles, shed
　　Their beams, and light
　　Us into Bed.

They are (indeed), our Pillar-fires
　　Seen as we go,
They are that Cities shining spires
　　We travel to ;

A swordlike gleame
Kept man for sin
First *Out*; this beame
Will guide him *In*.

Henry Vaughan

THE SAINTS

So tho' our Daystar from our sight be taken,
Gone from His brethren, hidden from His own,
Yet in His setting are we not forsaken,
Suffer not shadows of the dark alone.

Not in the west is Thine appearance ended,
Neither from night shall Thy renewal be,
Lo, for the firmament in spaces splendid
Lighteth her beacon-fires ablaze for Thee:

Holds them and hides and drowns them and discovers
Throngs them together, kindles them afar,
Showeth, O Love, Thy multitude of lovers,
Souls that shall know Thee and the saints that are.

Look what a company of constellations!
Say can the sky so many lights contain?
Hath the great earth these endless generations?
Are there so many purified thro' pain?

These thro' all glow and eminence of glory
Cry for a brighter, who delayeth long;
Star unto star the everlasting story
Peals in a mystic sanctity of song. . .

Hark what a sound, and too divine for hearing,
Stirs on the earth and trembles in the air!
Is it the thunder of the Lord's appearing?
Is it the music of His people's prayer?

Surely He cometh, and a thousand voices
Shout to the saints and to the deaf are dumb;
Surely He cometh, and the earth rejoices
Glad in His coming Who hath sworn, I come.

                                        F. W. H. Myers

TE MARTYRUM CANDIDATUS

Ah, see the fair chivalry come, the companions of Christ!
White Horsemen, who ride on white horses, the Knights of
          God!
They, for their Lord and their Lover who sacrificed
All, save the sweetness of treading, where He first trod!

These, through the darkness of death, the dominion of night,
Swept, and they woke in white places at morning tide:
They saw with their eyes, and sang for joy of the sight,
They saw with their eyes the Eyes of the Crucified.

Now, whithersoever He goeth, with Him they go:
White Horsemen, who ride on white horses, oh, fair to see!
They ride, where the rivers of Paradise flash and flow,
White Horsemen, with Christ their Captain: for ever He!

                                        Lionel Johnson

Let us now praise famous men, and our fathers that begat us.
The Lord hath wrought great glory by them through his
          great power from the beginning.
Such as did bear rule in their kingdoms, men renowned for
          their power, giving counsel by their understanding, and
          declaring prophecies :
Leaders of the people by their counsels, and by their know-
          ledge of learning meet for the people, wise and eloquent
          in their instructions :
Such as found out musical tunes, and recited verses in writing :
Rich men furnished with ability, living peaceably in their
          habitations :

All these were honoured in their generations, and were the glory of their times.

There be some of them, that have left a name behind them, that their praises might be reported.

And some there be, which have no memorial, who are finished, as though they had never been; and are become as though they had never been born; and their children after them.

But these were merciful men, whose righteousness hath not been forgotten . . . Their bodies are buried in peace; but their name liveth for evermore.

The people will tell of their wisdom, and the congregation will shew forth their praise . . . but . . . how can he get wisdom that holdeth the plough, and that glorieth in the goad, that driveth oxen, and is occupied in their labours, and whose talk is of bullocks?

He giveth his mind to make furrows; and is diligent to give the kine fodder.

So every carpenter and workmaster, that laboureth night and day: and they can cut and grave seals, and are diligent to make great variety, and give themselves to counterfeit imagery, and watch to finish a work:

The smith also sitting by the anvil and considering the iron work, the vapour of the fire wasteth his flesh, and he fighteth with the heat of the furnace: the noise of the hammer and the anvil is ever in his ears, and his eyes still look upon the pattern of the thing that he maketh; he setteth his mind to finish his work, and watcheth to polish it perfectly:

So doth the potter sitting at his work, and turning the wheel about with his feet, who is always carefully set at his work, and maketh all his work by number;

He fashioneth the clay with his arm, and boweth down his strength before his feet; he applieth himself to lead it over; and he is diligent to make clean the furnace:

All these trust to their hands: and every one is wise in his work.

Without these cannot a city be inhabited: and they shall not dwell where they will, nor go up and down:

They shall not be sought for in the publick counsel nor sit
     high in the congregation: they shall not sit on the
     judges' seat, nor understand the sentence of judgment:
     they cannot declare justice and judgment; and they shall
     not be found where parables are spoken.
But they will maintain the state of the world, and [all] their
     desire is in the work of their craft.

> *The Apocrypha The Book of Ecclesiasticus*

PHAEDO SPEAKS
OF HIS LAST HOUR WITH SOCRATES

I was indeed wonderfully affected by being present, for I was
not impressed with a feeling of pity, like one present at the
death of a friend, for the man appeared to me to be happy,
Echecrates, both from his manner and discourse, so fearlessly
and nobly did he meet his death: so much so, that it occurred
to me, that in going to Hades he was not going without
a divine destiny, but that when he arrived there he would be
happy, if any one ever was. For this reason I was entirely un-
influenced by any feeling of pity, as would seem likely to be
the case with one present on so mournful an occasion; nor
was I affected by pleasure from being engaged in philosophica
discussions, as was our custom, for our conversation was of tha
kind. But an altogether unaccountable feeling possessed me
a kind of unusual mixture compounded of pleasure and pai•
together, when I considered that he was immediately about to
die. And all of us who were present were affected in much
the same manner. . . .

Socrates speaks to Cebes of the immortality of the Soul

'Consider it also thus, that, when the soul and body are
together, nature enjoins the latter to be subservient and obey
the former to rule and exercise dominion. And in this way
which of the two appears to you to be like the divine, and

which the mortal? Does it not appear to you to be natural that the divine should rule and command, but the mortal obey and be subservient?'

'To me it does so.'

'Which, then, does the soul resemble?'

'It is clear, Socrates, that the soul resemble the divine, but the body, the mortal.' . . .

'Can the soul, then, which is invisible, and which goes to another place like itself, excellent, pure, and invisible, and therefore truly called the invisible world, to the presence of a good and wise God, (whither if God will, my soul also must shortly go), can this soul of ours, I ask, being such and of such a nature, when separated from the body be immediately dispersed and destroyed, as most men assert? Far from it, my dear Cebes and Simmias. But the case is much rather thus; if it is separated in a pure state, taking nothing of the body with it, as not having willingly communicated with it in the present life, but having shunned it and gathered itself within itself, as constantly studying this; but this is nothing else than to pursue philosophy aright, and in reality to study how to die easily; would not this be to study how to die?'

'Most assuredly.'

'Does not the soul, then, when in this state, depart to that which resembles itself, the invisible, the divine, immortal, and wise? and on its arrival there, is it not its lot to be happy, free from error, ignorance, fears, wild passions, and all the other evils to which human nature is subject, and, as is said of the initiated, does it not in truth pass the rest of its time with the gods? Must we affirm that it is so, Cebes, or otherwise?'

'So, by Jupiter,' said Cebes. . . .

'But it is right, my friends,' he said, 'that we should consider this, that if the soul is immortal, it requires our care not only for the present time, which we call life, but for all time; and the danger would now appear to be dreadful, if one should neglect it. For if death were a deliverance from every thing, it would be a great gain for the wicked, when they die, to be delivered at the same time from the body, and from their vices together with the soul: but now, since it appears to be immortal, it can have no other refuge from evils, nor safety, except by becoming as good and wise as possible. For the soul goes to Hades, possessing nothing else but its discipline and education, which are said to be of the greatest advantage or detriment to the dead, on the very beginning of his journey thither.' . . .

'We should use every endeavour, Simmias, so as to acquire virtue and wisdom in this life; for the reward is noble, and the hope great.'

Crito asks, 'How shall we bury you?' and Socrates replies

'Just as you please,' he said, 'if only you can catch me, and I do not escape from you.' And at the same time smiling gently, and looking round on us, he said : 'I cannot persuade Crito, my friends, that I am that Socrates who is now conversing with you, and who methodises each part of the discourse; but he thinks that I am he whom he will shortly behold dead, and asks how he should bury me. But that which I some time since argued at length, that when I have drunk the poison I shall no longer remain with you, but shall depart to some happy state of the blessed, this I seem to have urged to him in vain, though I meant at the same time to console both you and myself. Be ye then my sureties to Crito,' he said, 'in an obligation contrary to that which he made to the judges; for he undertook that I should remain; but do you be sureties that, when I die, I shall not remain, but shall depart, that Crito may more easily bear it, and when he sees my body either burnt or buried, may not be afflicted for me, as if I had suffered some dreadful thing, nor say at my interment that Socrates is laid out, or is carried out, or is buried. For be well assured,' he said, 'most excellent Crito, that to speak improperly is not only culpable as to the thing itself, but likewise occasions some injury to our souls. You must have a good courage then, and say that you bury my body, and bury it in such a manner as is pleasing to you, and as you think is most agreeable to our laws.'

'It is certainly both lawful and right to pray to the gods,

that my departure hence thither may be happy; which therefore I pray, and so may it be.' And as he said this he drank it off readily and calmly. Thus far, most of us were with difficulty able to restrain ourselves from weeping, but when we saw him drinking, and having finished the draught, we could do so no longer; but in spite of myself the tears came in full torrent, so that, covering my face, I wept for myself, for I did not weep for him, but for my own fortune, in being deprived of such a friend. But Crito, even before me, when he could not restrain his tears, had risen up. But Apollodorus even before this had not ceased weeping, and then bursting into an agony of grief, weeping and lamenting, he pierced the heart of every one present, except Socrates himself. But he said, 'What are you doing, my admirable friends? I indeed, for this reason chiefly, sent away the women, that they might not commit any folly of this kind. For I have heard that it is right to die with good omens. Be quiet, therefore, and bear up.'

When we heard this we were ashamed, and restrained our tears. But he, having walked about, when he said that his legs were growing heavy, laid down on his back; for the man so directed him. And at the same time he who gave him the poison, taking hold of him, after a short interval examined his feet and legs; and then having pressed his foot hard, he asked if he felt it : he said that he did not. And after this he pressed his thighs; and thus going higher, he showed us that he was growing cold and stiff. Then Socrates touched himself and said, that when the poison reached his heart he should then depart. But now the parts around the lower belly were almost cold; when uncovering himself, for he had been covered over, he said, and they were his last words, ' Crito, we owe a cock to Aesculapius; pay it, therefore, and do not neglect it '.

' It shall be done,' said Crito, ' but consider whether you have anything else to say.'

To this question he gave no reply; but shortly after he gave a convulsive movement, and the man covered him, and his eyes were fixed; and Crito, perceiving it, closed his mouth and eyes.

This, Echecrates, was the end of our friend, a man, as we may say, best of all of his time that we have known, and moreover, the most wise and just.

Phaedo   Five Dialogues of Plato   On Poetic Inspiration

THE SPEECH OF PERICLES

The bravest are surely those who have the clearest vision of what is before them, glory and danger alike, and yet notwithstanding go out to meet it . . . For even where life's previous record showed faults and failures it is just to weigh the last brave hour of devotion against them all . . . Counting the quest to avenge their citys' honour as the most glorious of all ventures, and leaving Hope, the uncertain goddess, to send them what she would, they faced the foe as they drew near him in the strength of their own manhood; and when the shock of battle came, they chose rather to suffer the uttermost then to win life by weakness. So their memory has escaped the reproaches of men's lips, but they bore instead on their bodies the marks of men's hands, and in a moment of time, at the climax of their lives, were rapt away from a world filled, for their dying eyes, not with terror but with glory. . . . So they gave their bodies to the commonwealth and received, each for his own memory, praise that will never die, and with it the grandest of all sepulchres, not that in which their mortal bones are laid, but a home in the minds of men, where their glory remains fresh to stir to speech or action as the occasion comes by. For the whole earth is the sepulchre of famous men; and their story is not graven only on stone over their native earth, but lives on far away, without visible symbol, woven into the stuff of other men's lives.

QUEEN ELIZABETH AT TILBURY, BEFORE THE ARMADA

On August 8th, 'full of princely resolution and more than feminine courage . . . she passed like some Amazonian empress through all her army '. ' Lord bless you all ', she cried, as the men fell on their knees and prayed for her. The following day, mounted on a stately steed, with a truncheon in her hands, she witnessed a mimic battle and afterwards reviewed the army. Nothing could surpass the felicity of the speech that she made to them :

'My loving people, we have been persuaded by some that are careful of our safety, to take heed how we commit ourselves to armed multitudes, for fear of treachery. But I assure you, I do not desire to live to distrust my faithful and loving people. Let tyrants fear. I have always so behaved myself that, under God, I have placed my chiefest strength and safety in the loyal hearts and good will of my subjects; and therefore I am come amongst you, as you see, at this time, not for my recreation and disport, but being resolved, in the midst and heat of the battle, to live or die amongst you all, to lay down for my God, and for my kingdom, and for my people, my honour and my blood, even in the dust. I know I have the body of a weak and feeble woman, but I have the heart and stomach of a king, and of a king of England too, and think foul scorn that Parma or Spain, or any prince of Europe should dare to invade the borders of my realm; to which, rather than any dishonour shall grow by me, I myself will take up arms, I myself will be your general, judge, and rewarder of every one of your virtues in the field. I know already for your forwardness you have deserved rewards and crowns; and we do assure you, on the word of a prince, they shall be duly paid you.'

The men gave a mighty shout. At noon that day, as Elizabeth was at dinner with Leicester, word was brought that Parma intended to come out on the spring tide. She therefore grew a conceit that she could not in honour return to London while there was a likelihood of the enemy arriving. ' Thus your Lordship seeth ', wrote Walsingham, ' that this place breedeth courage.'

J. E. Neale   Extract from ' Queen Elizabeth '

BY THE STATUE OF KING CHARLES
AT CHARING CROSS

Sombre and rich, the skies;
Great glooms, and starry plains.
Gently the night wind sighs;
Else a vast silence reigns.

The splendid silence clings
Around me: and around
The saddest of all kings
Crowned, and again discrowned.

Comely and calm, he rides
Hard by his own Whitehall:
Only the night wind glides:
No crowds, nor rebels, brawl.

Gone, too, his Court: and yet,
The stars his courtiers are:
Stars in their stations set;
And every wandering star.

Alone he rides, alone.
The fair and fatal king:
Dark night is all his own,
That strange and solemn thing.

Which are more full of fate:
The stars; or those sad eyes?
Which are more still and great:
Those brows; or the dark skies?

Although his whole heart yearn
In passionate tragedy:
Never was face so stern
With sweet austerity.

Vanquished in life, his death
By beauty made amends :
The passing of his breath
Won his defeated ends.

Brief life, and hapless? Nay :
Through death, life grew sublime.
Speak after sentence, Yea :
And to the end of time.

Armoured he rides, his head
Bare to the stars of doom :
He triumphs now, the dead,
Beholding London's gloom.

Our wearier spirit faints,
Vexed in the world's employ :
His soul was of the saints :
And art to him was joy.

King, tried in fires of woe!
Men hunger for thy grace :
And through the night I go,
Loving thy mournful face.

Yet, when the city sleeps;
When all the cries are still :
The stars and heavenly deeps
Work out a perfect will.

Lionel Johnson

THE TRULY GREAT

I think continually of those who were truly great.
Who, from the womb, remembered the soul's history
Through corridors of light where the hours are suns
Endless and singing. Whose lovely ambition
Was that their lips, still touched with fire,
Should tell of the Spirit clothed from head to foot in song.

And who hoarded from the Spring branches
The desires falling across their bodies like blossoms.

What is precious is never to forget
The essential delight of the blood drawn from ageless springs
Breaking through rocks in worlds before our earth.
Never to deny its pleasure in the morning simple light
Nor its grave evening demand for love.
Never to allow gradually the traffic to smother
With noise and fog the flowering of the spirit.

Near the snow, near the sun, in the highest fields
See how these names are fêted by the waving grass
And by the streamers of white cloud
And whispers of wind in the listening sky.
The names of those who in their lives fought for life
Who wore at their hearts the fire's centre.
Born of the sun they travelled a short while towards the sun,
And left the vivid air signed with their honour.

Stephen Spender

THE SOLDIER 1914-1918

If I should die, think only this of me:
That there's some corner of a foreign field
That is for ever England. There shall be
In that rich earth a richer dust concealed;
A dust whom England bore, shaped, made aware,
Gave, once, her flowers to love, her ways to roam,
A body of England's, breathing English air,
Washed by the rivers, blest by suns of home.

And think, this heart, all evil shed away,
A pulse in the eternal mind, no less
Gives somewhere back the thoughts by England given;
Her sights and sounds; dreams happy as her day;
And laughter, learnt of friends; and gentleness,
In hearts at peace, under an English heaven.

Rupert Brooke

THE SOLDIER 1939-1945

(this poem was blown by the wind into a slit trench at El
Agheila during a heavy bombardment and was first published
anonymously)

Stay with me, God. The night is dark
The night is cold : my little spark
Of courage dies. The night is long;
Be with me, God, and make me strong.

I love a game. I love a fight.
I hate the dark; I love the light.
I love my child; I love my wife.
I am no coward. I love Life,

Life with its change of mood and shade.
I want to live. I'm not afraid,
But me and mine are hard to part;
Oh, unknown God, lift up my heart.

You stilled the waters at Dunkirk
And saved Your Servants. All your work
Is wonderful, dear God. You strode
Before us down that dreadful road.

We were alone, and hope had fled;
We loved our country and our dead,
And could not shame them; so we stayed
The course, and were not much afraid.

Dear God, that nightmare road! And then
That sea! We got there—we were men.
My eyes were blind, my feet were torn,
My soul sang like a bird at dawn!

I knew that death is but a door.
I knew what we were fighting for :

Peace for the kids, our brothers freed,
A kinder world, a cleaner breed.

I'm but the son my mother bore,
A simple man and nothing more.
But—God of strength and gentleness,
Be pleased to make me nothing less.

Help me, O God, when Death is near
To mock the haggard face of fear,
That when I fall—if fall I must—
My soul may triumph in the Dust.

Gerald Kersh

THE AIRMAN 1939-1945

There was a heavy air-raid on. . . . I turned and looked on a
heap of bricks and mortar, wooden beams and doors, and one
framed picture, unbroken. It was the first time that I had
seen a building newly blasted. . . . We dug, or rather we
pushed, pulled, heaved, and strained, I somewhat ineffectually
because of my hands; I don't know for how long, but I suppose for a short enough while. And yet it seemed endless.
From time to time I was aware of figures round me: an
A.R.P. warden, his face expressionless under a steel helmet;
once a soldier swearing savagely in a quiet monotone; and
the taxi-driver, his face pouring sweat.

And so we came to the woman. It was her feet that we
saw first, and whereas before we had worked doggedly, now
we worked with a sort of frenzy, like prospectors at the first
glint of gold. She was not quite buried, and through the gap
between two beams we could see that she was still alive. We
got the child out first. It was passed back carefully and with an
odd sort of reverence by the warden, but it was dead. She
must have been holding it to her in the bed when the bomb
came.

Finally we made a gap wide enough for the bed to be
drawn out. The woman who lay there looked middle-aged.

She lay on her back and her eyes were closed. Her face, through the dirt and streaked blood, was the face of a thousand working women; her body under the cotton night-dress was heavy. The nightdress was drawn up to her knees and one leg was twisted under her. There was no dignity about that figure.

Around me I heard voices. 'Where's the ambulance?' 'For Christ's sake don't move her!' 'Let her have some air!'

I was at the head of the bed, and looking down into that tired, blood-streaked, work-worn face I had a sense of complete unreality. I took the brandy flask from my hip pocket and held it to her lips. Most of it ran down her chin but a little flowed between those clenched teeth. She opened her eyes and reached out her arms instinctively for the child. Then she started to weep. Quite soundlessly, and with no sobbing, the tears were running down her cheeks when she lifted her eyes to mine.

'Thank you, sir', she said, and took my hand in hers. And then, looking at me again, she said after a pause, 'I see they got you too'.

Very carefully I screwed the top on to the brandy flask, un-screwed it once and screwed it on again, for I had caught it on the wrong thread. I put the flask into my hip pocket and did up the button. I pulled across the buckle on my great coat and noticed that I was dripping with sweat. I pulled the cap down over my eyes and walked out into the street. . . . With difficulty I kept my pace to a walk, forcing myself not to run. For I wanted to run, to run anywhere away from that scene. . . . I was drowning, helpless in a rage that caught and twisted and hurled me on, mouthing in a blind unthink-ing frenzy. I heard myself cursing, the words pouring out, shrill, meaningless. . . . Her death was unjust, a crime, an outrage, a sin against mankind—weak inadequate words which even as they passed through my mind mocked me with their futility.

That that woman should so die was an enormity so great that it was terrifying in its implications, in its lifting of the veil on possibilities of thought so far beyond the grasp of the human mind. It was not just the German bombs, or the

German Air Force, or even the German mentality, but a feeling of the very essence of anti-life that no words could convey. This was what I had been cursing—in part, for I had recognised in that moment what it was that Peter and the others had instantly recognised as evil and to be destroyed utterly. I saw now that it was not crime; it was Evil itself—something of which until then I had not even sensed the existence. And it was in the end, at bottom, myself against which I had raged, myself I had cursed. With awful clarity I saw myself suddenly as I was. Great God, that I could have been so arrogant!

Richard Hillary   The Last Enemy

THE MISFIT 1939-1945

At the training depot that first morning
When the west-country draft came forth on parade—
Mechanics, labourers, men of trade
Handed with shouts like boneheaded cattle—
One stood out from the maul
Who least of them all
Looked metal for killing or meat for the butchery blade.

He wore a long black cutaway coat
Which should have been walking by blackthorn-fleeced
Hedges to church; and good as a feast
Was the spare, wild face much weather had flavoured.
A shepherd or ploughman
I thought, or a cowman—
One with a velvet hand for all manner of beast.

I cannot forget how he stood, bemused,
With the meek eye of a driven thing:
But a solitude old as cromlech ring
Was around him; a freeborn air of the downland,
A peace of deep combes
No world-anger consumes
Marked him off from the herd to be branded for soldiering.

I saw him not after. Is he now buried
Far from pastures buttercup-strewed,
Or tending his beasts again with the same rude
Rightness of instinct which then had brought him
So quaintly dressed
In his Sunday best
For the first step along the Calvary road?

C. Day Lewis

DIETRICH BONHOEFFER, AWAITING EXECUTION IN A CONCENTRATION CAMP, PRAYS FOR HIS FELLOW PRISONERS

O God, early in the morning do I cry unto Thee.
Help me to pray, and to think only of Thee.
I cannot pray alone.
In me there is darkness,
But with Thee there is light.

I am lonely
   but Thou leavest me not.
I am feeble in heart,
   but Thou leavest me not.
I am restless,
   but with Thee there is peace.
In me there is bitterness,
   but with Thee there is patience.
Thy ways are past understanding.
   but Thou knowest the way for me.

   Lord Jesus Christ,
Thou wast poor, and in misery,
   a captive and forsaken as I am.
Thou knowest all man's distress;
Thou abidest with me when all others have deserted me;
Thou wilt not forget me, Thou seekest me.
Thou willest that I should know Thee and turn to Thee.
Lord, I hear Thy call and follow Thee;
   do Thou help me.

O Holy Spirit,
Grant me the faith that will protect me from despair:
Deliver me from the lust of the flesh.
Pour into my heart such love for Thee and for all men
    that hatred and bitterness may be blotted out.
Grant me the hope that will deliver me from fear and timidity.

    O Holy and Merciful God,
    Creator and Redeemer,
    Judge and Saviour,
Thou knowest me and all that I do.
Thou hatest and dost punish evil without respect of persons
    In this world and the next.
Thou forgivest the sins of them that heartily pray for forgive-
    ness,
Thou lovest goodness and rewardest it on this earth with a
    clear conscience,
And in the world to come with a crown of righteousness.

I would remember before Thee
    all my loved ones,
    my fellow prisoners,
    and all who in this house perform their hard service.
    Lord have mercy.
Restore my liberty and enable me so to live that I may answer
    before Thee and before the world.

Lord, whatsoever this day may bring,
  -Thy name be praised.
Be gracious unto me and help me.
Grant me strength to bear whatsoever Thou dost send,
And let not fear overrule me.
I trust Thy grace, and commit my life wholly into Thy Hands.
Whether I live or whether I die, I am with Thee,
And Thou art with me,
        O my Lord and my God.
Lord, I wait for Thy salvation,
    and for the coming of Thy Kingdom.   Amen.

                  written Christmas 1943
    Dietrich Bonhoeffer   Letters and Papers from Prison

A WISH

That son of Cain, let him have no more power
to loose his fury on the unfettered spring
or deal death to the kiss.
Let hatred be restrained from flooding
the pristine margins of the air.
Let knives become
impotent against swallows, and the assassin
powerless to garrotte the dawn.
May war never again
batter the skulls of newborn babes, or sever
the exultant arteries of a man.
Let poisoned fangs and pistols
and slavering jaws be done away,
and nevermore let frenzy lash us
with its insensate waves.

Let nothing remain but a love
as vast as all the oceans,
pouring like a cataract across the pupils
of our eyes, flooding the planets,
filling the songs of poets everywhere.

Vidal de Nicolas   A Political Prisoner in Burgos Jail
Translated by Chloe Valliamy and Stephen Sedley

5 ORDINARY FOLK

CYNDDYLAN ON A TRACTOR IN SPRING

Ah, you should see Cynddylan on a tractor,
Gone the old look that yoked him to the soil;
He's a new man now, part of the machine,
His nerves of metal and his blood oil.

The clutch curses, but the gears obey
His least bidding, and lo, he's away
Out of the farmyard, scattering hens.
Riding to work now as a great man should,
He is the knight at arms breaking the fields'
Mirror of silence, emptying the wood
Of foxes and squirrels and bright jays,
The sun comes over the tall trees
Kindling all the hedges, but not for him
Who runs his engine on a different fuel.
And all the birds are singing, bills wide in vain,
As Cynddylan passes proudly up the lane.

                                    R. S. Thomas

THE SERMON

Like gript stick
Still I sit:
Eyes fixed on far small eyes,
Full of it;
On the old, broad face,
The hung chain;
Heavy arms, surplice
Worn through and worn thin.
Probe I the hid mind
Under the gross flesh:
Clutch at poetic words,
Follow their mesh
Scarce heaving breath.
Clutch, marvel, wonder,
Till the words end.

Stilled is the muttered thunder:
The hard few people wake,
Gather their books and go.
—Whether their hearts could break
How can I know?

                                    Richard Hughes

TO MY MOTHER

Most near, most dear, most loved and most far,
Under the window where I often found her
Sitting as huge as Asia, seismic with laughter,
Gin and chicken helpless in her Irish hand,
Irresistible as Rabelais, but most tender for
The lame dogs and hurt birds that surround her—
She is a procession no one can follow after
But be like a little dog following a brass band.

She will not glance up at the bomber, or condescend
To drop her gin and scuttle to a cellar,
But lean on the mahogany table like a mountain
Whom only faith can move, and so I send
O all my faith, and all my love to tell her
That she will move from mourning into morning.

                                    George Barker

FATHER AND SON

Only last week, walking the hushed fields
Of our most lovely Meath, now thinned by November,
I came to where the road from Laracor leads
To the Boyne river—that seemed more lake than river,
Stretched in uneasy light and stript of reeds.

And walking longside an old weir
Of my people's, where nothing stirs—only the shadowed
Leaden flight of a heron up the lean air—
I went unmanly with grief, knowing how my father,
Happy though captive in years, walked last with me there.

Yes, happy in Meath with me for a day
He walked, taking stock of herds hid in their own breathing;
And naming colts, gusty as wind, once steered by his hand;

Lightnings winked in the eyes that were half shy in greeting
Old friends—the wild blades, when he gallivanted the land.

For that proud, wayward man now my heart breaks—
Breaks for that man whose mind was a secret eyrie,
Whose kind hand was sole signet of his race,
Who curbed me, scorned my green ways, yet increasingly
   loved me
Till death drew its grey blind down his face.

Frederick Robert Higgins

*Mrs. Jakes, knowing that the hour has come when her son
is to be hanged for murder, has the courage to go about her
work as a charwoman*

She has dusted the ornaments, rubbed down the chairs,
   pried into hidden corners with the broom
a thousand times before, but now she stares
   as though she swept an unfamiliar room.

Nothing is changed or missing. The sun streams
   on carpets, pictures, and her restless hands
as carelessly as gold, indifferent dreams
   revisiting a sleeper. And still she stands

perplexed and waiting. From the busy street
   the sounds of London's summer rise, the roar
of cabs and carts, the steady stammer of feet,
   but she has often heard all this before.

And still it seems that something in the place
   vexes, and holds her motionless, as though
Rembrandt had charged her quiet ruined face
   with difficult beauty, and would not let her go.

A woman in a picture, she does not stir,
   save now and then to twitch her bonnet-tape,

as though an old dead poet had written her
   in broken rhyme, and she could not escape.

There are some late pale violets in a jar
   that she is watching sideways, cold, uncivil
blossoms, that match her glances, stare for stare,
   hinting at something old, and dark, and evil.

Her poor mind, coated with the grime of years,
   bent with ignoble care, with want distraught,
crouches behind her slow, unconscious tears
   that have the noble movement of a thought.

So patiently they fall, so without shame
   or wish of hers, beyond the hope of Art,
so silently they flood her cheek, the same
   that rose (it may be) in a slave-girl's heart,

when Agamemnon fell, and, while all those
   laughed one to other, she in her alien tongue
cried that there was no summer for the rose,
   that the great bow for ever was unstrung.

And no one knew or cared. So these slow tears,
   speaking with alien tongue, as though they were
in other lands addressed to other ears,
   interpreted her heart and spoke for her.
                    Humbert Wolfe The Uncelestial City

SŒUR MARIE EMILIE

Sœur Marie Emilie
is little and very old :
her eyes are onyx,
and her cheeks vermilion,
her apron wide and kind
and cobalt blue.

She comforts
generations and generations
of children,
who are ' new '
at the convent school.
When they are eight,
they are already up to her shoulder,
they grow up and go into the world,
she remains,
for ever,
always incredibly old,
but incredibly, never older.

Generations of children
sit in turn by her side,
and help her to shell the peas,
her dry and twisted fingers crackle,
snapping the green pods,
generations of children
sit in turn by her side,
helping to stone the plums,
that will be made into jam,
for the greater glory of God.

She has affinity with the hens,
when a hen dies,
she sits down on a bench and cries,
she is the only grown-up, whose tears
are not frightening tears.
Children can weep
without shame,
at her side.
She is simple as flax.
She collects the eggs,
they are warm and smooth,
and softly coloured,
ivory, ochre,
and brown and rose.
They fit the palm of her hand.

Her eyes kindle upon them,
the children, watching gravely,
understand
her dumb, untroubled love.

We have grown up,
and gone away,
'into the world'
and grown cold
in the service of God,
but we would love Him
even less than we do,
if we had never known
Sœur Marie Emilie,
with the green peas and the plums,
and the hens and the beautiful eggs,
and her apron as wide and kind
as skies on a summer day,
and as clean and blue.

Caryll Houselander

1 THE LOVE OF GOD

Who shall separate us from the love of Christ? shall tribula-
tion, or distress, or persecution, or famine, or nakedness,
or peril, or sword?
As it is written,
For thy sake we are killed all the day long;
We are accounted as sheep for the slaughter.
Nay, in all these things we are more than conquerors through
him that loved us.
For I am persuaded, that neither death, nor life, nor angels,
nor principalities, nor things present, nor things to come,
Nor height, nor depth, nor any other creature, shall be able
to separate us from the love of God, which is in Christ
Jesus our Lord.

Epistle to the Romans

Wherefore I ask that ye faint not at my tribulations for you,
which are your glory.
For this cause I bow my knees unto the Father of our Lord
Jesus Christ,
Of whom the whole family in heaven and on earth is named,
That he would grant you, according to the riches of his glory,
to be strengthened with might by his Spirit in the inner
man;
That Christ may dwell in your hearts by faith; that ye, being
rooted and grounded in love,
May be able to comprehend with all saints what is the breadth,
and length, and depth, and height;
And to know the love of Christ, which passeth knowledge,
that ye may be filled with all the fulness of God.

Now unto him that is able to do exceeding abundantly above
    all that we ask or think, according to the power that
    worketh in us,
Unto him be glory in the church by Christ Jesus throughout
    all ages, world without end. Amen.

Epistle to the Ephesians

O Lord, thou hast searched me, and known me.

Thou knowest my downsitting and mine uprising,
Thou understandest my thought afar off.

Thou compassest my path and my lying down,
And art acquainted with all my ways.

For there is not a word in my tongue,
But, lo, O Lord thou knowest it altogether.

Thou hast beset me behind and before,
And laid thine hand upon me.

Such knowledge is too wonderful for me;
It is high, I cannot attain unto it.

Whither shall I go from thy spirit?
Or whither shall I flee from thy presence?

If I ascend up into heaven, thou art there:
If I make my bed in hell, behold, thou art there.

If I take the wings of the morning,
And dwell in the uttermost parts of the sea;

Even there shall thy hand lead me,
And thy right hand shall hold me.

If I say, Surely the darkness shall cover me,
Even the night shall be light about me. . . .

Search me, O God, and know my heart:
Try me, and know my thoughts:

And see if there be any wicked way in me,
And lead me in the way everlasting.

Psalm 139

For the whole world before thee is as a little grain of the
balance, yea, as a drop of the morning dew that falleth down
upon the earth. But thou hast mercy upon all; for thou canst
do all things, and winkest at the sins of men, because they
should amend. For thou lovest all the things that are, and
abhorrest nothing which thou hast made : for never wouldst
thou have made anything, if thou hadst hated it. And how
could anything have endured, if it had not been thy will?
or been preserved, if not called by thee? But thou sparest all :
for they are thine, O Lord, thou lover of souls.

The Apocrypha The Book of Wisdom

From SAUL

*The boy David, longing to give the sick Saul not only the
glories of which he has sung but eternal life as well, and torn
by his love for the king, realises that if human love so longs
to give divine love in its perfection must far outstrip human
love, and receives the revelation of eternal life in Christ.*

. . . Saul . . . sat out my singing,—one arm round the tent-prop
    to raise
His bent head, and the other hung slack—till I touched on
    the praise
I foresaw from all men in all times, to the man patient there;
And thus ended, the harp falling forward. Then first I was
    'ware
That he sat, as I say, with my head just above his vast knees
Which were thrust out on each side around me, like oak roots
    which please

To encircle a lamb when it slumbers. I looked up to know
If the best I could do had brought solace: he spoke not, but
  slow
Lifted up the hand slack at his side, till he laid it with care
Soft and grave, but in mild settled will, on my brow: thro'
  my hair
The large fingers were pushed, and he bent back my head,
  with kind power—
All my face back, intent to peruse it, as men do a flower.
Thus held he me there with his great eyes that scrutinised
  mine—
And oh, all my heart how it loved him! but where was the
  sign?
I yearned—'Could I help thee, my father, inventing a bliss,
I would add to that life of the past, both the future and this;
I would give thee new life altogether, as good, ages hence,
As this moment,—had love but the warrant, love's heart to
  dispense!'

Then the truth came upon me. . . .
Do I find love so full in my nature, God's ultimate gift,
That I doubt his own love can compete with it? here, the
  parts shift?
Here, the creature surpass the Creator,—the end, what Began?
Would I fain in my impotent yearning do all for this man,
And dare doubt he alone shall not help him, who yet alone
  can?
Would it ever have entered my mind, the bare will, much less
  power,
To bestow on the Saul what I sang of, the marvellous dower
Of the life he was gifted and filled with? to make such a soul,
Such a body, and then such an earth for insphering the whole?
And doth it not enter my mind (as my warm tears attest)
These good things being given, to go on, and give one more,
  the best?
Ay, to save and redeem and restore him, maintain at the height
This perfection,—succeed with life's dayspring, death's minute
  of night?

Interpose at the difficult minute, snatch Saul the mistake,
Saul the failure, the ruin he seems now,—and bid him awake
From the dream, the probation, the prelude, to find himself set
Clear and safe in new light and new life,—a new harmony yet
To be run, and continued and ended—who knows?—or
    endure!
The man taught enough, by life's dream, of the rest to make
    sure;
By the pain-throb, triumphantly winning intensified bliss,
And the next world's reward and repose, by the struggle in
    this.

' I believe it! 'tis Thou, God, that givest, 'tis I who receive:
In the first is the last, in *thy* will is my power to believe.
All's one gift : thou canst grant it moreover, as prompt to my
    prayer
As I breathe out this breath, as I open these arms to the air.
From Thy will, stream the worlds, life and nature, the dread
    Sabaoth :
I will?—the mere atoms despise me! why am I not loth
To look that, even that in the face too? why is it I dare
Think but lightly of such impuissance? what stops my despair?
This;—'tis not what man Does which exalts him, but what
    man Would do!
See the King—I would help him but cannot, the wishes fall
    through.
Could I wrestle to raise him from sorrow, grow poor to enrich,
To fill up his life, starve my own out, I would—knowing
    which,
I know that my service is perfect. Oh, speak through me now!
Would I suffer for him that I love? So wouldst thou—so
    wilt thou!
So shall crown thee the topmost, ineffablest, uttermost crown—
And Thy love fill infinitude wholly, nor leave up nor down
One spot for the creature to stand in! It is by no breath,
Turn of eye, wave of hand, that salvation joins issue with
    death!
As thy love is discovered almighty, almighty be proved
Thy power, that exists with and for it, of being-Beloved!

He who did most, shall bear most; the strongest shall stand
    the most weak.
'Tis the weakness in strength, that I cry for! my flesh, that
    I seek
In the Godhead! I seek and I find it. O Saul, it shall be
A Face like my face that receives thee; a Man like to me,
Thou shalt love and be loved by, for ever: a Hand like this
    hand
Shall throw open the gates of new life to thee! See the Christ
    stand!'

Robert Browning

2 THE PRAISE OF CHRIST OUR LORD

He looked through the lattice of our flesh, and He spake us fair, He set us on fire, and we hasten on His scent . . . He built for Himself here below a lowly house of our clay, that by it He might bring down from themselves and bring up to Himself those who were to be made subject, healing the swollenness of their pride and fostering their love: so that their self-confidence might grow no further but rather diminish, seeing the deity at their feet, humbled by the assumption of our coat of human nature: to the end that weary at last they might cast themselves down upon His humanity and rise again in its rising. . . . Come, Lord, work upon us, set us on fire and clasp us close, be fragrant to us, draw us to Thy loveliness: let us love, let us run to Thee.

St Augustine   Confessions

> Jesu, I now begin
> To love Thee day and night.
> My soul from earth to wean
> I shall do all my might.
> 'Twas all my love to win
> Jesu became my knight.

Bodleian MS.

Long ago to Thee I gave
Body, soul, and all I have—
Nothing in the world I keep:

All that in return I crave
Is that Thou accept the slave:
Long ago to Thee I gave
Body, soul, and all I have.

Had I more to share or save,
I would give as give the brave,
Stooping not to part the heap;
Long ago to Thee I gave
Body, soul, and all I have—
Nothing in the world I keep.

*Rondel   Translated by Sir Henry Newbolt from
the French of Wenceslas, Duke of Brabant and Luxembourg*

CHRIST OUR LORD

Love bade me welcome; yet my soul drew back
        Guilty of dust and sin.
But quick-eyed Love observing me grow slack
        From my first entrance in,
Drew nearer to me, sweetly questioning
        If I lacked anything.

'A guest', I answered, 'worthy to be here':
        Love said, 'You shall be he'.
'I, the unkind, ungrateful? Ah, my dear,
        I cannot look on Thee.'
Love took my hand and smiling did reply,
        'Who made the eyes but I?'

'Truth, Lord; but I have marr'd them: let my shame
        Go where it doth deserve.'

'And know you not', says Love, 'Who bore the blame?'
  'My dear, then I will serve.'
'You must sit down', says Love, 'and taste my meat.'
  So I did sit and eat.

George Herbert

THE GUEST

Yet if His Majesty, our sovereign lord,
Should of his own accord
Friendly himself invite,
And say 'I'll be your guest to-morrow night',
How should we stir ourselves, call and command
All hands to work! 'Let no man idle stand!

'Set me fine Spanish tables in the hall;
See they be fitted all;
Let there be room to eat
And order taken that there want no meat.
See every sconce and candlestick made bright,
That without tapers they may give a light.

'Look to the presence: are the carpets spread,
The dazie o'er the head,
The cushions in the chair,
And all the candles lighted on the stair?
Perfume the chambers, and in any case
Let each man give attendance in his place!'

Thus, if a king was coming, would we do;
And 'twere good reason too;
For 'tis a duteous thing
To show all honour to an earthly king,
And after all our travail and our cost,
So he be pleased, to think no labour lost.

But at the coming of the King of Heaven
All's set at six and seven;

We wallow in our sin,
Christ cannot find a chamber in the inn.
We entertain Him always like a stranger,
And, as at first, still lodge Him in the manger.

Anonymous

LOVE UNKNOWN

My song is love unknown;
My Saviour's love to me;
Love to the loveless shown,
That they might lovely be.
O, who am I,
That for my sake
My Lord should take
Frail flesh, and die?

He came from his blest throne,
Salvation to bestow;
But men made strange, and none
The longed-for Christ would know.
But O, my friend,
My friend indeed,
Who at my need
His life did spend.

Sometimes they strew his way,
And his sweet praises sing;
Resounding all the day
Hosannas to their king.
Then 'Crucify!'
Is all their breath,
And for his death
They thirst and cry.

Why, what hath my Lord done?
What makes this rage and spite?

He made the lame to run,
He gave the blind their sight.
Sweet injuries!
Yet they at these
Themselves displease,
And 'gainst him rise.

They rise, and needs will have
My dear Lord made away;
A murderer they save,
The Prince of Life they slay.
Yet cheerful he
To suffering goes,
That he his foes
From thence might free.

In life, no house, no home
My Lord on earth might have;
In death, no friendly tomb
But what a stranger gave.
What may I say?
Heaven was his home
But mine the tomb
Wherein he lay.

Here might I stay and sing,
No story so divine;
Never was love, dear King!
Never was grief like thine.
This is my Friend,
In whose sweet praise
I all my days
Could gladly spend.

Samuel Crossman

THE WINDHOVER

To Christ our Lord

I caught this morning morning's minion, kingdom
    of daylight's dauphin, dapple-dawn-drawn Falcon, in his
    riding
  Of the rolling level underneath him steady air, and striding
High there, how he rung upon the rein of a wimpling wing
In his ecstasy! then off, off forth on swing,

  As a skate's heel sweeps smooth on a bow-bend: the hurl
    and gliding
  Rebuffed the big wind. My heart in hiding
Stirred for a bird,—the achieve of, the mastery of the thing!

Brute beauty and valour and act, oh, air, pride, plume, here
  Buckle! AND the fire that breaks from thee then, a billion
Times told lovelier, more dangerous, O my chevalier!

  No wonder of it: sheér plód makes plough down sillion
Shine, and blue-break embers, ah my dear,
  Fall, gall themselves, and gash gold-vermilion.

Gerard Manley Hopkins

From the WRECK OF THE DEUTSCHLAND

I
    THOU mastering me
   God! giver of breath and bread;
  World's strand, sway of the sea;
   Lord of living and dead;
Thou hast bound bones and veins in me, fastened me flesh,
And after it almost unmade, what with dread,
   Thy doing: and dost thou touch me afresh?
Over again I feel thy finger and find thee.

2

   I did say yes
   O at lightning and lashed rod;
  Thou heardst me truer than tongue confess
    Thy terror, O Christ, O God;
  Thou knowest the walls, altar and hour and night:
  The swoon of a heart that the sweep and the hurl of thee trod
    Hard down with a horror of height:
And the midriff astrain with leaning of, laced with fire of
  stress.

3

   The frown of his face
   Before me, the hurtle of hell
  Behind, where, where was a, where was a place?
    I whirled out wings that spell
  And fled with a fling of the heart to the heart of the Host.
  My heart, but you were dovewinged, I can tell,
    Carrier-witted, I am bold to boast,
To flash from the flame to the flame then, tower from the
  grace to the grace.

4

   I am soft sift
   In an hourglass—at the wall
  Fast, but mined with a motion, a drift,
    And it crowds and it combs to the fall;
  I steady as a water in a well, to a poise, to a pane,
  But roped with, always, all the way down from the tall
    Fells or flanks of the voel, a vein
Of the gospel proffer, a pressure, a principle, Christ's gift.

5

   I kiss my hand
   To the stars, lovely-asunder
  Starlight, wafting him out of it; and
    Glow, glory in thunder;

Kiss my hand to the dappled-with-damson west:
Since, tho' he is under the world's splendour and wonder,
   His mystery must be instressed, stressed;
For I greet him the days I meet him, and bless when I under-
   stand.

6

   Not out of his bliss
     Springs the stress felt
   Nor first from heaven (and few know this)
     Swings the stroke dealt—
Stroke and a stress that stars and storms deliver,
   That guilt is hushed by, hearts are flushed by and melt—
     But it rides time like riding a river
(And here the faithful waver, the faithless fable and miss)

7

   It dates from day
     Of his going in Galilee;
   Warm-laid grave of a womb-life grey;
     Manger, maiden's knee;
The dense and the driven Passion, and frightful sweat;
   Thence the discharge of it, there its swelling to be,
     Though felt before, though in high flood yet—
What none would have known of it, only the heart, being hard
   at bay.

8

   Is out with it! Oh,
     We lash with the best or worst
   Word last! How a lush-kept plush-capped sloe
     Will, mouthed to flesh-burst,
Gush!—flush the man, the being with it, sour or sweet,
   Brim, in a flash, full!—Hither then, last or first,
     To hero of Calvary, Christ's feet—
Never ask if meaning it, wanting it, warned of it—men go.

9

Be adored among men,
God, three-numberèd form;
Wring thy rebel, dogged in den,
Man's malice, with wrecking and storm.
Beyond saying sweet, past telling of tongue,
Thou art lightning and love, I found it, a winter and warm;
Father and fondler of heart thou hast wrung:
Hast thy dark descending and most art merciful then.

10

With an anvil-ding
And with fire in him forge thy will
Or rather, rather then, stealing as Spring
Through him, melt him but master him still:
Whether at once, as once at a crash Paul,
Or as Austin, a lingering-out swèet skill,
Make mercy in all of us, out of us all
Mastery, but be adored, but be adored King.

Gerard Manley Hopkins

From THE EVERLASTING MERCY

I did not think, I did not strive,
The deep peace burnt my me alive;
The bolted door had broken in,
I knew that I had done with sin.
I knew that Christ had given me birth
To brother all the souls on earth,
And every bird and every beast
Should share the crumbs broke at the feast.

. . . . . .

O wet red swathe of earth laid bare,
O truth, O strength, O gleaming share,
O patient eyes that watch the goal,
O ploughman of the sinner's soul.

O Jesus, drive the coulter deep
To plough my living man from sleep.

. . . . . .

O Christ who holds the open gate,
O Christ who drives the furrow straight,
O Christ, the plough, O Christ, the laughter
Of holy white birds flying after,
Lo, all my heart's field red and torn,
And Thou wilt bring the young green corn
The young green corn divinely springing,
The young green corn for ever singing;
And when the field is fresh and fair
Thy blessèd feet shall glitter there.
And we will walk the weeded field,
And tell the golden harvest's yield,
The corn that makes the holy bread
By which the soul of man is fed,
The holy bread, the food unpriced,
Thy everlasting mercy, Christ.

John Masefield

With this ambiguous earth
His dealings have been told us. These abide:
The signal to a maid, the human birth,
The lesson, and the young man crucified.

But not a star of all
The innumerable host of stars has heard
How He administered this terrestrial ball.
Our race have kept their Lord's entrusted Word.

Of His earth-visiting feet
None knows the secret, cherished, perilous,
The terrible, shamefast, frightened, whispered, sweet,
Heart-shattering secret of His way with us.

No planet knows but this
Our wayside planet, carrying land and wave,
Love and life multiplied, and pain and bliss,
Bears, as chief treasure, one forsaken grave.

Nor, in our little day,
May His devices with the heavens be guessed,
His pilgrimage to thread the Milky Way,
Or His bestowals there be manifest.

But, in the eternities,
Doubtless we shall compare together, hear
A million alien Gospels, in what guise
He trod the Pleiades, the Lyre, the Bear.

O be prepared, my soul!
To read the inconceivable, to scan
The million forms of God those stars unroll
When, in our turn, we show to them a Man.

Alice Meynell

A CHRISTMAS SERMON

We will speak of that which is older than our beginning, and
shall over-live our end, the mercy of God. Nay, to say that
mercy was first is but to post-date mercy; to prefer mercy
but so is to diminish mercy. The names of first or last derogate
from it, for first and last are but rags of time, and His mercy
hath no relation to time, no limitation in time. It is not first
nor last, but eternal, everlasting. Let the devil make me so far
desperate as to conceive a time when there was no mercy, and
he hath made me so far an atheist as to conceive a time when
there was no God. As long as there hath been love, and
God is love, there hath been mercy. And mercy, in the
practice and in the effect, began not at the helping of man
when he was fallen and became miserable, but at the making
of man, when man was nothing.

We ask our daily bread, and God never says, You should

have come yesterday. He never says, You must come again to-morrow. But ' to-day if you will hear His voice ', to-day He will hear you. If some king of the earth have so large an extent of dominion in north and south as that he hath winter and summer together in his dominions, so large an extent east and west as that he hath day and night together in his dominions, much more hath God mercy and judgement together. He brought light out of darkness, not out of a lesser light. He can bring thy summer out of winter though thou have no spring. Though in the ways of fortune, or misunderstanding, or conscience, thou have been benighted till now, wintred and frozen, clouded and eclipsed, damp and benumbed, smothered and stupified till now, now God comes to thee, not as 'in the dawning of the day, not as in the bud of the spring, but as the sun at noon, to banish all shadows; as the sheaves in harvest, to fill all penuries. All occasions invite His mercies, and all times are His seasons.

God made Sun and moon to distinguish seasons, and day and night; and we cannot have the fruits of the earth but in their seasons. But God hath made no decree to distinguish the seasons of His mercies. In Paradise the fruits were ripe the first minute, and in Heaven it is always autumn, His mercies are ever in their maturity.

God goes forward in His own ways, and proceeds as he began, in mercy. One of the most convenient hyroglyphics of God is a circle, and a circle is endless. Whom God loves He loves to the end; and not only to their own end, to their death, but to His end; and His end is, that He might love them still.

God is a circle, and He will make thee one; go not thou about to square either circle, to bring that which is equal in itself to angles and corners, into dark and sad suspicions of God, or of thyself : that God can give, or that thou canst receive, no more of mercy than thou hast already.

As the sun doth not set to any nation, but withdraws itself and returns again, so God, in the exercise of His mercy, doth not set to thy soul, though He benight it with an affliction. The blessed Virgin was overshadowed, but it was with the Holy Ghost. Thine understanding, thy conscience may be so too, and yet it may be the work of the Holy Ghost, Who moves in thy darkness and will bring light even out of that, will bring knowledge out of thine ignorance, clearness out of thy scruples, and consolation out of thy dejection of spirit. The sun is not weary with so many thousand years shining; God cannot be weary of doing good.

'God is thy portion', says David. David does not speak so narrowly, so penuriously as to say, God hath given thee thy portion, and thou must look for no more. But, 'God is thy portion', and as long as He is God He hath more to give, and as long as thou art His, thou hast more to receive.

John Donne   Sermons

3 THE REMEMBRANCE OF HIS BIRTH

CAROL

I sing of a maiden
   That is makeles;
King of all kings
   To her son she ches.

He came al so still
   There his mother was,
As dew in April
   That falleth on the grass.

He came al so still
   To his mother's bour,
As dew in April
   That falleth on the flour.

He came al so still
   There his mother lay,
As dew in April
   That falleth on the spray.

      Mother and maiden
         Was never none but she;
      Well may such a lady
         Goddes mother be.

                                        Anonymous

   And art Thou come, dear Saviour? Hath Thy love
Thus made Thee stoop, and leave Thy throne above
The lofty Heavens, and thus to dress
In dust to visit mortals! Could no less
A condenscension serve? And after all
The mean reception of a cratch—a stall!
Dear Lord, I'll fetch Thee hence, I have a room—
'Tis poor, but 'tis my best—if Thou wilt come
Within so small a cell, where I would fain
Mine and the world's Redeemer entertain,
I mean my heart. 'Tis filthy, I confess,
And will not mend Thy lodging, Lord, unless
Thou send before Thine harbinger—I mean
Thy pure and purging Grace—to make it clean
And sweep its inmost corners : then I'll try
To wash it also with a weeping eye.
And when 'tis swept and washed, I then will go
And with Thy leave, I'll fetch some flowers that grow
In Thine Own Garden—Faith and Love to Thee.
With these I'll dress it up, and there shall be
My Rosemary and Bays. Yet when my best
Is done, the room's not fit for such a Guest.
But here's a cure—Thy presence, Lord, alone
Can make the stall a Court, the cratch a Throne.

                                        Anonymous

From ON THE MORNING
OF CHRIST'S NATIVITY

The shepherds on the lawn,
Or ere the point of dawn,
  Sat simply chatting in a rustic row;
Full little thought they than
That the mighty Pan
Was kindly come to live with them below;
Perhaps their loves, or else their sheep,
Was all that did their silly thoughts so busy keep.

When such music sweet
Their hearts and ears did greet,
  As never was by mortal finger strook;
Divinely warbled voice
Answering the stringèd noise,
  As all their souls in blissful rapture took:
The air such pleasure loth to lose,
With thousand echoes still prolongs each heav'nly close.

At last surrounds their sight
A globe of circular light,
  That with long beams the shame-fac'd night array'd;
The helmèd cheribim
And sworded seraphim
  Are seen in glittering ranks with wings display'd,
Harping in loud and solemn quire,
With unexpressive notes to Heav'n's new-born Heir.

Such music (as 'tis said)
Before was never made,
  But when of old the sons of morning sung;
While the Creator Great
His constellations set,
  And the well-balanc'd world on hinges hung,
And cast the dark foundations deep,
And bid the welt'ring waves their oozy channel keep.

Ring out ye crystal spheres,
Once bless our human ears,
  (If ye have power to touch our senses so),
And let your silver chime
Move in melodious time;
  And let the base of Heav'ns deep organ blow;
And with your ninefold harmony
Make up full consort to th'angelic symphony.

For if such holy song
Enwrap our fancy long,
  Time will run back, and fetch the age of gold;
And speckl'd Vanity
Will sicken soon and die,
  And leprous Sin will melt from earthly mould;
And Hell itself will pass away,
And leave her dolorous mansions to the peering day.

But see the virgin blest,
Hath laid her Babe to rest.
  Time is our tedious song should here have ending:
Heav'n's youngest teeměd star,
Hath fix'd her polish'd car,
  Her sleeping Lord with handmaid lamp attending.
And all about the courtly stable,
Bright-harness'd angels sit in order serviceable.

John Milton

Verses from THE SHEPHERD'S HYMN

We saw Thee in Thy balmy nest,
  Young dawn of our eternal day;
We saw Thine eyes break from the East,
  And chase the trembling shades away:
We saw Thee, and we blest the sight,
We saw Thee by Thine own sweet light.

I saw the curl'd drops, soft and slow,
   Come hovering o'er the place's head,
Off'ring their whitest sheets of snow,
   To furnish the fair infant's bed.
Forbear, said I, be not too bold;
Your fleece is white, but 'tis too cold.

I saw th'obsequious seraphim
   Their rosy fleece of fire bestow,
For well they now can spare their wings,
   Since Heaven itself lies here below.
Well done, said I: but are you sure
Your down, so warm, will pass for pure?

No, no, your King's not yet to seek
   Where to repose His royal head;
See, see how soon His new-bloom'd cheek
   'Twixt mother's breasts is gone to bed!
Sweet choice, said we; no way but so,
Not to lie cold, yet sleep in snow!

Welcome—tho' not to those gay flies
   Gilded i' th' beams of earthly kings,
Slippery souls in smiling eyes—
   But to poor shepherds, homespun things,
Whose wealth's their flocks, whose wit's to be
Well read in their simplicity.

To Thee, meek Majesty, soft King
   Of simple graces and sweet loves!
Each of us his lamb will bring,
   Each his pair of silver doves!
At last, in fire of Thy fair eyes,
Ourselves become our own best sacrifice!
                                    Richard Crashaw

When love of us called Him to see
If we'd vouchsafe His company,
He left His Father's court, and came
Lightly as a lambent flame,
Leaping upon the hills, to be
The humble King of you and me.
Nor can the cares of His whole crown
(When one poor sigh sends for Him down)
Detain Him, but He leaves behind
The late wings of the lazy wind,
Spurns the tame laws of time and place,
And breaks thro' all ten heavens to our embrace.

Richard Crashaw

CHRISTMAS AT GRECIO

It happened in the third year before his death, that in order
to excite the inhabitants of Grecio to commemorate the nativity
of the Infant Jesus with great devotion, he determined to keep
it with all possible solemnity; and lest he should be accused
of lightness or novelty, he asked and obtained the permission
of the sovereign Pontiff. Then he prepared a manger, and
brought hay, and an ox and an ass to the place appointed.
The brethren were summoned, the people ran together, the
forest resounded with their voices, and that venerable night
was made glorious by many and brilliant lights and sonorous
psalms of praise. The man of God stood before the manger,
full of devotion and piety, bathed in tears and radiant with
joy; many Masses were said before it, and the Holy Gospel
was chanted by Francis, the Levite of Christ. Then he
preached to the people around of the nativity of the poor
King; and being unable to utter his Name for his tenderness
of his love, he called Him the Babe of Bethlehem. A certain
valiant and veracious soldier, Master John of Grecio, who,
for the love of Christ, had left the warfare of this world, and
become a dear friend of the holy man, affirmed that he beheld
an Infant marvellously beautiful sleeping in that manger,
Whom the blessed Father Francis embraced with both his

arms, as if he would awake Him from sleep. This vision of the devout soldier is credible, not only by reason of the sanctity of him that saw it, but by reason of the miracles which afterwards confirmed its truth. For the example of Francis, if it be considered by the world is doubtless sufficient to excite all hearts which are negligent in the faith of Christ; and the hay of that manger, being preserved by the people, miraculously cured all diseases of cattle, and many other pestilences; God thus in all things glorifying His servant, and witnessing to the great efficacy of his holy prayers by manifest prodigies and miracles.

Saint Bonaventure   Life of Saint Francis of Assisi

IN THE BLEAK MID-WINTER

In the bleak mid-winter
　　Frosty wind made moan,
Earth stood hard as iron,
　　Water like a stone;
Snow had fallen, snow on snow.
　　Snow on snow,
In the bleak mid-winter
　　Long ago.

Our God, Heaven cannot hold Him,
　　Nor earth sustain;
Heaven and earth shall flee away
　　When He comes to reign:
In the bleak mid-winter
　　A stable-place sufficed
The Lord God Almighty
　　Jesus Christ.

Enough for Him, whom cherubim
　　Worship night and day,
A breastful of milk
　　And a mangerful of hay;

Enough for Him, whom angels
  Fall down before,
The ox and ass and camel
  Which adore.

Angels and archangels
  May have gathered there,
Cherubim and seraphim
  Thronged the air;
But only His mother
  In her maiden bliss
Worshipped the Belovèd
  With a kiss.

What can I give Him,
  Poor as I am?
If I were a shepherd
  I would bring a lamb,
If I were a Wise Man
  I would do my part,—
Yet what I can I give Him,
  Give my heart.

Christina Georgina Rossetti

JOURNEY OF THE MAGI

'A cold coming we had of it,
Just the worst time of the year
For a journey, and such a long journey;
The ways deep and the weather sharp,
The very dead of winter.'
And the camels galled, sore-footed, refractory,
Lying down in the melting snow.
There were times we regretted
The summer palaces on slopes, the terraces,
And the silken girls bringing sherbet.
Then the camel men cursing and grumbling
And running away, and wanting their liquor and women,

And the night-fires going out, and the lack of shelters,
And the cities hostile and the towns unfriendly
And the villagers dirty and charging high prices:
A hard time we had of it.

At the end we preferred to travel all night,
Sleeping in snatches,
With the voices singing in our ears, saying
That this was all folly.
Then at dawn we came to a temperate valley,
Wet, below the snow line, smelling of vegetation;
With a running stream and a water-mill beating the darkness,
And three trees on the low sky,
And an old white horse galloping away in the meadow.

Then we came to a tavern with vine-leaves over the lintel,
Six hands at an open door dicing for pieces of silver,
And feet kicking the empty wine-skins.
But there was no information, and so we continued
And arrived at evening, not a moment too soon
Finding the place; it was (you may say) satisfactory.

All this was a long time ago, I remember,
And I would do it again, but set down
This set down
This: were we led all that way for
Birth or Death? There was a Birth, certainly,
We had evidence and no doubt. I had seen birth and death,
But had thought they were different; this Birth was
Hard and bitter agony for us, like Death, our death.
We returned to our places, these Kingdoms,
But no longer at ease here, in the old dispensation,
With an alien people clutching their gods.
I should be glad of another death.

                                        T. S. Eliot

TWELFTH NIGHT

No night could be darker than this night,
no cold so cold,
as the blood snaps like a wire,
and the heart's sap stills,
and the year seems defeated.

O never again, it seems, can green things run,
or sky birds fly,
or the grass exhale its humming breath
powdered with pimpernels,
from this dark lung of winter.

Yet here are lessons for the final mile
of pilgrim kings;
the mile still left when all have reached
their tether's end : that mile
where the Child lies hid.

For see, beneath the hand, the earth already
warms and glows;
for men with shepherd's eyes there are
signs in the dark, the turning stars,
the lamb's returning time.

Out of this utter death he's born again,
his birth our saviour;
from terror's equinox he climbs and grows,
drawing his finger's light across our blood—
the sun of heaven, and the son of God.

Laurie Lee

CHRISTMAS

The bells of waiting Advent ring,
   The Tortoise stove is lit again
And lamp-oil light across the night
   Has caught the streaks of winter rain
In many a stained-glass window sheen
From Crimson Lake to Hooker's Green.

The holly in the windy hedge
   And round the Manor House the yew
Will soon be stripped to deck the ledge,
   The altar, font and arch and pew,
So that villagers can say
'The Church looks nice' on Christmas Day.

Provincial public houses blaze
   And Corporation tramcars clang,
On lighted tenements I gaze
   Where paper decorations hang,
And bunting in the red Town Hall
Says 'Merry Christmas to you all'.

And London shops on Christmas Eve
   Are strung with silver bells and flowers
As hurrying clerks the City leave
   To pigeon-haunted classic towers,
And marbled clouds go scudding by
The many-steepled London sky.

And girls in slacks remember Dad,
   And oafish louts remember Mum,
And sleepless children's hearts are glad,
   And Christmas-morning bells say 'Come!'
Even to shining ones who dwell
Safe in the Dorchester Hotel.

And is it true? And is it true,
  This most tremendous tale of all,
Seen in a stained-glass window's hue,
  A Baby in an ox's stall?
The Maker of the stars and sea
Become a Child on earth for me?

And is it true? For if it is,
  No loving fingers tying strings
Around those tissued fripperies,
  The sweet and silly Christmas things,
Bath salts and inexpensive scent
And hideous tie so kindly meant,

No love that in a family dwells,
  No carolling in frosty air,
Nor all the steeple-shaking bells
  Can with this single Truth compare—
That God was Man in Palestine
And lives to-day in Bread and Wine.

John Betjeman

THAT BY THE CROSS CAME REDEMPTION

Then said our good Lord Jesus Christ: Art thou well pleased
that I suffered for thee? I said: Yea, good Lord, I thank
Thee: Yea, good Lord, blessed mayst Thou be. Then said
Jesus, our kind Lord: If thou art pleased, I am pleased: it is
a joy, a bliss, an endless satisfying to me that ever suffered
I Passion for thee; and if I might suffer more, I would suffer
more.

Wherefore we be not only His by His buying, but also by
the courteous gift of His Father, we be His bliss, we be His
meed, we be His worship, we be His crown. (And this was
a singular marvel and a full delectable beholding, that we be
His crown!) This that I say is so great bliss to Jesus that He
setteth at nought all His travail, and His hard Passion, and
His cruel and shameful death.

  Dame Julian of Norwich Revelations of Divine Love

Stanzas concerning CHRIST AND THE SOUL

A shepherd-boy his grief is brooding o'er,
Alone, uncomforted, disconsolate.
His thought is fix'd upon his heart's true mate;
His breast with love is stricken very sore.

He weeps not for some love-wound giv'n of yore,
For no such thing could pain and grieve him so,
E'en though it overcharg'd his heart with woe:
He weeps because she thinks of him no more.

And so, because she thinks of him no more
—That shepherd-maid of his, so fair to see—
He lets his alien foes treat cruelly
The breast that love had stricken very sore.

'Woe,' cried the shepherd-boy, 'woe be in store
For him that's come betwixt my love and me,
So that she wishes not to know or see
This breast that love has stricken very sore.'

Then climbs he slowly, when much time is o'er,
Into a tree, with fair arms wide outspread.
And, clinging to that tree, forthwith is dead.
For lo! his breast was stricken very sore.
    St. John of the Cross. Translated by E. Allison Peers

THE CROSS

Love, from the awful throne of patient power
In the wise heart, from the last giddy hour
Of dread endurance, from the slippery, steep,
And narrow verge of crag-like agony, springs
And folds over the world its healing wings . . .

To suffer woes which Hope thinks infinite;
To forgive wrongs darker than death or night;
To defy Power, which seems omnipotent;
To love, and bear; to hope till Hope creates
From its own wreck the thing it contemplates;
Neither to change, nor falter, nor repent;
This, like thy glory, Titan, is to be
Good, great and joyous, beautiful and free;
This is alone Life, Joy, Empire, and Victory.

Percy Bysshe Shelley   Prometheus

You are under the power of no other enemy, and held in no other captivity and want no other deliverance but from the power of your own earthly self. This is the one murderer of the divine life within you. It is your own Cain that murders your own Abel. Now everything that your earthly nature does is under the influence of self-will, self-love, and self-seeking, whether it carries you to laudable or blamable practices; all is done in the nature and spirit of Cain and helps you to such goodness as when Cain slew his brother. For every action and notion of self has the spirit of Antichrist and murders the divine life within you.

William Law   The Spirit of Love

Judas   I have sinned; I have betrayed the innocent blood.
Caiaphas   What is that to us?
Judas   Nothing at all,
 Brother, although you are part and part with me.
 There is no exchange in sin; when guilt is shared,
 It is only as two men share the same disease
 But cannot divide it; each has the whole disease,
 And cannot give it away, although he gives it.
 In death, you see, none can deliver his brother,
 And the brotherhood of Cain is of that kind.
 This guilt is yours and mine—altogether yours,
 Altogether mine; it cannot be called 'ours'—
 Sin cannot say that word.

Christ speaks　　　　　　　But I can say it,
Because our brotherhood is not in the sin
But in the blood—the fatherhood of God
And the motherhood of the first and the second Eve.
The yours and the mine can belong to both and either
By division or exchange, if you choose to make it so.
Say that the guilt is Mine; give it to Me,
And I will take it away to be crucified.
It is all so very much simpler than you think:
Give me the greedy heart and the little creeping treasons,
Give me the proud heart and the blind, obstinate eyes;
Give me the shallow heart, and the vain lust, and the folly;
Give me the coward heart and the spiritless refusals;
Give me the confused self that you can do nothing with;
I can do something.
　　　　　　　　Dorothy L. Sayers　The Just Vengeance

From GOOD FRIDAY

The wild duck, stringing through the sky,
Are south away.
Their green necks glitter as they fly,
The lake is gray.
So still, so lone, the fowler never heeds.
The wind goes rustle, rustle, through the reeds.

There they find peace to have their own wild souls.
In that still lake,
Only the moonrise or the wind controls
The way they take,
Through the gray reeds, the cocking moor-hen's lair,
Rippling the pool, or over leagues of air.

Not thus, not thus are the wild souls of men.
No peace for those
Who step beyond the blindness of the pen
To where the skies unclose.

A.B.O.C.　　　　　　　　　　　　　　　　　　　　F

For them the spitting mob, the cross, the crown of thorns,
The bull gone mad, the Saviour on his horns.

Beauty and peace have made,
No peace, no still retreat,
No solace, none.
Only the unafraid
Before life's roaring street
Touch Beauty's feet,
Know Truth, do as God bade,
Become God's son.

Darkness, come down, cover a brave man's pain,
Let the bright soul go back to God again.
Cover that tortured flesh, it only serves
To hold that thing which other power nerves.
Darkness, come down, let it be midnight here,
In the dark night the untroubled soul sings clear.

I have been scourged, blinded and crucified,
My blood burns on the stones of every street
In every town; wherever people meet
I have been hounded down, in anguish died.

The creaking door of flesh rolls slowly back
Nerve by red nerve the links of living crack,
Loosing the soul to tread another track.

Beyond the pain, beyond the broken clay,
A glimmering country lies
Where life is being wise,
All of the beauty seen by truthful eyes
Are lilies there, growing beside the way.
Those golden ones will loose the torted hands,
Smooth the scarred brow, gather the breaking soul,
Whose earthly moments drop like falling sands
To leave the spirit whole.
Now darkness is upon the face of the earth.

John Masefield

CHRIST IN THE HOSPITAL

Al Padre Evaristo, Carmelita Descalzo, Toledo

Ixions of the slow wheel of the day
They had come down at last, but not to stay,
And at the fall of night, with even sway,
Were slowly wheeling up the other way.

And he who felt the finest in the Ward
Was scarcely better than a broken stick;
His spine ran through him like a rusty sword
Rasping its meagre scabbard to the quick.

Through the dim pane he saw the stars take flight
Like pigeons scattered by the crash and groan
Of the great world, with pendulum of stone
Dingdonging in the steeple of the Night.

He heard, far off, the people stream their course
Whipped by their pleasures into frantic tops—
As the grey multitude (when twilight drops)
Goes out to trade its boredom for remorse.

The Moon, a soldier with a bleeding eye,
Returning to the war, beheld these things.
And long grey tom-cats crept across the sky
Between the chimneys where the wireless sings.

Never seemed anything so steep or tall
(Sierra, iceberg, or the tower of noon)
As what he saw when turning from the moon—
The bloody Christ that hung upon the wall!

Great Albatross, of every storm the Birth!—
His bleeding pinions bracketed a Night
Too small for His embrace; and from His height,
As from an Eagle's, cowered the plaintive Earth!

Roy Campbell

TO THE FAITHFUL

Listen now, whoever you may be,
if your soul is lit by the love of God:
You cannot leave this world all by yourself,
set out on the great path with empty hands,
arrive before the Gates of God—which your faith dreams
stand underneath the arch of the Eternal Home—
to say 'Lord, Lord, I have brought nothing with me;
give me a place in the love of your divine light.'

Because the Lord your God will answer 'Go.
Hack up your feet on red unending ice,
lean on the knotted stick of all your hatreds;
and you shall be a wanderer eternally unless
you find the palm of love which you refused to take
from the tree which was seeded by my blood.'

Marcos An
A Political Prisoner who was in Burgos Jail for twenty-tw
year
Translated by Chloe Valliamy and Stephen Sedle

GOOD FRIDAY

O heart, be lifted up; O heart be gay,
Because the Light was lifted up to-day—
Was lifted on the Rood, but did not die,
To shine eternally for such as I.

O heart, rejoice with all your humble might
That God did kindle in the world this Light,

Which stretching on the Cross could not prevent
From shining with continuous intent.

Why weep, O heart, this day? Why grieve you so?
If all the glory of the Light had lost its glow
Would the sun shine or earth put on her best—
Her flower-entangled and embroidered vest?

Look up, O heart; and then, O heart, kneel down
In humble adoration : give no crown
Nor golden diadem to your fair Lord,
But offer love and beauty by your word.

Let your faith burn, O heart : and let your eyes
Shine with such joy where deepest night still lies
In some too tired and over-burdened mind :
Let Christ be seen, wherever you are kind.

O heart, let your light shine so that all men
May see your works and glorify again
Your Father : and oh! let your light be gay,
And full of quiet laughter all the day.

The everlasting fire of love, O heart,
Has blazed in you and it will not depart.
Wherefore, O heart, exult and praises sing :
Lift up your voice and make the echoes ring.

Raise up your hands, O heart : your fingers raise
In adoration; and in bursting praise
Sing all your songs of beauty with delight,
You larks, exulting in the summer light.

O heart, rise up : O heart be lifted high.
Rejoice; for Light was slain to-day, yet did not die.

                                                    Anonymous

THE ROYAL WAY OF THE HOLY CROSS

He is gone before thee, carrying His cross, and He died for thee upon the cross, that thou mayest also bear thy cross, and love to die on the cross.

Because if thou be dead with Christ, thou shalt also live with Him; and if thou hast been His partner in the suffering, so shalt thou be also in the glory.

Behold in the cross is all, and all depends upon our dying; and there is no other way to life, and to true inward peace, but by the way of the holy cross, and of daily mortification.

Go where thou wilt, seek what thou wilt, and thou shalt not find a higher way above, nor a safer way below, than the way of the holy cross.

Dispose and order all things according as thou wilt, and as seems best to thee, and thou shalt still find something to suffer, either willingly or unwillingly, and so thou shalt always find the cross.

For thou shalt either feel pain in the body, or endure in the soul anguish of spirit.

Sometimes thou shalt be left by God, at other times thou shalt be afflicted by the neighbour; and what is more, thou shalt often be a trouble to thyself. . . .

The cross is always ready, and everywhere waits for thee.

Thou canst not escape it, whithersoever thou runnest; for whithersoever thou goest, thou carryest thyself with thee, and thou shalt always find thyself.

Upwards, downwards, outwards, inwards, turn thyself whither thou wilt, on all sides thou wilt find the cross.

And everywhere thou must needs have patience if thou desirest inward peace, and wouldst win an eternal crown.

If thou carry the cross willingly, it will carry thee, and bring thee to thy desired end; to wit, to that place where there will be an end of suffering, though there will be no end here. . . .

Set thyself then like a good and faithful servant of Christ, to bear manfully the cross of thy Lord, crucified out of love for thee. . . .

Drink of the cup of the Lord lovingly, if thou desirest to be His friend, and to have part with Him.

Leave consolations to God to do with them as best pleaseth him.

But set thou thyself to bear tribulations, and account them the greatest consolations; for the sufferings of this life, although thou alone couldst suffer them all, are not worthy to be compared with the glory which shall hereafter be revealed in us.

Thomas à Kempis   The Imitation of Christ

O my Lord, when I think in how many ways Thou hast suffered, and that Thou didst in no wise deserve it, I do not know what to say for myself, nor of what I am thinking when I shrink from suffering, nor where I am when I excuse myself. . . . O Jesus, Thou brightness of eternal glory, solace of the pilgrim soul, with Thee is my mouth without voice, and my silence speaks to Thee.

Saint Teresa of Avila and Thomas à Kempis
The Way of Perfection
and The Imitation of Christ

THE HARROWING OF HELL

A voice, loud in that light, to Lucifer crying,
'Princes of this place, open! Undo the doors
For here comes crowned He that is King of glory.'
Then Satan sighed and said to them all,
'Such was the light that against our leave fetched Lazarus
    forth;
Care and calamity are come upon us all.
If this King come in, He will capture mankind
And lead it whither He likes, and lodge us in bondage.
Patriarchs and prophets long have promised
That such a Lord and a light should lead them all hence.'
'Listen,' said Lucifer, 'I know this Lord,
Both the Lord and the light; long ago I knew them . . .

And now I see where a soul comes hitherwards, sailing
With glory and with great light, God it is, I well know.
Quick, take to flight,' said he, ' fast away with you,
For it were better not to have been than to abide His
  presence.'
. . . Then the Light bade unlock, and Lucifer answered,
' What Lord art Thou?' said Lucifer, ' Quis est iste?'
' Pax Gloriae,' the Light soon answered,
' And Lord of might and of main and all manner of virtues,
Dominus virtutum.
Dukes of this dim place, at once undo your gates
That Christ may come in, Son of the King of heaven!'
And with that breath, hell brake, and the bars of Belial,
For all the watch and the ward, wide went the gates.
Patriarchs and prophets, populus in tenebris,
Sang the song of Saint John, ' Ecce, Agnus Dei '.
Lucifer dared not look, being by Light blinded,
And those that Our Lord loved, He lifted into light.

> *William Langland Visions from Piers Plowman*
> *Translated into modern English by Nevill Coghill*

AMORETTI *Sonnet lxviii*

Most glorious Lord of life, that on this day
    didst make thy triumph over death and sin :
    and having harrowed hell, didst bring away
    captivity thence captive us to win :
This joyous day, dear Lord, with joy begin,
    and grant that we for whom thou diddest die
    being with thy dear blood clean washed from sin,
    may live for ever in felicity.
And that thy love we weighing worthily,
    may likewise love thee for the same again :
    and for thy sake that all like dear didst buy,
    with love may one another entertain.
So let us love, dear love, like as we ought,
    love is the lesson which the Lord us taught.

> *Edmund Spenser*

I got me flowers to strew Thy way,
   I got me boughs off many a tree;
But thou wast up by break of day,
   And brought'st Thy sweets along with Thee.

Yet though my flowers be lost, they say
   A heart can never come too late;
Teach it to sing Thy praise this day,
   And then this day my life shall date.
                                        George Herbert

THE FLOWER

How fresh, O Lord, how sweet and clean
Are Thy returns! ev'n as the flowers in spring:
To which, besides their own demean,
The late-past frosts tributes of pleasure bring.
         Grief melts away
         Like snow in May,
As if there were no such cold thing.

Who would have thought my shrivel'd heart
Could have recovered grennesse? It was gone
Quite underground: as flowers depart
To see their mother-root, when they have blown;
         Where they together
         All the hard weather
Dead to the world, keep house unknown.

These are Thy wonders, Lord of power,
Killing and quickening, bringing down to hell
And up to heaven in an houre;
Making the chiming of a passing-bell.
         We say amisse
         This or that is:
Thy word is all, if we could spell.

O that I once past changing were,
Fast in Thy Paradise, where no flower can wither!
Many a spring I shoot up fair,
Off'ring at heav'n, growing and growing thither:
    Nor doth my flower
    Want a spring-showre
My sinnes and I joining together.

But while I grow in a straight line,
Still upwards bent, as if heav'n were mine own
Thy anger comes, and I decline:
What frost to that? What pole is not the zone,
    Where all things burn
    When Thou dost turn,
And the least frown of Thine is shown?

And now in age I bud again,
After so many deaths I live and write;
I once more smell the dew and rain,
And relish versing: O my onely light,
    It cannot be
    That I am he
On whom Thy tempests fell all night.

These are Thy wonders, Lord of love,
To make us see we are but flowers that glide;
Which when we once can find and prove,
Thou hast a garden for us, where to hide.
    Who would be more
    Swelling through store
Forfeit their Paradise by their pride.

                    George Herbert

POEM FOR EASTER

Wrapped in his shroud of wax, his swoon of wounds,
still as a winter's star he lies with death.

Still as a winter's lake his stark limbs lock
the pains that run in stabbing frosts about him.

Star in the lake, grey spark beneath the ice,
candle of love snuffed in its whitened flesh,

I, too, lie bound within your dawn of cold
while on my breath the serpent mortal moans.

O serpent in the egg, become a rod,
crack the stone shell that holds his light in coil.

O grief within the serpent sink your root
and bear the flower for which our forked tongues wail.

Cold in this hope our mortal eyes forgather
wandering like moths about the tomb's shut mouth;

Waiting the word the riven rock shall utter,
waiting the dawn to fly its bird of god.

Laurie Lee

ASCEND AND LIVE

But our Life came down to this our earth and took away our
death, slew death with the abundance of His own life: and
He thundered, calling to us to return to Him into that secret
place from which He came forth to us—coming first into the
Virgin's womb, where humanity was wedded to Him, our
mortal flesh, though not always to be mortal; and thence like
a bridegroom coming out of his bride chamber, rejoicing as a
giant to run his course. For He did not delay but rushed on,
calling to us by what He said and what He did, calling to us
by His death, life, descent and ascension to return to Him.
And He withdrew from our eyes, that we might return to our
own heart and find Him. For He went away and behold He is
still here. He would not be with us long yet He did not leave
us. He went back to that place which He had never left, for

the world was made by Him. And he was in this world and
He came into this world to save sinners. O ye sons of men,
how long will ye be so slow of heart? Even now when Life
has come down to you, will you not ascend and live?

St. Augustine   Confessions
Translated by E. J. Sheed

4 THE HOLY SPIRIT, THE COMFORTER, AND HIS GIFTS

Come, Holy Ghost, our souls inspire;
And lighten with celestial fire.
Thou the anointing Spirit art,
Who dost Thy seven-fold gifts impart.
Thy blessed unction from above
Is comfort, life, and fire of love.
Enable with perpetual light
The dullness of our blinded sight,
Anoint and cheer our soiled face
With the abundance of Thy grace.
Keep far our foes, give peace at home:
When Thou art guide, no ill can come.
Teach us to know the Father, Son,
And Thee, of both, to be but One;
That, through the ages all along,
This may be our endless song:
    Praise to Thy eternal merit,
    Father, Son, and Holy Spirit.

Amen

Bishop J. Cosins
Based on Veni, Creator Spiritus

GOD'S GRANDEUR

The world is charged with the grandeur of God.
It will flame out, like shining from shook foil;
It gathers to a greatness, like the ooze of oil
Crushed. Why do men then now not reck his rod?
Generations have trod, have trod, have trod;
And all is seared with trade; bleared, smeared with toil;
And wears man's smudge and shares man's smell: the soil
Is bare now, nor can foot feel, being shod.
And for all this, nature is never spent;
There lives the dearest freshness deep down things;
And though the last lights off the black West went
Oh, morning, at the brown brink eastward, springs—
Because the Holy Ghost over the bent
World broods with warm breast and with ah! bright wings.

Gerard Manley Hopkins

THE HOLY SPIRIT

Come with birds' voices when the light grows dim
Yet lovelier in departure and more dear:
While the warm flush hangs yet at heavens' rim,
And the one star shines clear.

Though the swift night haste to approaching day
Stay Thou and stir not, brooding on the deep:
Thy secret love, Thy silent word let say
Within the senses' sleep.

Softer than dew. But where the morning wind
Blows down the world, O Spirit! show Thy power:
Quicken the dreams within the languid mind
And bring Thy seed to flower!

Evelyn Underhill   Letters of Evelyn Underhill

When we pray, 'Come, Holy Ghost, our souls inspire', we had better know what we are about. He will not carry us to easy triumphs and gratifying successes; more probably He will set us to some task for God in the full intention that we shall fail, so that others, learning wisdom by our failure, may carry the good cause forward. He may take us through loneliness, desertion by friends, apparent desertion even by God; that was the way Christ went to the Father. He may drive us into the wilderness to be tempted of the devil. He may lead us from the Mount of Transfiguration (if He ever lets us climb it) to the hill that is called the Place of a Skull. For if we invoke Him, it must be to help us in doing God's will, not ours. We cannot call upon the

Creator Spirit, by whose aid
The world's foundations first were laid

in order to use omnipotence for the supply of our futile pleasures or the success of our futile plans. If we invoke Him, we must be ready for the glorious pain of being caught by His power out of our petty orbit into the eternal purposes of the Almighty, in whose onward sweep our lives are as a speck of dust. The soul that is filled with the Spirit must have become purged of all pride or love of ease, all self-complacence and self-reliance; but that soul has found the only real dignity, the only lasting joy. Come then, Great Spirit, come. Convict the world; and convict my timid soul.

William Temple
Readings in St. John's Gospel

THE DOVE

The dove descending breaks the air
With flame of incandescent terror
Of which the tongues declare
The one discharge from sin and error.
The only hope, or else despair
    Lies in the choice of pyre or pyre—
    To be redeemed from fire by fire.

Who then devised the torment? Love.
Love is the unfamiliar Name.
Behind the hands that wove
The intolerable shirt of flame
Which human power cannot remove.
    We only live, only suspire
    Consumed by either fire or fire.
                T. S. Eliot   Little Gidding

GIFTS OF THE SPIRIT

A gift is properly an unreturnable giving . . . hence it is manifest that love has the nature of a first gift, through which all free gifts are given. So since the Holy Ghost proceeds as Love, He proceeds as the first gift. Gift . . . is the proper name of the Holy Ghost.
             St. Thomas Aquinas   Summa Theologica

O God the Father, who saidst at the beginning: Let there be light and it was so! Enlighten my eyes that I never sleep in death, lest at any time my enemy should say, I have prevailed against him.

O God the Son, Light of Light, the most true and perfect Light from whom this light of the sun and the day had their beginning: Thou that art the Light shining in darkness enlightening everyone that cometh into the world! expel from me all clouds of ignorance, and give me true understanding, that in Thee and by Thee I may know the Father: whom to know is to live, and to serve is to reign.

O God the Holy Ghost, the Fire that enlightens and warms our hearts! shed into me Thy most sacred light. . . . Ray Thyself into my soul, that I may see what an exceeding weight of Glory my enemy would bereave me of, for the mere shadows, and painting of this world.
         Henry Vaughan   The Mount of Olives

WISDOM

For wisdom, which is the worker of all things, taught me : for
in her is an understanding spirit, holy, one only, manifold, subtil, lively, clear, undefiled, plain, not subject to
hurt, loving the thing that is good, quick, which cannot
be letted, ready to do good.

Kind to man, stedfast, sure, free from care, having all power,
over-seeing all things, and going through all understanding, pure, and most subtil, spirits.

For wisdom is more moving than any motion : she passeth
and goeth through all things by reason of her pureness.

For she is the breath of the power of God, and a pure influence
flowing from the glory of the Almighty : therefore can
no defiled thing fall into her.

For she is the brightness of the everlasting light, the unspotted mirror of the power of God, and the image of his
goodness.

And being but one, she can do all things : and remaining in
herself, she maketh all things new : and in all ages
entering into holy souls, she maketh them friends of God,
and prophets.

For God loveth none but him that dwelleth with wisdom.

For she is more beautiful than the sun, and above all the
order of stars : being compared with the light, she is
found before it.

The Apocrypha   The Wisdom of Solomon

AGATHON SPEAKS OF LOVE

Love seems to me, O Phaedrus, a divinity the most beautiful
and the best of all, and the author to all others of the excel-
lencies with which his own nature is endowed. Nor can I
restrain the poetic enthusiasm which takes possession of my
discourse, and bids me declare that Love is the divinity who
creates peace among men, and calm upon the sea, the windless

silence of storms, repose and sleep in sadness. Love divests
us of all alienation from each other, and fills our vacant hearts
with overflowing sympathy; he gathers us together in such
social meetings as we now delight to celebrate, our guardian
and our guide in dances, and sacrifices, and feasts. Yes, Love,
who showers benignity upon the world, and before whose
presence all harsh passions flee and perish; the author of all
soft affections; the destroyer of all ungentle thoughts; merciful, mild; the object of the admiration of the wise, and the
delight of gods; possessed by the fortunate, and desired by the
unhappy, therefore unhappy because they possess him not;
the father of grace, and delicacy, and gentleness, and delight,
and persuasion, and desire; the cherisher of all that is good,
the abolisher of evil; our most excellent pilot, defence,
saviour and guardian in labour and in fear, in desire and in
reason; the ornament and governor of all things human and
divine; the best, the loveliest; in whose footsteps every one
ought to follow, celebrating him excellently in song, and bearing each his part in that divinest harmony which Love sings to
all things which live and are, soothing the troubled minds of
Gods and men.

The Banquet   Five Dialogues of Plato   On Poetic Inspiration

> Let me not to the marriage of true minds
> Admit impediments. Love is not love
> Which alters when it alteration finds,
> Or bends with the remover to remove;
> O, no! it is an ever-fixèd mark,
> That looks on tempests and is never shaken;
> It is the star to every wand'ring bark,
> Whose worth's unknown, although his height be taken.
> Love's not Time's fool, though rosy lips and cheeks
> Within his bending sickle's compass come;
> Love alters not with his brief hours and weeks,
> But bears it out even to the edge of doom:—
>   If this be error and upon me proved,
>   I never writ, nor no man ever loved.
>   *William Shakespeare   Sonnets*

LOVE

On all that the Lord laboured He lavished His love.
Love is the plant of peace, most precious of virtues;
All heaven could not hold it, so heavy in itself,
It fell in fulness forth on the field of earth
And of the folds of that field took flesh and blood;
No leaf thereafter on a linden-tree was ever lighter,
No needle-point so piercing or nimble to handle,
No armour can withhold it or high walls hinder.
Therefore is Love leader of the Lord's folk in heaven,
And, to know its nature, it is nurtured in power,
And in the heart is its home and fountain-head.
Instinctively at heart a strength is stirring
Flowing to the Father that formed us all,
Looked on us with love, and let His Son die,
Meekly, for our misdoings, to amend us all.
Yet appointed He no punishment for the pain they put Him to,
But meekly with His mouth besought mercy for them,
And pity for the people that were putting Him to death.
See it an example, only seen in Him,
That He was mighty and yet meek, and had mercy to grant
To those that hung Him on high and thrust Him through the
    heart.
So I recommend you rich ones to have pity on the poor,
To comfort the care-stricken, the sin-encumbered.
Love, the most pleasant thing that our Lord pleads for us,
Is also the ready roadway, running into heaven.

> *William Langland Visions from Piers Plowman*
> *Translated into modern English by Nevill Coghill*

LOVE

In short, my sisters, I will conclude with this advice : do no
build towers without a foundation, for our Lord does not care
so much for the importance of our works as for the love with

which they are done. When we do all we can, His Majesty
will enable us to do more every day. If we do not grow weary,
but during the brief time this life lasts (and perhaps it will
be shorter than any of you think) we give our Lord every
sacrifice we can, both interior and exterior, His Majesty
will unite them with that which He offered to His Father
for us on the Cross so that they may be worth the value given
them by our love, however mean the works themselves may
be. . . . Our Lord asks but two things of us : love for Him
and for our neighbour : . . . I think the most certain sign that
we keep these two commandments is that we have a genuine
love for others. We cannot know whether we love God although there may be strong reasons for thinking so, but there
can be no doubt about whether we love our neighbour or no.
Be sure that in proportion as you advance in fraternal charity,
you are increasing in your love of God, for His Majesty bears
so tender an affection for us that I cannot doubt He will
repay our love for others by augmenting, in a thousand different ways, that which we bear for Him. We should watch
most carefully over ourselves in this matter, for if we are
faultless on this point we have done all. I believe human
nature is so evil that we could not feel a perfect charity for our
neighbour unless it were rooted in the love of God.

Saint Teresa of Avila The Interior Castle
Translated by a Benedictine of Stanbrook

BREAD

Hunger was loneliness, betrayed
By the pitiless candour of the stars'
Talk, in an old byre he prayed

Not for food; to pray was to know
Waking from a dark dream to find
The white loaf on the white snow;

Not for warmth, warmth brought the rain's
Blurring of the essential point
Of ice probing his raw pain.

He prayed for love, love that would share
His rags' secret; rising he broke
Like sun crumbling the gold air

The live bread for the starved folk.

R. S. Thomas

ABU BEN ADHEM

Abu Ben Adhem (may his tribe increase!)
Awoke one night from a deep dream of peace,
And saw, within the moonlight in his room,
Making it rich, and like a lily in bloom,
An angel writing in a book of gold:—
Exceeding peace had made Ben Adhem bold,
And to the presence in the room he said,
   'What writest thou?'—The vision raised its head,
And with a look made of all sweet accord,
Answered, 'The names of those who love the Lord'.
   'And is mine one?' said Abu. 'Nay, not so',
Replied the angel. Abu spoke more low,
But cheerly still; and said, 'I pray thee, then,
Write me as one that loves his fellow men'.
   The angel wrote and vanish'd. The next night
It came again with a great wakening light,
And show'd the names whom love of God had blest,
And lo! Ben Adhem's name led all the rest.

Leigh Hunt

HOLY POVERTY

How St. Francis and Brother Masseo placed the bread they had begged upon a stone near a fountain; and how St. Francis praised the virtue of holy poverty

The wonderful servant and follower of Christ, St. Francis, wishing to be in all things conformed to his Master—Who, as the Gospel tells, sent His disciples two by two into all the cities and lands whither He intended to go to prepare the way for Him—after he had assembled his twelve companions, sent them forth two by two into the world to preach. In order to set them an example of holy obedience, he first began to act himself, like the Saviour Jesus Christ. Wherefore, having sent his companions to divers parts of the world, he took with him Brother Masseo, and set out towards the province of France. On arriving in a certain town, being very hungry, they went, according to the Rule, begging their bread for the love of God. St. Francis took one street, and Brother Masseo the other. St. Francis, being a little man, with a mean exterior, did not attract much attention, and gathered only a few bits of dry bread, whereas Brother Masseo, being tall and good-looking, received many large pieces of bread, with several whole loaves. When they had ended their task of begging, they met on a spot outside the city where there was a beautiful fountain and a large stone, on which each placed what he had collected. St. Francis, seeing that the pieces of bread which Brother Masseo had collected were much larger and better than those he had received, rejoiced greatly, and said: 'O Brother Masseo, we are not worthy of this great treasure': and he repeated these words several times. At this Brother Masseo answered: 'Father, how canst thou talk of a treasure where there is so much poverty, and indeed a lack of all things? for we have neither cloth, nor knife, nor dish, nor table, nor house to eat in, nor servant or maid to wait upon us'. St. Francis answered: 'This is indeed the reason why I account it a great treasure, because man has had no hand in it, but all has been given to us by divine providence, as we clearly see in this bread of charity, in this beautiful table of stone, and in this so clear fountain. Wherefore let us beg of God to make us love with all our hearts the treasure of Holy Poverty.' Having spoken thus, they returned thanks; and when they had refreshed themselves with the bread and water, they rose and went on their way to France.

The Little Flowers of St. Francis

HUMILITY

Once, while I was wondering why our Lord so dearly loved the virtue of humility, the thought suddenly struck me without previous reflection, that it is because God is the supreme Truth and humility is the *truth*, for it is most true that we have nothing good of ourselves but only misery and nothingness : whoever ignores this, lives a life of falsehood. They that realise this fact most deeply are the most pleasing to God, the supreme Truth, for they walk in the truth. God grant, sisters, that we may have the grace never to lose this self-knowledge! Amen.

Saint Teresa of Avila   The Interior Castle
Translated by a Benedictine of Stanbrook

THE SHEPHERD'S SONG

He that is down needs fear no fall,
    He that is low, no pride;
He that is humble ever shall
    Have God to be his guide.

I am content with what I have,
    Little be it or much :
And, Lord, contentment still I crave,
    Because Thou savest such.

Fullness to such a burden is
    That go on pilgrimage :
Here little, and hereafter bliss,
    Is best from age to age.

Pilgrim's Progress   John Bunyan

PEACE

When will you ever, Peace, wild wooddove, shy wings shut,
Your round me roaming end, and under be my boughs?
When, when Peace, will you, Peace? I'll not play hypocrite
To own my heart : I yield you do come sometimes ; but
That piecemeal peace is poor peace. What pure peace allows
Alarms of wars, the daunting wars, the death of it?

O surely, reaving Peace, my Lord should leave in lieu
Some good! And so he does leave Patience exquisite,
That plumes to Peace thereafter. And when Peace here does
    house
He comes with work to do, he does not come to coo,
    He comes to brood and sit.

Gerard Manley Hopkins

PATIENCE

Patience, hard thing! the hard thing but to pray,
But bid for, Patience is! Patience who asks
Wants war, wants wounds ; weary his times, his tasks ;
To do without, take tosses, and obey.
    Rare patience roots in these, and, these away,
Nowhere. Natural heart's ivy, Patience masks
Our ruins of wrecked past purpose. There she basks
Purple eyes and seas of liquid leaves all day.

We hear our hearts grate on themselves : it kills
To bruise them dearer. Yet the rebellious wills
Of us we do bid God bend to him even so.
    And where is he who more and more distils
Delicious kindness?—He is patient. Patience fills
His crisp combs, and that comes those ways we know.

Gerard Manley Hopkins

JOY

Put sadness away from thee, for truly sadness is the sister of
half-heartedness and bitterness. Array thee in the joy that
always finds favour in God's sight and is acceptable with him;
yea, revel thou therein. For everyone that is joyous worketh
and thinketh those things that are good, and despiseth sadness. But he that is sad doth always wickedly; first because he
maketh sad the Holy Spirit that hath been given to man for
joy; and secondly he worketh lawlessness, in that he neither
prays to God nor gives him thanks. Therefore cleanse thyself
from this wicked sadness, and thou shalt live with God. Yea,
unto God all they shall live who have cast out sadness from
themselves, and arrayed themselves in all joy.

From the Shepherd of Hermas

THE CELESTIAL SURGEON

If I have faltered more or less
In my great task of happiness;
If I have moved among my race
And shown no glorious morning face;
If beams from happy human eyes
Have moved me not; if morning skies,
Books, and my food, and summer rain
Knocked on my sullen heart in vain:—
Lord, Thy most pointed pleasure take
And stab my spirit broad awake;

Or, Lord, if too obdurate I,
Choose Thou, before that spirit die,
A piercing pain, a killing sin,
And to my dead heart run them in!
                    Robert Louis Stevenson

COURTESY

Of courtesy it is much less
Than courage of heart or holiness,
Yet in my walks it seems to me
That the Grace of God is in courtesy.

On monks I did in Storrington fall,
They took me straight into their hall;
I saw three pictures on a wall
And courtesy was in them all.

The first the Annunciation;
The second the Visitation;
The third the Consolation,
Of God that was Our Lady's Son.

The first was of Saint Gabriel;
On wings of flame from heaven he fell;
And as he went upon one knee
He shone with heavenly courtesy.

Our Lady out of Nazareth rode—
It was her month of heavy load;
Yet was her face both great and kind,
For Courtesy was in her mind.

The third, it was our little Lord,
Whom all the Kings in arms adored;
He was so small you could not see
His large intent of Courtesy.

Our Lord, that was Our Lady's Son,
Go bless you, People, one by one;
My Rhyme is written, my work is done.

Hilaire Belloc

KINDNESS

Kindness glides about my house,
Dame Kindness, she is so nice!
The blue and red jewels of her rings smoke
In the windows, the mirrors
Are filling with smiles.

What is so real as the cry of a child?
A rabbit's cry can be wilder
But it has no soul.
Sugar can cure everything, so Kindness says.
Sugar is a necessary fluid,

It crystals a little poultice.
O kindness, kindness
Sweetly picking up pieces!
My Japanese silks, desperate butterflies,
May be pinned any minute, anaesthetized.

And here you come, with a cup of tea
Wreathed in steam.
The blood jet is poetry,
There is no stopping it.
You hand me two children, two roses.

Sylvia Plath

5 THE SEARCH

Console thyself, thou wouldst not seek Me, if thou hadst not found Me.

Blaise Pascal   Pensées

As the hart panteth after the water brooks, so panteth my
   soul after Thee, O God. . . .
O God, thou art my God; early will I seek Thee: my soul
   thirsteth for Thee, my flesh longeth for Thee in a dry
   and thirsty land, where no water is. . . .
Glory ye in His Holy name: let the heart of them rejoice
   that seek the Lord. Seek the Lord, and his strength:
   seek His face evermore.

The Psalms

Ask, and it shall be given you; seek, and ye shall find;
   knock, and it shall be opened unto you. For every one
   that asketh receiveth; and he that seeketh findeth; and
   to him that knocketh it shall be opened.

The Gospel of St. Luke

Late have I loved Thee, O Beauty so ancient and so new; late
have I loved Thee! For behold Thou wert within me, and I
outside; and I sought Thee outside and in my loneliness fell
upon those lovely things that Thou hast made. Thou wert
with me and I was not with Thee. I was kept from Thee by
those things, yet had they not been in Thee, they would not
have been at all. Thou didst call and cry to me and break open
my deafness: and Thou didst send forth Thy beams and
shine upon me and chase away my blindness: Thou didst
breathe fragrance upon me, and I drew in my breath and do

now pant for Thee: I tasted Thee, and now hunger and
thirst for Thee: Thou didst touch me, and I have burned
for thy peace.

St. Augustine   Confessions
Translated by E. J. Sheed

THE SEARCH

Whither hast vanishèd,
Belovèd, and hast left me full of woe,
And like the hart hast sped,
Wounding, ere thou didst go,
Thy love, who follow'd, crying, high and low?

Ye shepherds, soon to be
Among those sheepcotes on the hillside high,
If ye perchance should see
Him that I love pass by,
Say to him that I suffer, grieve and die.

I'll seek my love straightway
Over yon hills, down where yon streamlets flow.
To pluck no flowers I'll stay;
No fear of beasts, I'll know;
Past mighty men, o'er frontier-grounds I'll go.

Yon forest, thicket, dene,
Which my belovèd set in close array;
Yon meadow-land so green,
Spangled with blossoms gay,
Tell me, oh, tell me, has he pass'd your way?

Rare gifts he scatterèd
As through these woods and groves he pass'd apace,
Turning, as on he sped,
And clothing every place
With loveliest reflection of his face.

O that my griefs would end!
Come, grant me thy fruition full and free!
And henceforth do thou send
No messenger to me,
For none but thou my comforter can be. . . .

End thou my torments here,
Since none but thou canst remedy my plight;
And to these eyes appear,
For thou art all their light
And save for thee I value not their sight.

Reveal thyself, I cry,
Yea, though the beauty of thy presence kill,
For sick with love am I,
And naught can cure my ill
Save only if of thee I have my fill.

O crystal spring so fair,
Might now within thy silvery depths appear,
E'en as I linger there,
Those features ever dear
Which on my soul I carry graven clear! . . .

Ah, scorn me not, I pray,
For if, in truth, uncomely once was I,
Thy beauty came one day,
And clothed my misery:
Look then on me, thus shrouded, as I cry.

     St. John of the Cross   The Spiritual Canticle
       Translated by E. Allison Peers

THE OBSCURE NIGHT OF THE SOUL

Upon an obscure night,
Fevered with love in love's anxiety,
(O hapless-happy plight!)
I went, none seeing me,
Forth from my house where all things quiet be.

By night, secure from sight,
And by the sacred stair, disguisedly,
(O hapless-happy plight!)
By night, and privily,
Forth from my house where all things quiet be.

Blest night of wandering,
In secret, where by none might I be spied,
Nor I see anything;
Without a light or guide,
Save that which in my heart burnt in my side.

That light did lead me on,
More surely than the shining of noontide,
Where well I knew that one
Did for my coming bide;
Where he abode might none but he abide.

O night that didst lead thus,
O night more lovely than the dawn of light,
O night that broughtest us,
Lover to lover's sight,
Lover with loved in marriage of delight!

Upon my flowery breast,
Wholly for him, and save himself for none,
There did I give sweet rest
To my beloved one;
The fanning of the cedars breathed thereon.

When the first moving air
Blew from the tower, and waved his locks aside,
His hand with gentle care,
Did wound me in the side,
And in my body all my senses died.

All things I then forgot,
My cheeks on him who for my coming came;
All ceased and I was not,
Leaving my cares and shame
Among the lilies, and forgetting them.
  St. John of the Cross   Translated by Arthur Symons

NIGHT

Dear night! this world's defeat,
The stop to busy fools, care's check and curb,
The day of spirits; my soul's calm retreat
Which none disturb!
Christ's progress, and his prayer-time,
The hours to which high heaven doth chime.

God's silent, searching flight,
When my Lord's head is filled with dew, and all
His locks are wet with the clear drops of night;
His still, soft call,
His knocking time, the soul's dumb watch,
When spirits their fair kindred catch.

Were all my loud, evil days
Calm and unhaunted as is thy dark tent,
Whose peace but by some angel's wing or voice
Is seldom rent,
Then I in heaven all the long year
Would keep and never wander here.

But living where the sun
Doth all things wake, and where all mix and tyre
Themselves and others, I consent and run
To every myre;
And by the world's ill-guiding light
Erre more than I can do by might.

There is in God, some say,
A deep, but dazzling darkness : as men here
Say it is late and dusky, because they
See not all clear.
O for that night! when I in him
Might live invisible and dim.

Henry Vaughan

MY SPIRIT LONGETH FOR THEE

My spirit longeth for Thee,
    Within my troubled breast
Altho' I be unworthy
    Of so divine a Guest.

Of so divine a Guest,
    Unworthy tho' I be,
Yet has my heart no rest,
    Unless it come from Thee.

Unless it come from Thee,
    In vain I look around;
In all that I can see,
    No rest is to be found.

No rest is to be found,
    But in Thy blessed love;
O! let my wish be crown'd,
    And send it from above!

John Byrom

IF IT IS NOT MY PORTION

If it is not my portion to meet thee in this my life then let me ever feel that I have missed thy sight—let me not forget for a moment, let me carry the pangs of this sorrow in my dreams and in my wakeful hours.

As my days pass in the crowded market of this world and my hands grow full with the daily profits, let me ever feel that I have gained nothing—let me not forget for a moment, let me carry the pangs of this sorrow in my dreams and in my wakeful hours.

When I sit by the roadside, tired and panting, when I spread my bed low in the dust, let me ever feel that the long journey is still before me—let me not forget for a moment, let me carry the pangs of this sorrow in my dreams and in my wakeful hours.

When my rooms have been decked out and the flutes sound and the laughter there is loud, let me ever feel that I have not invited thee to my house—let me not forget for a moment, let me carry the pangs of this sorrow in my dreams and in my wakeful hours.

Rabindranath Tagore   Gitanjali

6 THE FINDING

Flee we to our Lord and we shall be comforted, touch we Him and we shall be made clean, cleave we to Him and we shall be sure, and safe from all manner of peril.

For our courteous Lord willeth that we should be as homely with him as heart may think or soul may desire. But let us beware that we take not so recklessly this homeliness as to leave courtesy. For our Lord Himself is sovereign homeliness, and as homely as He is, so courteous He is: for He is very courteous. And the blessed creatures that shall be in heaven with Him without end, He will have them like to Himself in all things. And to be like our Lord perfectly, it is our very salvation and our full bliss. . . .

God, of Thy Goodness, give me Thyself : for Thou art enough to me, and I may nothing ask that is less than may be full worship to Thee;. and if I ask anything that is less, ever me wanteth,—but only in Thee I have all.

Dame Julian of Norwich   Revelations of Divine Love

Pray remember what I have recommended to you, which is, to think often of God, by day, by night, in your business, and even in your diversions. He is always near you and with you; leave Him not alone. You would think it rude to leave a friend alone who came to visit you : why then must God be neglected? Do not then forget Him, but think on Him often, adore Him continually, live and die with Him; this is the glorious employment of a Christian; in a word, this is our profession; if we do not know it we must learn it. I will endeavour to help you with my prayers.

A letter of Brother Lawrence
The Practice of the Presence of God

Wherever thou goest, whatever thou dost, at home or abroad, in the field or at church, do all in a desire of union with Christ, in imitation of His tempers and inclinations, and look upon all as nothing but that which exercises the Spirit and life of Christ in the soul. From morning to night keep Jesus in thy heart, long for nothing, desire nothing, hope for nothing, but to have all that is within thee changed into the Spirit and temper of the holy Jesus.

William Law   The Spirit of Prayer

FINDING GOD IN OUR WORK

God does not deflect our gaze prematurely from the work He Himself has given us, since He presents Himself to us as attainable through that very work. Nor does He blot out, in His intense light, the detail of our earthly aims, since the closeness of our union with Him is in fact determined by the exact fulfilment of the least of our tasks. . . . God, in all that is most living and incarnate in Him, is not far away from us, altogether apart from the world we see, touch, hear, smell and taste about us. Rather He awaits us every instant in our action, in the work of the moment. There is a sense in which He is at the tip of my pen, my spade, my brush, my needle—of my heart and of my thought. By pressing the stroke, the line, or the stitch, on which I am engaged, to its ultimate natural finish, I shall lay hold of the last end towards which my innermost will tends. . . . Try, with God's help, to perceive the connection—even physical and natural—which binds your labour with the building of the Kingdom of Heaven; try to realise that heaven itself smiles upon you and, through your works, draws you to itself; then, as you leave church for the noisy streets, you will remain with only one feeling, that of continuing to immerse yourself in God. . . . Never, at any time . . . consent to do anything without first of all realising its significance and constructive value in Christo Jesu, and pursuing it with all your might. This is not simply a commonplace precept for salvation : it is the very path to sanctity for each man according to his state and calling. For what is sanctity in a creature if not to adhere to God with the maximum of his strength?—and what does that maximum adherence to God mean if not the fulfilment—in the world organised around Christ—of the exact function, be it lowly or eminent, to which that creature is destined both by natural endowment and by supernatural gift?

Pierre Teilhard de Chardin   Le Milieu Divin

ST. PAUL SPEAKS

Oh could I tell, ye surely would believe it!
Oh could I only say what I have seen!
How should I tell or how can ye receive it,
How, till He bringeth you where I have been? . . .

Whoso has felt the Spirit of the Highest
Cannot confound nor doubt Him nor deny:
Yea with one voice, O world, tho' thou deniest,
Stand thou on that side, for on this am I.

Rather the earth shall doubt when her retrieving
Pours in the rain and rushes from the sod,
Rather than he for whom the great conceiving
Stirs in his soul to quicken into God. . . .

Who that one moment has the least descried Him,
Dimly and faintly, hidden and afar,
Doth not despise all excellence beside Him,
Pleasures and powers that are not and that are. . . .

Yea thro' life, death, thro' sorrow and thro' sinning
He shall suffice me, for He hath sufficed:
Christ is the end, for Christ was the beginning,
Christ the beginning, for the end is Christ.

                                  F. W. H. Myers

QUICKNESS

False life! a foil and no more, when
        Wilt thou be gone?
Thou foul deception of all men
That would not have the true come on.

Thou art a Moon-like toil; a blinde
    Self-posing state;
A dark contest of waves and winde;
A mere tempestuous debate.

Life is a fix'd discerning light,
    A knowing Joy;
No chance, or fit : but ever bright,
And calm and full, yet doth not cloy.

'Tis such a blissful thing, that still
    Doth vivifie,
And shine and smile, and hath the skill
To please without Eternity.

Thou art a tiresome Mole, or less
    A moving mist,
But life is, what none can express,
A quickness, which my God hath kist.
                Henry Vaughan

OUR GOD FINDS US

Now of that long pursuit
Comes on at hand the bruit;
That Voice is round me like a bursting sea;
' And is thy earth so marred,
Shattered in shard on shard?
Lo, all things fly thee, for thou fliest Me!
    Strange, piteous, futile thing!
Wherefore should any set thee love apart?
Seeing none but I makes much of naught' (He said),
' And human love needs human meriting :
    How hast thou merited—
Of all man's clotted clay the dingiest clot?
    Alack, thou knowest not
How little worthy of any love thou art!

Whom wilt thou find to love ignoble thee,
    Save Me, save only Me?
All which I took from thee I did but take,
    Nor for thy harms,
But just that thou might'st seek it in My arms.
    All which thy child's mistake
Fancies as lost, I have stored for thee at home :
    Rise, clasp My hand, and come!'
    Halts by me that footfall :
    Is my gloom, after all,
Shade of His hand, outstretched caressingly?
    ' Ah, fondest, blindest, weakest,
    I am He Whom thou seekest !
Thou dravest love from thee, who dravest Me.'
        Francis Thompson   The Hound of Heaven

The Pantheist's God does nothing, demands nothing. He is
there if you wish for Him, like a book on a shelf. He will not
pursue you. There is no danger that at any time heaven and
earth should flee away at His glance. If He were the truth,
then we could really say that all the Christian images of
kingship were a historical accident of which our religion
ought to be cleansed. It is with a shock that we discover them
to be indispensable. You have had a shock like that before, in
connection with smaller matters—when the line pulls at your
hand, when something breathes beside you in the darkness.
So here; the shock comes at the precise moment when the
thrill of *life* is communicated to us along the clue we have
been following. It is always shocking to meet life where we
thought we were alone. ' Look out!' we cry, ' it's *alive*.' And
therefore this is the very point at which so many draw back—
I would have done so myself if I could—and proceed no
further with Christianity. An 'impersonal God'—well and
good. A subjective God of beauty, truth and goodness, inside
our own heads—better still. A formless life-force surging
through us, a vast power which we can tap—best of all. But
God Himself, alive pulling at the other end of the cord,

perhaps approaching at an infinite speed, the hunter, king, husband—that is quite another matter. There comes a moment when the children who have been playing at burglars hush suddenly : was that a *real* footstep in the hall? There comes a moment when people who have been dabbling in religion ('Man's search for God'!) suddenly draw back. Supposing we really found Him? We never meant it to come to *that*! Worse still, supposing He found us?

So it is a sort of Rubicon. One goes across; or not. But if one does, there is no manner of security against miracles. One may be in for *anything*.

C. S. Lewis   Miracles

THE MYSTICS

For, just as mediaeval explorers brought home the news that there existed lands which their fellow-countrymen had never seen, and probably never would see, but the existence of which they would henceforward take on trust, so the mystics, one after another, with a unanimity independent of age, creed or race, bring us reports from a country, more difficult to chart than any on earth, which, but for their testimony, might be supposed to exist only in the imagination. The time has passed when intelligent Christians could reject the cumulative evidence of all the mystics, or dismiss it as of no concern to them : few thinking people can deliberately do that to-day, and even these few are sometimes overborne by the weight of evidence. No one has charted more of this spiritual land than St. John of the Cross. And, though it may never be our 'happy chance' to make the journey, the knowledge that the goal exists is surely an invitation to us to tighten up our spiritual life and nerve ourselves to set out for at least a small part of the way. Nay, even the most humdrum routine of our lowly workaday lives must be illumined by the knowledge that far above us, other souls—elect, heroic souls indeed, but 'subject to like passions as we are'—are receiving supernatural graces. To know that there is a beauty greater than any

we ourselves have seen or can imagine should not make us
discontented with the drabness of our own lives but help us
to appreciate more deeply such beauty as may be given to us
either now or in the future. To know that God gives Himself
on earth to those who can lay aside every weight and struggle
upward till they meet Him should fill us with praise for His
goodness and determination to struggle ourselves for as much
of the way as we can.

E. Allison Peers   Spirit of Flame
A Study of St. John of the Cross

ST. FRANCIS RECEIVES THE STIGMATA

The day before the Feast of the Most Holy Cross, as St.
Francis was praying secretly in his cell, an angel of God
appeared to him, and spake to him thus from God : ' I am
come to admonish and encourage thee, that thou prepare thyself to receive in all patience and humility that which God
will give and do to thee.'

St. Francis replied : ' I am ready to bear patiently whatsoever my Lord shall be pleased to do to me '; and so the
angel departed. On the following day—being the Feast of
the Holy Cross—St. Francis was praying before daybreak at
the entrance of his cell, and turning his face towards the
east, he prayed in these words : ' O Lord Jesus Christ, two
graces do I ask of Thee before I die; the first, that in my
lifetime I may feel, as far as possible, both in my soul and
body, that pain which Thou, sweet Lord, didst endure in the
hour of Thy most bitter Passion; the second, that I may feel
in my heart as much as possible of that excess of love by
which Thou, O Son of God, was inflamed to suffer so cruel
a Passion for us sinners.' And continuing a long time in that
prayer, he understood that God had heard him, and that, so
far as is possible for a mere creature, he should be permitted
to feel these things.

Having then received this promise, St. Francis began to
contemplate most devoutly the Passion of Jesus Christ and

His infinite charity; and so greatly did the fervour of devotion increase within him, that he was all transformed into Jesus by love and compassion.

And being thus inflamed in that contemplation, on that same morning he beheld a seraph descending from heaven with six fiery and resplendent wings; and this seraph with rapid flight drew nigh unto St. Francis, so that he could plainly discern him, and perceive that he bore the image of one crucified; and the wings were so disposed, that two were spread over the head, two were outstretched in flight, and the other two covered the whole body. And when St. Francis beheld it, he was much afraid, and filled at once with joy and grief and wonder. He felt great joy at the gracious presence of Christ, who appeared to him thus familiarly, and looked upon him thus lovingly, but, on the other hand, beholding Him thus crucified, he felt exceeding grief and compassion. He marvelled much at so stupendous and unwonted a vision, knowing well that the infirmity of the Passion accorded ill with the immortality of the seraphic spirit. And in that perplexity of mind it was revealed to him by Him who thus appeared, that by divine providence this vision had been thus shown to him that he might understand that, not by martyrdom of the body, but by a consuming fire of the soul, he was to be transformed into the express image of Christ crucified in that wonderful apparition . . . Then, after long and secret conference together, that marvellous vision disappeared, leaving in the heart of St. Francis an excessive fire and ardour of divine love, and on his flesh a wonderful trace and image of the Passion of Christ. For upon his hands and his feet began immediately to appear the figures of the nails, as he had seen them on the body of Christ crucified, Who had appeared to him in the likeness of a seraph.

Little Flowers of St. Francis

Saint Teresa of Avila tries to describe
THE LIGHT OF HEAVEN

I never saw with my bodily eyes . . . but only with the eyes of the soul. . . .

It is like most pellucid water running in a bed of crystal, reflecting the rays of the sun, compared with most muddy water on a cloudy day, flowing on the surface of the earth. Not that there is anything like the sun present here, nor is the light like that of the sun : this light seems to be natural; and, in comparison with it, every other light is something artificial. It is a light which knows no night; but rather, as it is always light, nothing ever disturbs it. In short, it is such that no man, however gifted he may be, can ever, in the whole course of his life, arrive at any imagination of what it is. God puts it before us so instantaneously, that we could not open our eyes in time to see it, if it were necessary for us to open them at all. But whether our eyes be open or shut, it makes no difference whatever; for when our Lord wills, we must see it, whether we will or not. No distraction can shut it out, no power can resist it, nor can we attain to it by any diligence or efforts of our own. I know this by experience.

The Life of Saint Teresa of Avila by Herself
Translated from the Spanish by David Lewis

On the night of January 23rd 1655, when he was thirty-two, Blaise Pascal had an experience which changed his life. Nothing would have been known of it had not a piece of paper telling of it been found after his death sewn into the lining of his coat. At the head and foot of the paper he had drawn a cross.

Feast of S. Clement, Pope and Martyr, and others of the Martyrology.

From about half-past ten in the evening to about half-past twelve.

FIRE

God of Abraham, God of Isaac, God of Jacob,
Not of philosophers and scholars.
Certainty, Joy, Certainty, Feeling, Vision, Joy.
     God of Jesus Christ.
     My God and thy God.
     Thy God shall be my God.
Oblivion of the world and of everything save God.
He is only to be found in the ways that are shown in the
     Gospel.
     ' The GRANDEUR of the human soul.'
O righteous Father, the world has not known Thee, but I have
     known Thee.
          Joy, Joy, and tears of Joy.
     I have fallen away from Him,
' They have forsaken me, the fountains of living waters.'
     My God, wilt thou forsake me?
May I not be separated from Him eternally.
' This is life eternal that they may know Thee, and Jesus
     Christ Whom Thou has sent.'
          Jesus Christ.
          Jesus Christ.
I have become separated from Him, I have fled Him, denied
     Him, crucified Him.
May I never be separated from Him.
He is only to be kept by the ways taught in the Gospel.
Total and sweet renunciation.
Total submission to Jesus Christ and to my director.
Eternally in joy for one day's trial upon earth.
I will not forget Thy word. Amen.

Taken from Jacqueline Pascal and her Brother
by M. V. Woodgate

From THE PRISONER

He comes with western winds, with evening's wandering airs,
With that clear dusk of heaven that brings the thickest stars.
Winds take a pensive tone, and stars a tender fire,
And visions rise, and change, and kill me with desire.

Desire for nothing known in my maturer years,
When Joy grew mad with awe, at counting future tears.
When, if my spirit's sky was full of flashes warm,
I knew not whence they came, from sun or thunderstorm.

But, first, a hush of peace—a soundless calm descends;
The struggle of distress and fierce impatience ends;
Mute music soothes my breast—unuttered harmony,
That I could never dream, till Earth was lost to me.

Then dawns the Invisible; the Unseen its truth reveals;
My outward sense is gone, my inward essence feels:
Its wings are almost free—its home, its harbour found,
Measuring the gulf, it stoops—and dares the final bound.

O! dreadful is the check—intense the agony—
When the ear begins to hear, and the eye begins to see;
When the pulse begins to throb, the brain to think again;
The soul to feel the flesh, and the flesh to feel the chain.

Yet I would lose no sting, would wish no torture less;
The more that anguish racks, the earlier it will bless;
And robed in fires of hell, or bright with heavenly shine,
If it but herald death, the vision is divine!

Emily Brontë

THE VISIONARY

Silent is the house: all are laid asleep:
One alone looks out o'er the snow-wreaths deep,
Watching every cloud, dreading every breeze
That whirls the wildering drift, and bends the groaning trees.

Cheerful is the hearth, soft the matted floor;
Not one shivering gust creeps through pane or door;
The little lamp burns straight, its rays shoot strong and far:
I trim it well, to be the wanderer's guilding-star.

Frown, my haughty sire! chide, my angry dame;
Set your slaves to spy; threaten me with shame:
But neither sire nor dame, nor prying serf shall know,
What angel nightly tracks that waste of frozen snow.

What I love shall come like visitants of air,
Safe in secret power from lurking human snare;
What loves me, no word of mine shall e'er betray,
Though for faith unstained my life must forfeit pay.

Burn, then, little lamp, glimmer straight and clear—
Hush! a rustling wing stirs, methinks, the air;
He for whom I wait thus ever comes to me;
Strange Powers! I trust thy might; trust thou my constancy!

Emily Brontë

I had a heightened perception of everything, and everything
was perceived as beautiful and good. But it was more than a
perception; it was a meeting, for which I had gone out to
the other and for which the other had gone out to me: a
meeting with everything's self which at the same time was
my self, but was nevertheless of a difference in selfhood which
alone made the meeting a possibility. But the going out and
the meeting were not different things but the same thing, not
successive but simultaneous; which is to say that they were not

in time but in eternity. And the meeting, I say again, was
with everything. With the greenness, the freshness, the
slenderness, the littleness, the gentleness, the strength, the
taperingness, the sun-acceptingness, the daisy-and-buttercup-
enclosingness, of the benign and far-stretching grass. With the
trees in their various species, and with every branch and every
twig and every leaf of them. With stones and mould and
air and sun and a deck-chair in the garden and a car down the
lane and a spire on the downs and the wall of our house as I
come in for lunch at one. And with people. Not specially
with people—it would be easy but untrue to say that—but
equally with people. I would sit, going up to London, in a
crowded railway-compartment, and know myself as in every
one of my fellow travellers, and know every one of them as
in me.

> *Victor Gollancz   Extract from My Dear Timothy*

I was in an underground train, a crowded train in which all
sorts of people jostled together, sitting and strap-hanging—
workers of every description going home at the end of the
day. Quite suddenly I saw with my mind, but as vividly as a
wonderful picture, Christ in them all. But I saw more than
that; not only was Christ in every one of them, living in
them, dying in them, rejoicing in them, sorrowing in them—
but because He was in them, and because they were here, the
whole world was here too, here in this underground train;
not only the world as it was at that moment, not only all the
people in all the countries of the world, but all those people
who had lived in the past, and all those yet to come.

I came out into the street and walked for a long time in
the crowds. It was the same here, on every side, in every
passer-by, everywhere—Christ. . . .

I saw too the reverence that everyone must have for a
sinner; instead of condoning his sin, which is in reality his
utmost sorrow, one must comfort Christ who is suffering in
him. And this reverence must be paid even to those sinners
whose souls seem to be dead, because it is Christ, who is the

life of the soul, who is dead in them : they are His tombs, and Christ in the tomb is potentially the risen Christ. For the same reason, no one of us who has fallen into mortal sin himself must ever lose hope. . . .

After a few days the ' vision ' faded. People looked the same again, there was no longer the same shock of insight for me each time I was face to face with another human being. Christ was hidden again; indeed, through the years to come I would have to seek for Him, and usually I would find Him in others—and still more in myself—only through a deliberate and blind act of faith. But if the ' vision ' had faded, the knowledge had not; on the contrary, that knowledge, touched by a ray of the Holy Spirit, is like a tree touched by the sun— it puts out leaf and flowers, bearing fruit and blossom from splendour to splendour.

Caryll Houselander   A Rocking Horse Catholic

IV. COMFORT IN TRIBULATION

Hast thou not known? hast thou not heard, that the everlasting God, the Lord, the Creator of the ends of the
earth, fainteth not, neither is weary? there is no searching of his understanding.

He giveth power to the faint; and to him that hath no might
he increaseth strength.

Even the youths shall faint and be weary, and the young men
shall utterly fall:

But they that wait upon the Lord shall renew their strength;
they shall mount up with wings as eagles; they shall
run, and not be weary; they shall walk, and not
faint. . . .

Sing, O heavens; and be joyful, O earth; and break forth
into singing, O mountains: for the Lord hath comforted
his people, and will have compassion upon his afflicted.

But Zion said, Jehovah hath forsaken me, and the Lord hath
forgotten me.

Can a woman forget her sucking child, that she should not
have compassion on the son of her womb? yea, these may
forget, yet will not I forget thee.

Behold, I have graven thee upon the palms of my hands.

The Book of Isaiah

My son, if thou come to serve the Lord, prepare thy soul for
temptation.

Set thy heart aright, and constantly endure, and make not
haste in time of trouble.

Cleave unto him, and depart not away, that thou mayest
be increased at thy last end.

Whatsoever is brought upon thee take cheerfully, and be
patient when thou art changed to a low estate.

For gold is tried in the fire, and acceptable men in the furnace
of adversity.

Believe in him, and he will help thee; order thy way aright,
and trust in him.

Ye that fear the Lord, wait for his mercy; and go not aside,
lest ye fall.

Ye that fear the Lord, believe him; and your reward shall not
fail.

Ye that fear the Lord, hope for good, and for everlasting joy
and mercy.

Look at the generations of old, and see; did ever any trust
in the Lord, and was confounded? or did any abide in
his fear, and was forsaken? or whom did he ever despise,
that called upon him?

For the Lord is full of compassion and mercy, longsuffering,
and very pitiful, and forgiveth sins, and saveth in time
of affliction.

The Apocrypha   The Book of Ecclesiasticus

CHRIST SPEAKS TO US
WHEN WE ARE FRIGHTENED

Pluck up thy courage, faint heart; what though thou be
fearful, sorry and weary, and standeth in great dread of most
painful torments, be of good comfort; for I myself have
vanquished the whole world, and yet felt I far more fear,
sorrow, weariness, and much more inward anguish too, when
I considered my most bitter, painful Passion to press so fast
upon me. He that is strong-hearted may find a thousand
glorious valiant martyrs whose ensample he may right joyously
follow. But thou now, O timorous and weak, silly sheep,
think it sufficient for thee only to walk after me, which am
thy shepherd and governor, and so mistrust thyself and put
thy trust in me. Take hold on the hem of my garment, therefore; from thence shalt thou perceive such strength and relief
to proceed. . . .

Sir Thomas More   Treatise on the Passion

SEED-TIME AND HARVEST

There is time of weeping and there is time of laughing. But
as you see, he setteth the weeping time before, for that is ye
time of this wretched world and the laughing time shall come
after in heaven. There is also a time of sowing, and a time of
reaping too. Now must we in this world sow, that we may in
the other world reap : and in this short sowing time of this
weeping world, must we water our seed with the showers of
our tears, and then shall we have in heaven a merry laughing harvest for ever.

Sir Thomas More   A Dialogue of Comfort in Tribulation

1 IN ILLNESS

COMFORT AND COURAGE IN ILLNESS

The first day they got only as far as S. Damian's and here
Francis had to rest for more than eight weeks, during the
whole of which he was totally blind. Then in February 1225
they managed to go on to Rieti where a lay friend kindly put
them up in his house. As Francis lay there in pain and darkness he suddenly conceived the idea that he would like to
hear some music, so he called one of the friars who had been
a lute-player before he joined the Order, and bade him
borrow a lute and sing to him. But the poor friar, torn
between love of S. Francis and, perhaps, fear of Elias, asked
to be excused since he was afraid that the people of the town
would criticise him. So Francis let the matter drop. 'But,'
says Brother Leo, 'the following night, about midnight,
Francis was lying awake, and lo, close to the house where he
lay, he heard a minstrel playing the sweetest music which he
had ever heard in the whole of his life. And as he played
he went up and down, going first so far away as to be almost

inaudible and then coming back, but always playing. And this continued for a full hour. Wherefore the blessed Francis, knowing that this was a work of God, not of man, was filled with the greatest joy and with gladness of heart praised God with all his strength in that He had been pleased to cheer his soul with such consolation.'

Francis had come to Rieti in order to have some treatment for his eyes and preparations were now made for the operation. The method was that of cauterisation, which meant the burning with a hot iron of his face from the jaw to the eyebrow with the purpose apparently of 'opening the veins'. It sounds barbaric to us, but in those days was thought to be efficacious, and the surgeon really believed that it would eventually relieve the pain. Francis submitted because Brother Elias wished it and had taken great trouble to prepare for it, but even his gallant spirit quailed when he saw the iron put into the fire to be heated up. For a moment he thought he would faint, but, summoning all his strength, he addressed the fire in these words : 'My Brother Fire, noble and useful among all creatures, be kind to me in this hour, for I have always loved thee for the love of Him who created thee. But I pray our Creator who created us, that He will so temper thy heat that I may be able to bear it.' Then he made the sign of the cross over the fire and the surgeon took the red-hot iron and plunged it into the flesh. The sight was so terrible that all the friars who were present fled from the room, but when they returned Francis reproved them for their lack of courage and assured them that he had felt no pain whatsoever.

St Francis of Assisi   by John R. H. Moorman

If we were well accustomed to the exercise of the presence of God, all bodily diseases would be much alleviated thereby. God often permits that we should suffer a little to purify our souls, and oblige us to continue with him.

Take courage, offer Him your pains incessantly, pray to Him for strength to endure them. Above all, get a habit of entertaining yourself often with God, and forget Him the least you can. Adore Him in your infirmities, offer yourself to Him

from time to time; and, in the height of your sufferings, be-
seech him humbly and affectionately (as a child his father) to
make you conformable to His holy will. I shall endeavour
to assist you with my poor prayers.

God has many ways of drawing us to Himself, He sometimes hides Himself from us; but faith alone, which will not
fail us in time of need, ought to be our support, and the
foundation of our confidence, which must be all in God.

I know not how God will dispose of me. I am always
happy. All the world suffer; and I, who deserve the severest
discipline, feel joys so continual and so great that I can scarce
contain them.

I would willingly ask of God a part of your sufferings, but
that I know my weakness, which is so great that if He left me
one moment to myself I should be the most wretched man
alive. And yet I know not how He can leave me alone, because faith gives me as strong a conviction as sense can do
that He never forsakes us until we have first forsaken Him.
Let us fear to leave Him. Let us be always with Him. Let us
live and die in His presence. Do you pray for me as I for
you.

A Letter of Brother Lawrence
The Practice of the Presence of God

HYMN TO GOD MY LOVE, IN MY SICKNESS

Since I am coming to that holy room,
    Where, with thy choir of saints for evermore,
I shall be made thy music; as I come
    I tune the instrument here at the door,
    And what I must do then, think here before.

Whilst my physicians by their love are grown
    Cosmographers, and I their map, who lie
Flat on this bed, that by them may be shown
    That this is my south-west discovery
    Per fretum febris, by these straits to die,

I joy, that in these straits, I see my west;
　For, though their currents yield return to none,
What shall my west hurt me? As west and east
　In all flat maps (and I am one) are one,
　So death doth touch the resurrection.

Is the pacific sea my home? Or are
　The eastern riches? Is Jerusalem?
Anyan, and Magellan, and Gibraltar,
All straits, and none but straits, are ways to them,
Whether where Japhet dwelt, or Cham, or ·Sem.

We think that Paradise and Calvary,
　Christ's Cross and Adam's tree, stood in one place;
Look Lord, and find both Adams met in me;
　As the first Adam's sweat surrounds my face,
　May the last Adam's blood my soul embrace.

So, in his purple wrapp'd receive me, Lord,
　By these his thorns give me his other crown;
And as to other's souls I prech'd thy word,
　Be this my text, my sermon to mine own,
　Therefore that he may raise the Lord throws down.
                                                    John Donne

ON HIS BLINDNESS

When I consider how my light is spent,
　Ere half my days, in this dark world and wide,
　And that one talent which is death to hide,
　Lodg'd with me useless, though my Soul more bent
To serve therewith my Maker, and present
　My true account, lest he returning chide,
　'Doth God exact day-labour, light deni'd';
　I fondly ask: But Patience to prevent

That murmur, soon replies, ' God doth not need
   Either man's work or his own gifts; who best
   Bear his mild yoke, they serve him best, his State
Is Kingly; thousands at his bidding speed
   And post o'er Land and Ocean without rest:
   They also serve who only stand and wait '.

John Milton

From THE SERMON IN THE HOSPITAL

But yet one thought has often stayed by me
In the night watches, which has brought at least
The patience for the hour, and made the pain
No more a burden which I groaned to leave,
But something precious which I feared to lose. . . .

But if, impatient, thou let slip thy cross,
Thou wilt not find it in this world again,
Nor in another; here, and here alone,
Is given thee to *suffer* for God's sake.
In other worlds we shall more perfectly
Serve Him and love Him, praise Him, work for Him,
Grow near and nearer Him with all delight;
But then we shall not any more be called
To suffer, which is our appointment here.
Canst thou not suffer then one hour,—or two?
If He should call thee from thy cross to-day,
Saying, It is finished!—that hard cross of thine
From which thou prayest for deliverance,
Thinkest thou not some passion of regret

Would overcome thee? Thou wouldst say, ' So Soon?
Let me go back, and suffer yet awhile
More patiently;—I have not yet praised God.' . . .

And while we suffer, let us set our souls
To suffer perfectly : since this alone,
The suffering, which is this world's special grace,
May here be perfected and left behind.
> *Harriet Eleanor Hamilton King   The Disciples*

COMFORT FOR THE SLEEPLESS

I woke up with foreboding, and despair
Lurked in the gloomy shadows of the night;
But very weak and foolish is my care
    If Jesus Christ was right.

All the grim puzzles of the universe
Compassed me round, all nature's endless fight;
But I shall see a blessing, not a curse,
    If Jesus Christ was right.

And most of all, longing for those who died
Smote at my heart with overwhelming might;
But I shall see them and be satisfied
    If Jesus Christ was right.

Lord, unto Thee in the old words I cry,
'Illumine my dark spirit with Thy light'.
Oh save me from the sin of accidie,
    And let me know Thee right.
> *H. C. Bradby*

We all know instances of really saintly people who are suffering constantly from physical disabilities that bring them great
pain. . . . Once you have reached the point of real supremacy
over your body, it is at least possible that the spiritual power
may be increased by its constant exercise against something
physical which to others would seem to be weakening and
debilitating. . . . The causes of health, as the causes of sickness, are very many, but among the forces which will tend to

keep us in health will be a faith which is extended to a real expectation of God's goodness in every department of our being. That will bring us either actual health or a greater power of triumphing over ill-health, and either of these is a great blessing. Moreover, when we triumph in the way that I have described over ill-health, the result, is, in fact, that our health is somewhat better than if we were merely lying passive in the grip of our disease, because owing to the exaltation of mind there is a real access of vitality which tends to combat the disease itself. The way in which faith, as I think, chiefly promotes health, is precisely by the creation of peace of mind beyond what can be reached in any other way, and especially beyond what can be reached by those who have much to distract them, whether in their circumstances or in their bodily condition.

William Temple

In His Mental Illness, William Cowper
Finds He is not Alone

I was a stricken deer, that left the herd
  Long since; with many an arrow deep infixt
My panting side was charg'd, when I withdrew
To seek a tranquil death in distant shades.
There was I found by one who had himself
Been hurt by th'archers. In his side he bore,
And in his hands and feet, the cruel scars.
With gentle force soliciting the darts,
He drew them forth, and heal'd, and bade me live.
Since then, with few associates, in remote
  And silent woods, I wander, far from those
My former partners of the peopled scene;
With few associates, and not wishing more.

William Cowper   The Task

2 IN OLD AGE

THE OLD WHOM GOD LOVES
The aged St. John speaks of what he has known

' If I live yet, it is for good, more love
Through me to men : be nought but ashes here
That keep awhile my semblance, who was John,—
Still, when they scatter, there is left on earth
No one alive who knew (consider this!)
—Saw with his eyes and handled with his hands
That which was from the first, the Word of Life.
How will it be when none more saith " I saw "? . . .

' And how shall I assure them? Can they share
—They, who have flesh, a veil of youth and strength
About each spirit, that needs must bide its time,
Living and learning, still as years assist
Which wear the thickness thin, and let man see—
With me who hardly am withheld at all,
But shudderingly, scarce a shred between,
Lie bare to the universal prick of light?
Is it for nothing we grow old and weak,
We whom God loves? When pain ends, gain ends too.
To me, that story—ay, that Life and Death
Of which I wrote " it was "—to me, it is;
—Is, here and now : I apprehend nought else.
Is not God now i' the world His power first made?
Is not His love at issue still with sin,
Closed with and cast and conquered, crucified
Visibly when a wrong is done on earth?
Love, wrong, and pain, what see I else around?
Yea, and the Resurrection and Uprise
To the right hand of the throne—what is it beside,

When such truth, breaking bounds, o'erfloods my soul,
And, as I saw the sin and death, even so
See I the need yet transiency of both,

The good and glory consummated thence?
I saw the Power; I see the Love, once weak,
Resume the Power: and in this word "I see",
Lo, there is recognized the Spirit of both
That, moving o'er the spirit of man, unblinds
His eye and bids him look . . . .

' Then stand before that fact, that Life and Death,
Stay there at gaze, till it dispart, dispread,
As though a star should open out, all sides,
And grow the world on you, as it is my world.

' For life, with all it yields of joy and woe,
And hope and fear,—believe the aged friend,—
Is just our chance o' the prize of learning love,
How love might be, hath been indeed, and is;
And that we hold thenceforth to the uttermost
Such prize despite the envy of the world,
And, having gained truth, keep truth : that is all.'

Robert Browning   From, Death in the Desert

*The Old Pope is Comforted by the Thought of the
Young Pompilia, who has gone ahead of him to Paradise*

                                  First of the first,
Such I pronounce Pompilia, then as now
Perfect in whiteness : stoop thou down, my child,
Give one good moment to the poor old Pope
Heart-sick at having all his world to blame—
Let me look at thee in the flesh as erst,
Let me enjoy the old clean linen garb,
Not the new splendid vesture ! Armed and crowned,
Would Michael, yonder, be, nor crowned nor armed,

The less pre-eminent angel? Everywhere
I see in the world the intellect of man,
That sword, the energy his subtle spear,
The knowledge which defends him like a shield—
Everywhere; but they make not up, I think,
The marvel of a soul like thine, earth's flower
She holds up to the softened gaze of God!
It was not given Pompilia to know much,
Speak much, to write a book, to move mankind,
Be memorised by who records my time.
Yet if in purity and patience, if
In faith held fast despite the plucking fiend,
Safe like the signet stone with the new name
That saints are known by,—if in right returned
For wrong, most pardon for worst injury,
If there be any virtue, any praise,—
Then will this woman-child have proved—who knows?—
Just the one prize vouchsafed unworthy me,
Seven years a gardener of the untoward ground,
I till,—this earth, my sweat and blood manure
All the long day that barrenly grows dusk:
At least one blossom makes me proud at eve
Born 'mid the briers of my enclosure! . . . Go past me
And get thy praise,—and be not far to seek
Presently when I follow if I may!

       Robert Browning   From, The Ring and the Book

From 'SAMSON AGONISTES'

All is best, though we oft doubt,
What th' unsearchable dispose
Of highest wisdom brings about,
And ever best found in the close.
Oft he seems to hide his face,
But unexpectedly returns
And to his faithful Champion hath in place
Bore witness gloriously; whence Gaza mourns

And all that band them to resist
His uncontrollable intent.
His servants he with new acquist
Of true experience from this great event
With peace and consolation hath dismist,
And calm of mind all passion spent.

John Milton

A FAREWELL TO ARMS

His golden locks Time hath to silver turn'd;
   O Time too swift, O swiftness never ceasing!
His youth 'gainst time and age hath ever spurn'd,
   But spurn'd in vain; youth waneth by increasing:
Beauty, strength, youth, are flowers but fading seen;
Duty, faith, love, are roots, and ever green.

His helmet now shall make a hive for bees;
   And, lovers' sonnets turn'd to holy psalms,
A man-at-arms must now serve on his knees,
   And feed on prayers, which are Age his alms;
But though from court to cottage he depart,
His Saint is sure of his unspotted heart.

And when he saddest sits in homely cell,
   He'll teach his swains this carol for a song,—
'Blest be the hearts that wish my sovereign well,
   Curst be the souls that think her any wrong.'
Goddess, allow this aged man his right
To be your beadsman now that was your knight.

George Peele

OLD AGE

The seas are quiet when the winds give o'er;
So calm are we when passions are no more.
For then we know how vain it was to boast
Of fleeting things, so certain to be lost.

Clouds of affection from our younger eyes
Conceal that emptiness which age descries.

The soul's dark cottage, batter'd and decay'd,
Lets in new light through chinks that Time hath made:
Stronger by weakness, wiser men become
As they draw near to their eternal home.
Leaving the old, both worlds at once they view
That stand upon the threshold of the new.

Edmund Waller

He requires no great matters of us; a little remembrance of
Him from time to time, a little adoration: sometimes to pray
for His grace, sometimes to offer Him your sufferings, and
sometimes to return Him thanks for the favours He has given
you, and still gives you, in the midst of your troubles, and to
console yourself with Him the oftenest you can. Lift up your
heart to Him, sometimes even at your meals, and when you
are in company: the least little remembrance will always be
acceptable to Him. You need not cry very loud; He is nearer
to us than we are aware of.

It is not necessary for being with God to be always at
church; we may have an oratory of our heart, wherein to
retire from time to time, to converse with Him in meekness,
humility, and love. Every one is capable of such familiar
conversation with God, some more, some less: He knows
what we can do. Let us begin then; perhaps He expects but
one generous resolution on our part. Have courage. We have
but little time to live; you are near sixty-four, and I am almost
eighty. Let us live and die with God: sufferings will be
sweet and pleasant to us while we are with Him; and the
greatest pleasures will be, without Him, a cruel punishment to
us. May He be blessed for all. Amen.

From a letter of Brother Lawrence
The Practice of the Presence of God

AMOR DEI

Give me to be Thy child, and learn for ever at Thy knee.
Give me to grow weak and grey-headed, since Thou willst it so.
Bid me aside
Lay all the pleasures of my youth and pride,
Gladness as well,
Sweet ardours and bright hopes—I'll not rebel.

Only, I pray, keep me beside Thee all the night and day,
Only for all Thou takest give Thyself and past recall!
And when youth's gone
As men count going, twixt us two alone
Still let me be
Thy little child, left learning at Thy knee.

Anonymous

Something of the boy always remained in him. He said,
' The soul of the old man who plods his last stage slowly and
with bent head, laughs inwardly at being taken for a shadow
of something that was once alive. He knows he is the very
same boy who went as if he had wings and used to see
wonders.' And he notes how the kindness of youth to old
age is an unlooked for delight. ' Youth does not understand
that the Christian soul does not grow old. The one thing that
the old man cannot forget is his youth, for his youth is himself. Often he catches its sparkle and hears its good laughter
in his solitary soul when you think he dozes.' Once during
the South African war he received from his younger, very
youthful nephew, who was fighting there, a letter which he
could not read. ' But do not let him know this, or perhaps he
will not write to me again. How precious is a letter from
youth to age, even if age cannot decipher it.' Old age, he
used to say, has the same capacity and hunger for joy as youth
' and an even deeper need of Christ '.

Two panaceas he had for old age—love and prayer. ' It is

not years that make souls grow old, but having nothing to love, nothing to hope for.'

'If I cannot work or rise from my chair or my bed, love remains to me; I can pray.'

'If we are old and uninteresting, it is so to the world which is passing away moment by moment. To God, who made each of us for Himself, we are not uninteresting. And what we are to Him, that is what we really are. If our life is hid with Christ in God, however silently the years pass, we shall grow in humility in that secret place; our stillness will be full of happiness because full of love. "He that loveth dwelleth in God and God in him", and the soul that dwelleth in God must be ever growing in love, for God is love.'

'There is the testing of solitude; it means that Christ trusts us alone. When He was left alone upon the cross He never wavered in His witness; He maintained it by a solitary direct appeal to the eternal Father.'

'The soul whose prayer is its life lives in peace.'

Taken from, Father Congreve of Cowley
by Mildred Woodgate

3 WHEN FACING BEREAVEMENT AND DEATH

The souls of the righteous are in the hand of God, and there shall no torment touch them.

In the sight of the unwise they seemed to die: and their departure is taken for misery.

And their going from us to be utter destruction: but they are in peace.

For though they be punished in the sight of men, yet is their hope full of immortality.

And having been a little chastised, they shall be greatly rewarded: for God proved them, and found them worthy for himself.

As gold in the furnace hath he tried them, and received them
    as a burnt offering.
And in the time of their visitation they shall shine, and run to
    and fro like sparks among the stubble.
They shall judge the nations, and have dominion over the
    people, and their Lord shall reign for ever.
They that put their trust in him shall understand the truth :
    and such as be faithful in love shall abide with him :
    for grace and mercy is to his saints, and he hath care for
    his elect.

The Apocrypha   The Wisdom of Solomon

Though I walk through the valley of the shadow of death, I
    will fear no evil : for thou art with me; Thy rod and
Thy staff comfort me.

The Psalms

And one of the malefactors which were hanged railed on him,
    saying, If thou be the Christ, save thyself and us.
But the other answering rebuked him, saying, Dost not thou
    fear God, seeing thou art in the same condemnation?
    And we indeed justly; for we receive the due reward
    of our deeds : but this man hath done nothing amiss.
And he said unto Jesus, Lord, remember me when thou
    comest into thy kingdom.
And Jesus said unto him, Verily I say unto thee, Today thou
    shalt be with me in Paradise.

St. Luke's Gospel

THEY ARE ALL GONE INTO
THE WORLD OF LIGHT

They are all gone into the world of light !
    And I alone sit ling'ring here;
Their very memory is fair and bright,
    And my sad thoughts doth clear.

It glows and glitters in my cloudy breast
   Like stars upon some gloomy grove,
Or those faint beams in which this hill is dress'd,
    After the sun's remove.

I see them walking in an air of glory,
   Whose light doth trample on my days:
My days, which are at best but dull and hoary,
    Mere glimmering and decays.

O holy hope! and high humility,
   High as the Heavens above!
These are your walks, and you have show'd them me
    To kindle my cold love,

Dear, beauteous death! the Jewel of the Just,
   Shining nowhere, but in the dark;
What mysteries do lie beyond thy dust;
    Could man outlook that mark!

He that hath found some fledg'd bird's nest, may know
   At first sight, if the bird be flown;
But what fair well, or grove he sings in now,
    That is to him unknown.

And yet, as angels in some brighter dreams
   Call to the soul, when man doth sleep:
So some strange thoughts transcend our wonted themes,
    And into glory peep.

If a star were confin'd into a tomb
   Her captive flames must need burn there;
But when the hand that lock'd her up, gives room,
    She'll shine through all the sphere.

O Father of eternal life, and all
   Creator glories under thee!
Resume thy spirit from this world of thrall
    Into true liberty.

A.B.O.C.   H

Either disperse these mists, which blot and fill
  My perspective (still) as they pass,
Or else remove me hence unto that hill,
    Where I shall need no glass.
            Henry Vaughan   From Silex Scintillans

From LYCIDAS

*A Lament for a friend drowned in his passage from
Chester on the Irish Seas, 1637*

Weep no more, woeful Shepherds weep no more,
For Lycidas your sorrow is not dead,
Sunk though he be beneath the watry floar,
So sinks the day-star in the Ocean bed,
And yet anon repairs his drooping head,
And tricks his beams, and with new spangled Ore,
Flames in the forehead of the morning sky:
So Lycidas sunk low, but mounted high,
Through the dear might of him that walk'd the waves
Where other groves, and other streams along,
With Nectar pure his oozy Lock's he laves,
And hears the unexpressive nuptiall Song,
In the blest Kingdom meek of joy and love,
There entertain him all the Saints above,
In solemn troops, and sweet Societies
That sing, and singing in their glory move,
And wipe the tears for ever from his eyes,
Now Lycidas the Shepherds weep no more;
Hence forth thou art the Genius of the shore,
In thy large recompense, and shalt be good
To all that wander in that perilous flood.
    Thus sang the uncouth Swain to th'Okes and rills,
While the still morn went out with Sandals gray,
He touch'd the tender stops of various Quills,
With eager thought warbling his Dorick lay:

And now the Sun had stretch'd out all the hills,
And now was dropt into the Western bay;
At last he rose, and twitch'd his Mantle blew:
To morrow to fresh Woods, and Pastures new.

John Milton

He has outsoared the shadow of our night;
Envy and calumny and hate and pain,
And that unrest which men miscall delight,
Can touch him not and torture not again;
From the contagion of the world's slow stain
He is secure, and now can never mourn
A heart grown cold, a head grown gray in vain;
Nor, when the Spirit's self has ceased to burn,
With sparkless ashes load an unlamented urn. . . .

He is made one with Nature: there is heard
His voice in all her music, from the moan
Of thunder to the song of night's sweet bird;
He is a presence to be felt and known
In darkness and in light, from herb and stone,
Spreading itself where'er that Power may move
Which has withdrawn his being to its own;
Which wields the world with never-wearied love,
Sustains it from beneath, and kindles it above.

He is a portion of the loveliness
Which once he made more lovely: he doth bear
His part, while the one Spirit's plastic stress
Sweeps through the dull dense world, compelling there
All new successions to the forms they wear;
Torturing th'unwilling dross that checks its flight
To its own likeness, as each mass may bear;
And bursting in its beauty and its might
From trees and beasts and men into the Heaven's light . . .

The One remains, the many change and pass;
Heaven's light forever shines, Earth's shadows fly;

Life, like a dome of many-coloured glass,
Stains the white radiance of Eternity,
Until Death tramples it to fragments.—Die,
If thou wouldst be with that which thou dost seek!
Follow where all is fled!—. . . .

                    Percy Bysshe Shelley   From Adonais

IN MEMORIAM

Now fades the last long streak of snow,
    Now burgeons every maze of quick
    About the flowering squares, and thick
By ashen roots the violets blow.

Now rings the woodland loud and long,
    The distance takes a lovelier hue,
    And drown'd in yonder living blue
The lark becomes a sightless song.

Now dance the lights on lawn and lea,
    The flocks are whiter down the vale,
    And milkier every milky sail
On winding stream or distant sea;

Where now the seamew pipes, or dives
    In yonder greening gleam, and fly
    The happy birds, that change their sky
To build and brood; that live their lives

From land to land; and in my breast
    Spring wakens too; and my regret
    Becomes an April violet,
And buds and blossoms like the rest.

Love is and was my Lord and King,
    And in his presence I attend
    To hear the tidings of my friend,
Which every hour his couriers bring.

Love is and was my King and Lord,
　　And will be, tho' as yet I keep
　　Within his court on earth, and sleep
Encompass'd by his faithful guard,

And hear at times a sentinel
　　Who moves about from place to place,
　　And whispers to the worlds of space,
In the deep night, that all is well.

Lord Tennyson

ETERNAL LIFE

There is nothing in the world of which I feel so certain. I have no idea what it will be like, and I am glad that I have not, as I am sure it would be wrong. I do not want it for myself as mere continuance, but I want it for my understanding of life. And moreover 'God is love' appears to me nonsense in view of the world He has made, if there is no other.

William Temple

SOCRATES SPEAKS TO A FRIEND OF THE LIGHT BEYOND THE SHADOW OF THE CAVE

Imagine a number of men living in an underground cavernous chamber, with an entrance open to the light, extending along the entire length of the cavern, in which they have been confined, from their childhood, with their legs and necks so shackled, that they are obliged to sit still and look straight forwards, because their chains render it impossible for them to turn their heads round : and imagine a bright fire burning some way off, above and behind them, and an elevated roadway passing between the fire and the prisoners, with a low wall built along it, like the screens which conjurors put up in front of their audience, and above which they exhibit their wonders.

I have it, he replied.

Also figure to yourself a number of persons walking behind this wall, and carrying with them statues of men, and images of other animals, wrought in wood and stone and all kinds of materials, together with various other articles, which overtop the wall; and, as you might expect, let some of the passers-by be talking, and others silent.

You are describing a strange scene, and strange prisoners.

They resemble us, I replied. For let me ask you, in the first place, whether persons so confined could have seen anything of themselves or of each other, beyond the shadows thrown by the fire upon the part of the cavern facing them?

Certainly not, if you suppose them to have been compelled all their lifetime to keep their heads unmoved.

And is not their knowledge of the things carried past them equally limited?

Unquestionably it is.

And if they were able to converse with one another, do you not think that they would be in the habit of giving names to the objects which they saw before them?

Doubtless they would.

Again: if their prison-house returned an echo from the part facing them, whenever one of the passers-by opened his lips, to what, let me ask you, could they refer the voice, if not to the shadow which was passing?

Unquestionably they would refer it to that.

Then surely such persons would hold the shadows of those manufactured articles to be the only realities.

Without a doubt they would.

Now consider what would happen if the course of nature brought them a release from their fetters, and a remedy for their foolishness, in the following manner. Let us suppose that one of them has been released, and compelled suddenly to stand up, and turn his neck round and walk with open eyes towards the light; and let us suppose that he goes through all these actions with pain, and that the dazzling splendour renders him incapable of discerning those objects of which he used formerly to see the shadows. What answer should you expect him to make, if some one were to tell him that in those days he was watching foolish phantoms, but that now he is somewhat nearer to reality, and is turned towards things more real, and sees more correctly; above all, if he were to point out to him the several objects that are passing by, and question him, and compel him to answer what they are? Should you not expect him to be puzzled, and to regard his old visions as truer than the objects now forced upon his notice?

Yes, much truer.

And if he were further compelled to gaze at the light itself, would not his eyes, think you, be distressed, and would he not shrink and turn away to the things which he could see distinctly, and consider them to be really clearer than the things pointed out to him?

Just so.

And if some one were to drag him violently up the rough and steep ascent from the cavern, and refuse to let him go till he had drawn him out into the light of the sun, would he not, think you, be vexed and indignant at such treatment, and on reaching the light, would he not find his eyes so dazzled by the glare as to be incapable of making out so much as one of the objects that are now called true?

Yes, he would find it so at first.

Hence, I suppose, habit will be necessary to enable him to perceive objects in that upper world. At first he will be most successful in distinguishing shadows; then he will discern the reflections of men and other things in water, and afterwards the realities; and after this he will raise his eyes to encounter the light of the moon and stars, finding it less difficult to study the heavenly bodies and the heaven itself by night, than the sun and the sun's light by day.

Doubtless.

Last of all, I imagine, he will be able to observe and contemplate the nature of the sun, not as it *appears* in water or on alien ground, but as it *is* in itself in its own territory.

Of course.

His next step will be to draw the conclusion, that the sun

is the author of the seasons and the years, and the guardian of all things in the visible world, and in a manner the cause of all those things which he and his companions used to see.

Obviously, this will be his next step.

What then? When he recalls to mind his first habitation, and the wisdom of the place, and his old fellow-prisoners, do you not think he will congratulate himself on the change, and pity them?

Assuredly he will.

And if it was their practice in those days to receive honour and commendations one from another, and to give prizes to him who had the keenest eye for a passing object, and who remembered best all that used to precede and follow and accompany it, and from these data divined most ably what was going to come next, do you fancy that he will covet these prizes, and envy those who receive honour and exercise authority among them? Do you not rather imagine that he will feel what Homer describes, and wish extremely

'To drudge on the lands of a master,
Under a Portionless wight,'

and be ready to go through anything, rather than entertain those opinions, and live in that fashion?

For my own part, he replied, I am quite of that opinion. I believe he would consent to go through anything rather than live in that way.

And now consider what would happen if such a man were to descend again and seat himself on his old seat? Coming so suddenly out of the sun, would he not find his eyes blinded with the gloom of the place?

Certainly, he would.

And if he were forced to deliver his opinion again, touching the shadows aforesaid, and to enter the lists against those who had always been prisoners, while his sight continued dim, and his eyes unsteady,—and if this process of initiation lasted a considerable time,—would he not be made a laughing-stock, and would it not be said of him, that he had gone up

only to come back again with his eyesight destroyed, and that
it was not worth while even to attempt the ascent? And if any
one endeavoured to set them free and carry them to the light,
would they not go so far as to put him to death, if they could
only manage to get him into their power?

Yes.

The Republic of Plato   Book VII

THE AUTHOR'S EPITAPH,
MADE BY HIMSELFE

Even such is Time, which takes in trust
Our youth, our joys, and all we have,
And pays us but with age and dust;
Who in the dark and silent grave,
When we have wandered all our ways,
Shuts up the story of our days:
And from which earth, and grave, and dust,
The Lord shall raise me up I trust.

Sir Walter Raleigh

FIDELE

Fear no more the heat o' the sun,
    Nor the furious winter's rages;
Thou thy worldly task hast done,
    Home art gone, and ta'en thy wages:
Golden lads and girls all must,
As chimney-sweepers, come to dust.

Fear no more the frown o' the great,
    Thou art past the tyrant's stroke;
Care no more to clothe and eat;
    To these the reed is as the oak:
The sceptre, learning, physic, must
All follow this, and come to dust.

Fear no more the lightning-flash,
　　Nor the all-dreaded thunder-stone;
Fear not slander, censure rash;
　　Thou hast finish'd joy and moan:
All lovers young, all lovers must
Consign to thee, and come to dust.

No exorciser harm thee!
Nor no witchcraft charm thee!
Ghost unlaid forbear thee!
Nothing ill come near thee!
Quiet consummation have;
And renownèd be thy grave!

William Shakespeare

NEVER WEATHER-BEATEN SAIL

Never weather-beaten Sail more willing bent to shore,
Never tired Pilgrim's limbs affected slumber more,
Than my wearied sprite now longs to fly out of my troubled
　　breast.
　O come quickly, sweetest Lord, and take my soul to rest.

Ever-blooming are the joys of Heav'n's high paradise,
Cold age deafs not there our ears, nor vapour dims our eyes:
Glory there the sun outshines, whose beams the blessed only
　　see;
　O come quickly, glorious Lord, and raise my sprite to thee.

Thomas Campion

LIFE AND DEATH

Frail Life! in which, through mists of human breath
　We grope for truth, and make our progress slow,
Because by passion blinded; till, by death
　Our passions ending, we begin to know.

O reverend Death! whose looks can soon advise
E'en scornful youth, while priests their doctrine waste;
Yet mocks us too; for he does make us wise,
When by his coming our affairs are past.

O harmless Death! whom still the valiant brave,
The wise expect, the sorrowful invite,
And all the good embrace, who know the grave
A short dark passage to eternal light.

Sir William Davenant

ON TIME

Fly envious *Time*, till thou run out thy race,
Call on the lazy leaden-stepping hours,
Whose speed is but the heavy plummet's pace;
And glut thyself with what thy womb devours,
Which is no more than what is false and vain,
And merely mortal dross;
So little is our loss,
So little is thy gain.
For when as each thing bad thou hast entomb'd,
And last of all, thy greedy self consum'd,
Then long Eternity shall greet our bliss
With an individual kiss;
And joy shall overtake us as a flood,
When everything that is sincerely good
And perfectly divine,
With truth, and peace, and love shall ever shine
About the supreme Throne
Of him, t'whose happy making sight alone,
When once our heav'nly-guided soul shall climb,
Then all this earthly grossness quit,
Attir'd with stars, we shall for ever sit,
Triumphing over death, and chance, and thee, O Time.

John Milton

DEATH

Death, be not proud, though some have callèd thee
Mighty and dreadful, for thou art not so:
For those whom thou think'st thou dost overthrow
Die not, poor Death; nor yet canst thou kill me.
From Rest and Sleep, which but thy picture be,
Much pleasure, then from thee much more must flow;
And soonest our best men with thee do go—
Rest of their bones and souls' delivery!
Thou'rt slave to fate, chance, kings, and desperate men,
And dost with poison, war, and sickness dwell;
And poppy or charms can make us sleep as well
And better than thy stroke. Why swell'st thou then?
One short sleep past, we wake eternally,
And Death shall be no more: Death, thou shalt die!

John Donne

Almighty Father, Thy love is like a great sea that girdles the
earth. Out of the deep we come to float awhile upon its surface. We cannot sound its depth nor tell its greatness, only
we know it never faileth. The winds that blow over us are
the breathing of Thy Spirit; the sun that lights and warms
us is Thy truth. Now Thou does suffer us to sail calm seas;
now Thou dost buffet us with storms of trouble; on the crest
of waves of sorrow Thou dost raise us, but it is Thy love that
bears us up; in the trough of desolation Thou dost sink us,
that we may see nought but Thy love on every side. And when
we pass into the deep again the waters of Thy love encompass
and enfold us. The foolish call them the waters of misery
and death; those who have heard the whisper of Thy Spirit
know them for the boundless ocean of eternal life and love.

Anonymous

CHRIST SPEAKS

To him who ever thought with love of me
    Or ever did for my sake some good deed
    I will appear, looking such charity
    And kind compassion, at his life's last need
    That he will out of hand and heartily
    Repent he sinned and all his sins be freed.
                                    Gerard Manley Hopkins

LAST LINES

    No coward soul is mine,
No trembler in the world's storm-troubled sphere:
    I see Heaven's glories shine,
And Faith shines equal, arming me from fear.

    O God within my breast,
Almighty, ever-present Deity!
    Life—that in me has rest,
As I—undying Life—have power in Thee!

    Vain are the thousand creeds
That move men's hearts: unutterably vain;
    Worthless as withered weeds,
Or idlest froth amid the boundless main,

    To waken doubt in one
Holding so fast by Thine infinity;
    So surely anchored on
The steadfast rock of immortality

    With wide-embracing love
Thy Spirit animates eternal years,
    Pervades and broods above,
Changes, sustains, dissolves, creates, and rears.

Though earth and man were gone,
And suns and universes ceased to be,
   And Thou were left alone,
Every existence would exist in Thee.

There is not room for Death,
Nor atom that his might could render void:
   Thou—THOU art Being and Breath,
And what THOU art may never be destroyed.

Emily Brontë

I HAVE GOT MY LEAVE

I have got my leave. Bid me farewell, my brothers! I bow
to you all and take my departure.

Here I give back the keys of my door—and I give up all
claims to my house. I only ask for last kind words from you.

We were neighbours for long, but I received more than I
could give. Now the day has dawned and the lamp that lit my
dark corner is out. A summons has come and I am ready for
my journey.

Rabindranath Tagore   Gitanjali

GOD BE IN MY HEAD

God be in my head,
   And in my understanding;
God be in mine eyes,
   And in my looking;
God be in my mouth
   And in my speaking;
God be in my heart,
   And in my thinking;
God be at my end and at my departing.

Anonymous

4 IN DARKNESS AND ARIDITY

A thing of beauty is a joy for ever:
Its loveliness increases; it will never
Pass into nothingness; but still will keep
A bower for us, and a sleep
Full of sweet dreams, and health, and quiet breathing.
Therefore, on every morrow, are we wreathing
A flowery band to bind us to the earth,
Spite of despondence, of the inhuman dearth
Of noble natures, of the gloomy days,
Of all the unhealthy and o'er-darken'd ways
Made for our searching: yes, in spite of all,
Some shape of beauty moves away the pall
From our dark spirits. Such the sun, the moon,
Trees old and young, sprouting a shady boon
For simple sheep; and such are daffodils
With the green world they live in; and clear rills
That for themselves a cooling covert make
'Gainst the hot season; the mid forest brake,
Rich with a sprinkling of fair musk-rose blooms:
And such too is the grandeur of the dooms
We have imagined for the mighty dead;
All lovely tales that we have heard or read:
An endless fountain of immortal drink,
Pouring unto us from the heaven's brink.

    Nor do we merely feel these essences
For one short hour; no, even as the trees
That whisper round a temple become soon
Dear as the temple's self, so does the moon,
The passion poesy, glories infinite,
Haunt us till they become a cheering light
Unto our souls, and bound to us so fast,
That, whether there be shine, or gloom o'ercast,
They always must be with us, or we die.

John Keats   From Endymion

CARRION COMFORT

Not, I'll not, carrion comfort, Despair, not feast on thee;
Not untwist-slack they may be-these last strands of man
In me, ór, most weary, cry *I can no more.* I can;
Can something, hope, wish day come, not choose not to be.
But ah, but O thou terrible, why wouldst thou rude on me
Thy wring-world right foot rock? lay a lionlimb against me?
    scan
With darksome devouring eyes my bruisèd bones? and fan,
O in turns of tempest, me heaped there; me frantic to avoid
    thee and flee?

   Why? That my chaff might fly; my grain lie, sheer and
    clear.
Nay in all that toil, that coil, since (seems) I kissed the rod,
Hand rather, my heart lo! lapped strength, stole joy, would
    laugh, chéer.
Cheer whom though? the hero whose heaven-handling flung
    me, fóot tród
Me? or me that fought him? O which one? is it each one?
    That night, that year
Of now done darkness I wretch lay wrestling with (my God!)
    my God.

                                        Gerard Manley Hopkins

   My own heart let me more have pity on; let
Me live to my sad self hereafter kind,
Charitable; not live this tormented mind
With this tormenting mind tormenting yet.

   I cast for comfort I can no more get
By groping round my comfortless, than blind
Eyes in their dark can day or thirst can find
Thirst's all-in-all in all a world of wet.

Soul, self; come, poor Jackself, I do advise
You, jaded, let be; call off thoughts awhile
Elsewhere; leave comfort root-room; let joy size
At God knows when to God knows what; whose smile
's not wrung, see you; unforeseen times rather-as skies
Betweenpie mountains-lights a lovely mile.

Gerard Manley Hopkins

A PRAYER IN DARKNESS

This much, O heaven—if I should brood or rave
Pity me not, but let the world be fed.
Yea, in my madness if I strike me dead
Heed you the grass that grows upon my grave.

If I dare snarl between this sun and sod,
Whimper and clamour, give me grace to own
In sun and rain and fruit in season shown,
The shining silence of the scorn of God.

Thank God the stars are set beyond my power;
If I must travail in a night of wrath,
Thank God my tears will never vex a moth
Nor any curse of mine cut down a flower.

Men say the sun was darkened, yet I had
Thoughts it beat brightly, even on Calvary:
And He that hung upon the torturing Tree
Heard all the crickets singing, and was glad.

A very early poem by G. K. Chesterton

IN DARKNESS AND ARIDITY

Out of the depths have I cried unto thee, O Lord.

Lord, hear my voice:
Let thine ears be attentive
To the voice of my supplications.

If thou, Lord, shouldst mark iniquities,
O Lord, who shall stand?

But there is forgiveness with thee,
That thou mayest be feared.

I wait for the Lord, my soul doth wait,
And in his word do I hope.

My soul looketh for the Lord,
More than watchmen look for the morning;
Yea, more than watchmen for the morning.

O Israel, hope in the Lord;
For with the Lord there is mercy,
And with him is plenteous redemption.

And he shall redeem Israel
From all his iniquities.

The Psalms

ST. TERESA'S BOOKMARK

Let nothing disturb thee;
Let nothing dismay thee;
All things pass :
God never changes.
Patience attains
All that it strives for.
He who has God
Finds he lacks nothing :
God alone suffices.

Translated by E. Allison Peers

It is easier to be angry than to pity,
    it is easier to condemn than to understand,
easier to find the Uncelestial City
    than the dim counties of the Holy Land.

I too have raged, I too have sullenly rated,
   I too have judged men, being judged by these.
And I have loved far less than I have hated,
   and was proud of this, like all the Pharisees.

Shall not I, therefore, now that the day is over,
   remember, if men sinned, that they have suffered,
come back at nightfall an unfaithful lover,
   who would not understand the love they offered?

Shall I not see that to live is to have relinquished
   beauty to the sequestration of the dark,
and yet that the spirit of man, benighted, vanquished
   has folded wings, and shall use them as the lark

into the sun beyond the cold clouds flinging
her desperate hope, not reaching where she has
   striven,
but soaring forever beyond herself, and singing
   high above earth as she is low in heaven?

Shall I not confess that mine own evil humour
   and not man's failure forged this black despair,
and, while I wept, high up the golden rumour
   of the lark ascending fringed the quiet air?

Oh, I will listen to that, and when I falter,
   hold up my hands above me in my blindness,
you ancient virtues, man's immortal shelter,
   faith, and the courage to fail in all but kindness.

Hold up my hands! And, while the battle sways
   beneath the least of the watchers on the hill,
let me remember that, though my heart betrays
   the cause of man, you are his angels still;

that, while you watch, although the night descend,
   you uphold it in your hands, like the silk woof

of some black Sultan's palanquin, and bend
it vastly over the head of man for a roof

powdered with stars, and with the moon for a lamp,
confronting God, rejoinder to the tomb,
giving the soul of man, though the last trump
blare through the curtains, the right to his own room.
                        The Uncelestial City   Humbert Wolfe

ARIDITY

My heart is empty. All the fountains that should run
With longing, are in me
Dried up. In all my countryside there is not one
That drips to find the sea.
I have no care for anything thy love can grant
Except the moment's vain
And hardly noticed filling of the moment's want
And to be free of pain.
Oh, thou that art unwearying, that dost neither sleep
Nor slumber, who didst take
All care for Lazarus in the careless tomb, oh keep
Watch for me while I wake.
If thou think for me what I cannot think, if thou
Desire for me what I
Cannot desire, my soul's interior Form, though now
Deep-buried, will not die,
—No more than the insensible dropp'd seed which grows
Through winter ripe for birth
Because, while it forgets, the heaven remembering throws
Sweet influence still on earth,
—Because the heaven, moved moth-like by thy beauty, goes
Still turning round the earth.
                        C. S. Lewis   The Pilgrim's Regress

ARIDITY

O Soul, canst thou not understand
Thou art not left alone,
As a dog to howl and moan
His master's absence? Thou art as a book
Left in a room that He forsook,
But returns to by and by,
A book of His dear choice,—
That quiet waiteth for His Hand,
That quiet waiteth for His Eye,
That quiet waiteth for His Voice.

Michael Field

COMFORT WHEN WORK SEEMS DIFFICULT

They helped every one his neighbour; and everyone said to
his brother, Be of good courage. So the carpenter encouraged
the goldsmith, and he that smootheth with the hammer him
that smote the anvil, saying, It is ready for the sodering: and
he fastened it with nails, that it should not be moved. . . .
Thou art my servant; I have chosen thee and not cast thee
away. Fear thou not; for I am with thee: be not dismayed;
for I am thy God: I will strengthen thee; yea, I will uphold
thee.

The Book of Isaiah

TO A FRIEND
WHOSE WORK HAS COME TO NOTHING

Now all the truth is out,
Be secret and take defeat
From any brazen throat
For how can you compete,

Being honour bred, with one
Who, were it proved he lies,
Were neither shamed in his own
Nor in his neighbours' eyes?
Bred to a harder thing
Than Triumph, turn away
And like a laughing string
Whereon mad fingers play
Amid a place of stone,
Be secret and exult,
Because of all things known
That is most difficult.

William B. Yeats

I HAVE LOST MYSELF

Then first I knew the delight of being lowly; of saying to myself, 'I am what I am, nothing more'. 'I have failed,' I said, 'I have lost myself—would it had been my shadow.' I looked round : the shadow was nowhere to be seen. Ere long, I learned that it was not myself, but only my shadow, that I had lost. I learned that it is better, a thousand-fold, for a proud man to fall and be humbled, than to hold up his head in his pride and fancied innocence. I learned that he that will be a hero, will barely be a man; that he that will be nothing but a doer of his work, is sure of his manhood. In nothing was my ideal lowered, or dimmed, or grown less precious; I only saw it too plainly, to set myself for a moment beside it. Indeed, my ideal soon became my life; whereas, formerly, my life had consisted in a vain attempt to behold, if not my ideal in myself, at least myself in my ideal. Now, however, I took, at first, what perhaps was a mistaken pleasure, in despising and degrading myself. Another self seemed to arise, like a white spirit from a dead man, from the dumb and trampled self of the past. Doubtless, this self must again die and be buried, and again, from its tomb, spring a winged child; but of this my history as yet bears

not the record. Self will come to life even in the slaying of
self; but there is even something deeper and stronger than it,
which will emerge at last from the unknown abysses of the
soul : will it be as a solemn gloom, burning with eyes? or a
clear morning after the rain? or a smiling child, that finds
itself nowhere, and everywhere?

George Macdonald   Phantastes

PRAYER FOR RICH AND POOR

Now Lord, send them summer, some manner of joy,
Heaven after hence-going, that here have such default!
And have pity on the rich that relieve no prisoners
From the good things Thou hast given, the ungrateful many;
But, God, in Thy goodness, give them grace to amend.
But poor people, Thy prisoners Lord, in the pit of mischief,
Comfort those creatures that suffer many cares,
Through dearth or drought, all their days here,
Woe in winter-time, for want of clothing,
And in summer-time, seldom a full supper;
Comfort Thy care-stricken, Christ in Thy Kingdom.

William Langland   Visions from Piers Plowman
Translated into modern English by Nevill Coghill

O God that art the sole hope of the world,
The only refuge for unhappy men,
Abiding in the faithfulness of Heaven,
Give me a strong succour in this testing-place,
O King, protect Thy man from utter ruin,
Lest the weak flesh surrender to the tyrant,
Facing innumerable blows alone.
Remember I am dust and wind and shadow,
And life as fleeting as the flower of the grass.
But may the eternal mercy which hath shone from time of old
Rescue Thy servant from the jaws of the lie.

Thou Who didst come from on high in the cloak of the flesh,
Strike down the dragon with the two-edged sword
Whereby our mortal flesh can war with the winds
And break down strongholds, with our Captain, God. Amen.
      The Venerable Bede   Translated by Helen Waddell

Lord, since Thou hast taken from me all that I had of Thee,
yet of Thy grace leave me the gift which every dog has by
nature: that of being true to Thee in my distress, when I am
deprived of all consolation. This I desire more fervently than
Thy heavenly Kingdom. Amen.
                              Mechthild of Magdeburg

5 THE COMFORT OF REPENTANCE AND FORGIVENESS

All the paths of the Lord are loving-kindness and truth
Unto such as keep his covenant and his testimonies. . . .

Mine eyes are ever toward the Lord;
For he shall pluck my feet out of the net.

Turn thee unto me, and have mercy upon me;
For I am desolate and afflicted.

The troubles of my heart are enlarged:
O bring thou me out of my distresses. . . .

Have mercy upon me, O God, according to thy loving
      kindness:
According to the multitude of thy tender mercies blot out
      my transgressions.

Wash me thoroughly from mine iniquity,
And cleanse me from my sin.

For I acknowledge my transgressions:
And my sin is ever before me. . . .

Hide thy face from my sins,
And blot out all mine iniquities.

Create in me a clean heart, O God;
And renew a right spirit within me.

Cast me not away from thy presence;
And take not thy holy spirit from me.

Restore unto me the joy of thy salvation:
And uphold me with a free spirit. . . .

The sacrifices of God are a broken spirit:
A broken and contrite heart, O God, thou wilt not despise. . . .

Bless the Lord, O my soul;
And all that is within me, bless his holy name.

Bless the Lord, O my soul,
And forget not all his benefits:

Who forgiveth all thine iniquities;
Who healeth all thy diseases;

Who redeemeth thy life from destruction;
Who crowneth thee with loving-kindness and tender
    mercies: . . .

The Lord is full of compassion and gracious,
Slow to anger, and plenteous in mercy.

He will not always chide,
Neither will he keep his anger for ever.

He hath not dealt with us after our sins,
Nor rewarded us after our iniquities.

For as the heaven is high above the earth,
So great is his mercy toward them that fear him.

As far as the east is from the west,
So far hath he removed our transgressions from us.

Like us a father pitieth his children,
So the Lord pitieth them that fear him.

The Psalms

And he said, A certain man had two sons : and the younger
of them said to his father, Father, give me the portion of
goods that falleth to me. And he divided unto them his
living. And not many days after the younger son gathered all
together, and took his journey into a far country, and there
he wasted his substance with riotous living. And when he had
spent all, there arose a mighty famine in that land; and he
began to be in want. And he went and joined himself to one
of the citizens of that country; and he sent him into his fields
to feed swine. And he would fain have been filled with the
husks that the swine did eat : and no man gave unto him.
And when he came to himself, he said, How many hired
servants of my father's have bread enough and to spare, and I
perish here with hunger ! I will arise and go to my father,
and will say unto him, Father, I have sinned against heaven,
and before thee, I am no more worthy to be called thy son :
make me as one of thy hired servants. And he arose, and
came to his father. But when he was yet a great way off, his
father saw him, and had compassion, and ran, and fell on his
neck, and kissed him. And the son said unto him, Father,
I have sinned against heaven, and in thy sight, and am no
more worthy to be called thy son. But the father said to his
servants, Bring forth the best robe, and put it on him; and
put a ring on his hand, and shoes on his feet : and bring
the fatted calf, and kill it, and let us eat, and make merry :
for this my son was dead, and is alive again; he was lost and
is found. And they began to be merry.

Gospel of St. Luke

Our Lord of His mercy sheweth us our sin and our feebleness by the very sweet gracious light of Himself; for our sin is so vile and so horrible that He of His courtesy will not shew it to us but by the light of His grace and mercy. . . .

But our courteous Lord willeth not that His servants despair, for often nor for grievous falling: for our falling hindereth not Him to love us. . . .

He willeth that we be like Him in wholeness of endless love to ourself and to our even-Christians: no more than His love is broken to us for our sin, no more willeth He that our love be broken to ourself and to our even-Christians: but that we endlessly hate the sin and endlessly love the soul, as God loveth it. Then shall we hate sin like as God hateth it, and love the soul as God loveth it. And this word that He said is an endless comfort: *I keep thee securely.* . . .

And when we fall, hastily He raiseth us by His lovely calling and gracious touching. . . .

For it needeth us to fall, and it needeth us to see it. For if we never fell, we should not know how feeble and how wretched we are of our self, and also we should not fully know that marvellous love of our Maker. For we shall see verily in heaven, without end, that we have grievously sinned in this life, and notwithstanding this, we shall see that we were never hurt in His love, we were never the less of price in His sight. And by the assay of this falling we shall have an high, marvellous knowing of love in God, without end. For strong and marvellous is that love which may not, nor will not, be broken for trespass. . . .

And what time that we fall into sin and leave the mind of Him and the keeping of our own soul, then keepeth Christ alone all the charge; and thus standeth He sorrowfully and moaning.

Then belongeth it to us for reverence and kindness to turn us hastily to our Lord and leave Him not alone. He is here alone with us all: that is to say, only for us He is here. And what time I am strange to Him by sin, despair or sloth, then I let my Lord stand alone, in as much as it is in me. And thus it fareth with us all which be sinners. But though it be so that we do thus often times, His Goodness suffereth us never to be alone, but lastingly He is with us, and tenderly He excuseth us, and ever shieldeth us from blame in his sight. . . .

But all shall be well, and all shall be well, and all manner of thing shall be well.

Dame Julian of Norwich   *Revelations of Divine Love*

HE HATH GIVEN ME REST BY HIS SORROW, AND LIFE BY HIS DEATH

Now I saw in my dream, that the highway up which Christian was to go was fenced on either side by a wall, and the wall was called Salvation. Up this way, therefore, did burdened Christian run, but not without great difficulty, because of the load on his back.

He ran thus till he came to a place somewhat ascending; and upon that place stood a Cross, and a little below, in the bottom, a sepulchre. So I saw in my dream that just as Christian came up with the Cross, his burden loosed from off his shoulders, and fell off his back, and began to tumble, and so continued to do till it came to the mouth of the sepulchre, where it fell in, and I saw it no more.

Then was Christian glad and lightsome, and said with a merry heart, ' He hath given me rest by His sorrow, and life by His death '. Then he stood still a while to look and wonder; for it was very surprising to him that the sight of the Cross should thus ease him of his burden. He looked therefore, and looked again, even till the springs that were in his head sent the waters down his cheeks. Now as he stood looking and weeping, behold, three shining ones came to him, and saluted him with ' Peace be to thee '. So the first said to him, ' Thy sins be forgiven thee '; the second stripped him of his rags, and clothed him with a change of raiment; the third also set a mark on his forehead; and gave him a roll with a seal upon it, which he bid him look on as he ran, and that he should give it in at the celestial gate; so they went their way. Then Christian gave three leaps for joy, and went on singing.

John Bunyan   *The Pilgrim's Progress*

A HYMN TO GOD THE FATHER

Wilt Thou forgive that sin where I begun,
Which was my sin, though it were done before?
Wilt thou forgive that sin, through which I run,
And do run still : though still I do deplore?
When Thou hast done, Thou hast not done,
 For I have more.

Wilt Thou forgive that sin which I have won
Others to sin? and made my sin their door?
Wilt Thou forgive that sin which I did shun
A year, or two, but wallowed in, a score?
When Thou hast done, Thou hast not done,
 For I have more.

I have a sin of fear, that when I have spun
My last thread, I shall perish on the shore;
But swear by Thyself, that at my death Thy Son
Shall shine as He shines now, and heretofore :
And, having done that, Thou hast done,
 I fear no more.

John Donne

A LITANY

Drop, drop, slow tears,
 And bathe those beauteous feet
Which brought from Heaven
 The news and Prince of Peace :
Cease not, wet eyes,
 His mercy to entreat;
To cry for vengeance
 Sin doth never cease.

In your deep floods
    Drown all my faults and fears;
Nor let His eye
    See sin, but through my tears.

Phineas Fletcher

Bad I am, but yet thy child.
Father, be thou reconciled,
Spare thou me, since I see
With thy might that thou art mild.

I have life before me still
And thy purpose to fulfil;
Yea a debt to pay thee yet:
Help me, Sir, and so I will

Gerard Manley Hopkins

6 THE COMFORT OF THE WORD, AND OF PRAYER

Heaven and earth shall pass away, but my words shall not pass away.

St. Matthew's Gospel

From one Word are all things, and this one all things speak, and this is the beginning that speaks also to us.

Without this Word no one understands or judges rightly.

He to whom all things are one, and who reduceth all to one, and seeth all things in one, may be steadfast in his heart and abide in peace with God.

O Truth, my God! make me one with Thee in everlasting charity.

Thomas à Kempis   The Imitation of Christ

Wonderful is the depth of Thy words; whose surface, see, is
before us, gently leading on the little ones : and yet a wonderful deepness, O my God, a wonderful deepness. It is awe to
look into it; even an awfulness of honour, and a trembling of
love.

St. Augustine Confessions
Translated by E. J. Sheed

Whatsoever things were written aforetime were written for
our learning; that we through patience and comfort of the
Scriptures, might have hope.

Epistle to the Romans

For the Goodness of God is the highest prayer, and it cometh
down to the lowest part of our need. It quickeneth our soul
and bringeth it on life, and maketh it for to waxen in grace
and virtue. It is nearest in nature; and readiest in grace : for
it is the same grace that the soul seeketh, and ever shall seek
till we know verily that He hath us all in Himself enclosed.

For he hath no despite of that He hath made, nor hath He
any disdain to serve us at the simplest office that to our body
belongeth in nature, for love of the soul that He hath made to
His own likeness.

For as the body is clad in the cloth, and the flesh in the
skin, and the bones in the flesh, and the heart in the whole,
so are we, soul and body, clad in the Goodness of God, and
enclosed.

Beseeching is a true, gracious, lasting will of the soul,
owned and fastened into the will of our Lord by the sweet
inward work of the Holy Ghost. Our Lord Himself, He is the
first receiver of our prayer, as to my sight, and taketh it full
thankfully and highly enjoying; and He sendeth it up
above and setteth it in the Treasure, where it shall never
perish. It is there afore God with all His Holy continually
received, ever speeding [the help of] our needs; and when
we shall receive our bliss it shall be given us for a degree of
joy, with endless worshipful thanking from Him.

Full glad and merry is our Lord of our prayer; and He looketh thereafter and He willeth to have it because with His grace He maketh us like to Himself in condition as we are in kind: and so is His blissful will. Therefore he saith thus: *Pray inwardly, though thee thinketh it savour thee not (for it is profitable, though thou feel not, though thou see nought) yea, though thou think thou canst not. For in dryness and in barrenness, in sickness and in feebleness, then is thy prayer well-pleasant to me, though thee thinketh it savour thee nought but little. And so is all thy believing prayer in my sight.* For the meed and the endless thanks that He will give us, therefore He is covetous to have us pray continually in His sight. God accepteth the goodwill and travail of His servant, howsoever we feel: wherefore it pleaseth Him that we work both in our prayers and in good living, by His help and His grace, reasonably with discretion keeping our powers turned to Him, till when that we have Him that we seek, in fullness of joy: that is, Jesus.

And also to prayer belongeth thanking. Thanking is a true inward knowing, with great reverence and lovely dread turning ourselves with all our mights unto the working that our good Lord stirreth us to, enjoying and thanking inwardly. And sometimes, for plenteousness it breaketh out with voice, and saith: *Good Lord, I thank Thee! Blessed mayst Thou be!* And sometime when the heart is dry and feeleth not, or else by temptation of our enemy,—then it is driven by reason and by grace to cry upon our Lord with voice, rehearsing His blessed Passion and His great Goodness; and the virtue of our Lord's word turneth into the soul and quickeneth the heart and entereth it by His grace into true working, and maketh it pray right blisfully. And truly to enjoy our Lord, it is a full blissful thanking in His sight.

　　Dame Julian of Norwich　Revelations of Divine Love

COMFORT FOR THE MARTHAS

God does not conduct us all by the same way. It may chance that those who think themselves to be lower than all may be the most exalted in the eyes of the Lord; and though every soul . . . is called to prayer, it does not follow that all must be contemplatives. It is impossible, and she who is not contemplative might be greatly discouraged if she did not understand this truth : that contemplation is the gift of God, and it is not necessary for salvation, nor is it required of us as a condition of our reward, nor are we to think that anyone will demand it of us. . . . Saint Martha was holy, though we are not told that she was contemplative; and what more do you want than to become such as was this blessed woman, who deserved so often to entertain Christ, our Lord, and to give Him sustenance, to serve Him, and to eat at His table? If she had been like the Magdalene, rapt in contemplation, there would have been no-one to give to eat to this divine Guest . . . . Remember, it is necessary that some-one should cook the food, and think yourselves happy in serving with Martha; recollect that true humility largely consists in being very ready to be satisfied with what the Lord wishes to make of us; and always to consider ourselves unworthy to be called His servants.

Saint Teresa of Avila   The Way of Perfection
Translated by a Discalced Carmelite

PRAYER

Prayer, the Church's banquet, Angels' age,
    God's breath in man returning to his birth,
The soul in paraphrase, heart in pilgrimage,
    The Christian plummet sounding heav'n and earth;

Engine against th'Almighty, sinner's tower,
  Reversèd thunder, Christ-side-piercing spear,
The six-days-world transposing in an hour,

Softness, and peace, and joy, and love, and bliss,
  Exalted Manna, gladness of the best,
  Heaven in ordinary, man well dressed,
The milky way, the bird of Paradise,

    Church-bells beyond the stars heard, the soul's blood,
    The land of spices, something understood.
                                        George Herbert

Reading is good, hearing is good, conversation and meditation
are good; but then, they are only good at times and occasions,
in a certain degree, and must be used and governed with such
caution as we eat and drink and refresh ourselves, or they will
bring forth in us the fruits of intemperance. But the spirit of
prayer is for all times and all occasions, it is a lamp that is to
be always burning, a light to be ever shining; everything calls
for it, everything is to be done in it and governed by it,
because it is and means and wills nothing else but the whole
totality of the soul, not doing this or that, but wholly, incessantly given up to God to be where and what and how
He pleases.
                                William Law Letters

THE MORNING WATCH

O joys! Infinite sweetness! with what flowers,
And shoots of glory, my soul breaks, and buds!
    All the long hours
    Of night, and rest
    Through the still shrouds
    Of sleep, and clouds,
    This dew fell on my breast;
    O how it bloods,

And spirits all my earth! Hark! In what rings,
And hymning circulations the quick world
　　Awakes, and sings;
　　The rising winds,
　　And falling springs,
　　Birds, beasts, all things
　　Adore him in their kinds.
　　Thus all is hurled
In sacred hymns, and order, the great chime
And symphony of Nature. Prayer is
　　The world in tune,
　　A spirit voice,
　　And vocal joys
　　Whose echo is heaven's bliss.
　　O let me climb
When I lie down! The pious soul by night
Is like a clouded star, whose beams though said
　　To shed their light
　　Under some cloud
　　Yet are above,
　　And shine, and move
　　Beyond that misty shroud.
　　So in my bed
That curtained grave, though sleep, like ashes, hide
My lamp, and life, both shall in thee abide.

Henry Vaughan

From THE RIME OF
THE ANCIENT MARINER

'Beyond the shadow of the ship,
I watch'd the water-snakes:
They moved in tracks of shining white,
And when they rear'd, the elfish light
Fell off in hoary flakes.

Within the shadow of the ship
I watch'd their rich attire:
Blue, glossy green, and velvet black,
They coil'd and swam; and every track
Was a flash of golden fire.

O happy living things! no tongue
Their beauty might declare:
A spring of love gush'd from my heart,
And I bless'd them unaware:
Sure my kind saint took pity on me,
And I bless'd them unaware.

The selfsame moment I could pray;
And from my neck so free
The Albatross fell off, and sank
Like lead into the sea.

Farewell, farewell! but this I tell
To thee, thou Wedding-Guest!
He prayeth well, who loveth well
Both man and bird and beast.

He prayeth best, who loveth best
All things both great and small;
For the dear God who loveth us,
He made and loveth all.'

Samuel Taylor Coleridge

V. THE COMFORT WE HAVE IN LIVING IN THE WORLD OF THE IMAGINATION

1 HEAVEN

THE HEAVEN OF ANCIENT EGYPT

I have heard those songs which are inscribed in the ancient sepulchres and what they tell in praise of life on earth and belittling the region of the dead. Yet wherefore do they this in regard to the land of Eternity, the just and the fair, where fear is not? Wrangling is its abhorrence, nor does any there gird himself against his fellow. That land, free of enemies!— all our kinsmen from the earliest days of time rest within it. The children of millions of millions come thither, every-one. For none may tarry in the land of Egypt; none there is that passeth not thither. The span of our earthly deeds is as a dream; but fair is the welcome that awaits him who has reached the hills of the West.

Neferhotep

DANTE'S HEAVEN

All that he can say is only a shadow of what he has seen.

'The glory of Him who moves all things soe'er
  Impenetrates the universe, and bright
  The splendour burns, more here and lesser there.

'Within that heav'n which most receives His light
  Was I, and saw such things as man nor knows
  Nor skills to tell, returning from that height;

'For when our intellect is drawing close
    To its desire, its paths are so profound
    That memory cannot follow where it goes.

'Yet now, of that blest realm whate'er is found
    Here in my mind still treasured and possessed
    Must set the strain for all my song to sound. . . .

'O power divine, grant me in song to show
    The blest realm's image—shadow though it be—
    Stamped on my brain. . . .'

THE CELESTIAL ROSE

The saints in heaven form the petals of a snow-white rose.

'So, as I looked to greater joyances
    The gems and flowers were changed, and I beheld
    Both courts of Heaven in true appearances.

'Splendour of God, whereby these eyes beheld
    Thy true realm's triumph, grant me power to say
    How that exalted triumph I beheld.

'In yonder heaven the *lumen gloriae*
    Reveals the Maker to created mind
    Which in His sight alone finds peace for aye.

'In figure of a circle it doth wind
    So wide and far that its circumference
    About the sun itself would loosely bind.

'The whole is fashioned from a radiance
    Shone from above the *Primum mobile*,
    Which draws vitality and virtue hence.

'As water by a mountain's foot may be
    A glass wherein it sees itself so fair,
    Decked out in grass and flowers luxuriantly,

' So, mirrored in that light, tier upon tier,
    On myriad thrones, rising on every side,
    Those who from here returned I gazed on there.

' If in its inmost petals can reside
    So vast a light, in such a rose as this
    What width immense must in the rim abide?

' My sight, being undismayed, ne'er went amiss
    In all that amplitude and height, but knew
    The full extent and nature of such bliss. . . .

' So now, displayed before me as a rose
    Of snow-white purity, the sacred might
    I saw, whom with His blood Christ made His spouse

' But the other, winging ever in His sight,
    Chants praises to the glory it adores,
    Its Maker's good extolling in delight.

' As bees ply back and forth, now in the flowers
    Busying themselves, and now intent to wend
    Where all their toil is turned to sweetest stores,

' So did the host of Angels now descend
    Amid the Flower of the countless leaves,
    Now rise to where their love dwells without end.

' Their glowing faces were as fire that gives
    Forth flame, golden their wings; the purest snow
    The whiteness of their raiment ne'er achieves.

' Down floating to the Flower, from row to row,
    Each ministered the peace and burning love
    They gathered in their waftings to and fro.

' Between the Flower and that which blazed above
    The volant concourse interposed no screen
    To dim the splendour and the sight thereof;

' For God's rays penetrate with shafts so keen
   Through all the universe, in due degree,
   There's naught can parry them or intervene.

' Drawn from the new age of antiquity,
   This realm of saints, whose joy no dangers mar,
   Gazed on one sign in love and unity.

' O trinal light, which shining as one star
   It fills them with delight to gaze on there,
   Look down on us, storm-driven as we are.'

*St. Bernard prays to the Virgin that Dante may be granted
grace to behold God, and all the saints in heaven join with
him in prayer for one man.*

' " High noon of charity to those in bliss,
   And upon earth, to men in mortal plight,
   A living spring of hope, thy presence is.

' " Lady, so great thou art and such thy might,
   The seeker after grace who shuns thy knee
   May aim him prayer, but fails to wing the flight.

' " Not only does thy succour flow out free
   To him who asks, but many a time the aid
   Fore-runs the prayer, such largesse is in thee.

' " All ruth, all mercy are in thee displayed,
   And all munificence; in thee is knit
   Together all that's good in all that's made.

' " This man, who witnessed from the deepest pit
   Of all the universe, up to this height,
   The souls' lives one by one, doth now entreat

' " That thou, by grace, may grant to him such might
   That higher yet in vision he may rise
   Towards the final source of bliss and light.

' " And I who never burned for my own eyes
    More than I burn for his, with all my prayers
    Now pray to thee, and pray they may suffice,

' " That of all mortal clouding which impairs,
    Thine own prayers may possess the power to clean
    His sight, till in the highest bliss it shares.

' " And further do I pray thee, heavenly Queen,
    Who canst all that thou wilt, keep his heart pure
    And meet, when such great vision he has seen.

' " With thy protection render him secure
    From human impulse; for this boon the saints,
    With Beatrice, thronging fold hands and implore." '

THE VISION

' Henceforth my vision mounted to a height
    Where speech is vanquished and must lag behind,
    And memory surrenders in such plight.

' As from a dream one may awake to find
    Its passion yet imprinted on the heart,
    Although all else is cancelled from the mind,

' So of my vision now but little part
    Remains, yet in my inmost soul I know
    The sweet instilling which it did impart.

' So the sun melts the imprint on the snow,
    Even so the Sybil's wisdom that was penned
    On light leaves vanished on the winds that blow.

' O Light supreme, by mortal thought unscanned,
    Grant that Thy former aspect may return,
    Once more a little of Thyself relend.

‘ Make strong my tongue that in its words may burn
    One single spark of all Thy glory's light
    For future generations to discern.

‘ For if my memory but glimpse the sight
    Whereof these lines would now a little say,
    Men may the better estimate Thy might.

‘ The piercing brightness of the living ray
    Which I endured, my vision had undone,
    I think, if I had turned my eyes away.

‘ And I recall this further led me on,
    Wherefore my gaze more boldness yet assumed
    Till to the Infinite Good it last had won.

‘ O grace abounding, whereby I presumed
    So deep the eternal light to search and sound
    That my whole vision was therein consumed!

‘ In that abyss I saw how love held bound
    Into one volume all the leaves whose flight
    Is scattered through the universe around;

‘ How substance, accident, and mode unite
    Fused, so to speak, together, in such wise
    That this I tell of is one simple light.

‘ Yea, of this complex I believe mine eyes
    Beheld the universal form—in me,
    Even as I speak, I feel such joy arise.

‘ One moment brings me deeper lethargy
    Than twenty-five centuries brought the quest that
        dazed
    Neptune when Argo's shadow crossed the sea.

‘ And so my mind, bedazzled and amazed,
    Stood fixed in wonder, motionless, intent,
    And still my wonder kindled as I gazed.

'That light doth so transform a man's whole bent
 That never to another sight or thought
 Would he surrender, with his own consent;

'For everything the will has ever sought
 Is gathered there, and there is every quest
 Made perfect, which apart from it falls short.

'Now, even what I recall will be exprest
 More feebly than if I could wield no more
 Than a babe's tongue, yet milky from the breast;

'Not that the living light I looked on wore
 More semblances than one, which cannot be,
 For it is always what it was before;

'But as my sight by seeing learned to see,
 The transformation which in me took place
 Transformed the single changeless form for me.

'That light supreme, within its fathomless
 Clear substance, showed to me three spheres, which
   bare
 Three hues distinct, and occupied one space;

'The first mirrored the next, as though it were
 Rainbow from rainbow, and the third seemed flame
 Breathed equally from each of the first pair.

'How weak are words, and how unfit to frame
 My concept—which lags after what was shown
 So far, 'twould flatter it to call it lame!

'Eternal light, that in Thyself alone
 Dwelling, alone dost know Thyself, and smile
 On Thy self-love, so knowing and so known!

'The sphering thus begot, perceptible
 In Thee like mirrored light, now to my view—
 When I had looked on it a little while—

'Seemed in itself, and in its own self-hue
  Limned with our image; for which cause mine eyes
  Were altogether drawn and held thereto.

' As the geometer his mind applies
  To square the circle, nor for all his wit
  Finds the right formula, howe'er he tries,

' So strove I with that wonder—how to fit
  The image to the sphere; so sought to see
  How it maintained the point of rest in it.

' Thither my own wings could not carry me.
  But that a flash my understanding clove,
  Whence its desire came to it suddenly.

' High phantasy lost power and here broke off;
  Yet, as a wheel moves smoothly, free from jars,
  My will and my desire were turned by love,

' The love that moves the sun and the other stars.'
                    Dante   The Divine Comedy
  Translated by Dorothy L. Sayers and Barbara Reynolds

HEAVEN

Sing me the men ere this
Who, to the gate that is
A cloven pearl uprapt,
The big white bars between
With dying eyes have seen
The sea of jasper, lapt
About with crystal sheen;

And all the far pleasance
Where linkèd Angels dance,
With scarlet wings that fall

Magnifical, or spread
Most sweetly over-head,
In fashion musical,
Of cadenced lutes instead.

Sing me the tower they saw
Withouten fleck or flaw,
Aflame, more fine than glass
Of fair Abbayes the boast,
More glad than wax of cost
Doth make at Candlemas
The Lifting of the Host:

When many Knights and Dames,
With new and wondrous names,
One great Laudatè Psalm
Go singing down the street;—
'Tis peace upon their feet,
In hand 'tis pilgrim palm
Of Goddes Land so sweet:—

Where Mother Mary walks
In silver lily stalks,
Star-tirèd, moon-bedight;
When Cecily is seen,
With Dorothy in green,
And Magdelen all white,
The maidens of the Queen.

Sing on—the Steps untrod,
The Temple that is God,
Where incense doth ascend,
Where mount the cries and tears
Of all the dolorous years,
With moans that ladies send
Of durance and sore fears:—

And Him who sitteth there,
The Christ of purple hair,
And great eyes deep with ruth,
Who is of all things fair
That shall be, or that were,
The sum, and very truth.
Then add a little prayer,

That since all these be so,
Our Liege, who doth us know,
Would fend from Sathanas,
And bring us, of His grace,
To that His joyous place:
So we the Doom may pass,
And see Him in the Face.

   Dolben He would have his lady sing

GENERAL WILLIAM BOOTH
ENTERS HEAVEN

Booth led boldly with his big bass drum—
(Are you washed in the blood of the Lamb?)
The saints smiled gravely, and they said, 'He's come'.
(Are you washed in the blood of the Lamb?)
Walking lepers followed, rank on rank,
Lurching bravoes from the ditches dank,
Drabs from the alley-ways and drug-fiends pale—
Minds still passion-ridden, soul-powers frail!
Vermin-eaten saints with mouldy breath
Unwashed legions from the ways of death—
(Are you washed in the blood of the Lamb?)

Every slum had sent its half-a-score
The round world over—Booth had groaned for more.
Every banner that the wide world flies
Bloomed with glory and transcendant dyes.
Big-voiced lassies made their banjos bang!
Tranced, fanatical, they shrieked and sang,
(Are you washed in the blood of the Lamb?)

Hallelujah! It was queer to see
Bull-necked convicts with that land make free!
Loons with trumpets blowing blare, blare, blare,—
On, on, upward through the golden air!
(Are you washed in the blood of the Lamb?)

Booth died blind, and still by faith he trod,
Eyes still dazzled by the ways of God.
Booth led boldly, and he looked the chief:
Eagle countenance in sharp relief,
Beard a-flying, air of high command
Unabated in that Holy Land.
Jesus came out from the Court-House door,
Stretched his hand above the passing poor.

Booth saw not, but led his queer ones there
Round and round the mighty Court-House square.
Yet in an instant all that blear review
Marched on spotless, clad in raiment new.
The lame were straightened, withered limbs uncurled
And blind eyes opened on a new sweet world.

Drabs and vixens in a flash made whole!
Gone was the weasel-head, the snout, the jowl;
Sages and sibyls now, and athletes clean,
Rulers of empires, and of forests green!

The hosts were sandalled and the wings were fire!—
(Are you washed in the blood of the Lamb?)
But their noise played havoc with the angel choir.
(Are you washed in the blood of the Lamb?)

O, short Salvation! It was good to see
Kings and princes by the Lamb set free.
The banjos rattled and the tambourines
Jing-jing-jingling in the hands of queens!

And when Booth halted by the curb for prayer
He saw his Master through the flag-filled air.

Christ came gently with a robe and crown
For Booth the soldier, while the throng knelt down.
He saw King Jesus—they were face to face,
And he knelt a-weeping in that holy place!
(Are you washed in the blood of the Lamb?)

Vachel Lindsay

THE PEACE OF HEAVEN

My soul, there is a country
  Far beyond the stars,
Where stands a wingèd sentry
  All skilful in the wars :
There, above noise and danger,
  Sweet Peace sits crown'd with smiles,
And One born in a manger
  Commands the beauteous files.
He is thy gracious Friend,
  And—O my soul, awake!—
Did in pure love descend
  To die here for thy sake.
If thou canst get but thither,
  There grows the flower of Peace,
The Rose that cannot wither,
  Thy fortress, and thy ease.
Leave then thy foolish ranges;
  For none can thee secure
But One who never changes—
  Thy God, thy life, thy cure.

Henry Vaughan

You cannot traffick in peace,
and you cannot quote it as priced
in the Stock Exchange list. For Christ
(or whatever name is given
to the secret kingdom of heaven

in which we are and have
this shadow of life, that shadow of the grave)
to those who remain has said,
'Leave the dead to bury the dead!'
Rich though they be, you cannot sell
or buy their miracle,
nor be enriched by it, nor in Jerusalem,
sweet with the bugles blowing over them,
set up your market-place and have increase—Not thus comes
    peace,
nor freedom thus. But, slowly
making more holy what is holy
from the guarded pool
of the spirit, swift, cold, and beautiful,
in mists diaphanous his rain
a god draws back again;
and, as the sun builds with the clouds, of these
he builds his city of peace—
those stoneless streets at whose sweet end
friend meets with friend,
those star-hung towers in which the light of the sun
with the moon's light is one,
and love as visible and exquisite
as the little lamps with which the yew is lit,
so luminously red in the translucent green
of that deep air the lanterns of love are seen—
and the music of the meeting and the trumpet at the gate
sounding, 'All ye who enter here, abandon hate'.
Thus freedom comes, thus peace.

Humbert Wolfe   The Uncelestial City

THE CHILDLESS WOMAN IN HEAVEN

The children she had missed,
That never yet had birth,
Unwarmed, unfed, unkissed,
Soured all her joy on earth.

But when her day was done
And none were desolate,
Dusty and all alone,
She knocked at Heaven's gate.

Birds from a parapet
Called to her clear and shrill;
With 'Mother! Mother!' so wild and sweet,
And they were never still.

They were no birds at all,
But children small and bright;
When she came past the high wall
They were as birds in flight.

One was clasping her hand;
One was hugging her gown;
The littlest one of all the band
She lifted nor set him down.

Her hungry heart and cold
Was filled full and to spare:
One had her feet to hold,
One was kissing her hair.

The heart in her side
Forgot the ancient wrong:
When 'Mother! Mother! Mother!' they cried,
It soared like a bird's song.

Her arms were full of children,
As they were in the nest.
The littlest one crept softly in,
So he lay in her breast.

God's people passing by,
They smiled at her heart's ease;
'The mother of many children,
Her flowers grown to her knees'.

They dance, they laugh, they run,
She laughs with them at play;
Their pleasures are not done
Nor their sweet holiday.

When they lie down at night,
Soft pillows, downiest beds,
Her arms are full of her birds bright,
Dark heads and golden heads.

She draws them close to her,
Lest haply it should seem
That the new life in some wild fear
Was a dream, but a dream.

Katharine Tynan

PROMISE

Be not so desolate
Because thy dreams have flown
And the hall of the heart is empty
And silent as stone,
As age left by children
Sad and alone.

Those delicate children,
Thy dreams, still endure:
All pure and lovely things
Wend to the Pure.
Sigh not: unto the fold
Their way is sure.

The gentlest dreams, thy frailest,
Even those that were
Born and lost in a heart-beat,
Shall meet thee there.
They are become immortal
In shining air.

The unattainable beauty
The thought of which was pain,
That flickered in eyes and on lips
And vanished again:
That fugitive beauty
Thou shalt attain.

The lights innumerable
That led thee on and on,
The Masque of Time ended,
Shall glow into one.
It shall be with thee for ever
Thy travel done.

A E. (George William Russell)

IN SLEEP, A FORETASTE OF THE MERRY LAND

O Lord Jesus Christ, our Watchman and Keeper, take us to Thy care: grant that, our bodies sleeping, our minds may watch in Thee, and be made merry by some sight of that celestial and heavenly life, wherein Thou art the King and Prince, together with the Father and the Holy Spirit, where Thy angels and holy souls be most happy citizens. Oh purify our souls, keep clean our bodies, that in both we may please Thee, sleeping and waking, for ever. Amen.

Anonymous   Christian Prayers

CLOSE, MORTAL EYES

Close, mortal eyes: open, my eyes, in heaven.
On consolations that the poor devise,
On the clay image and the candles seven
    Close, mortal eyes.

Open upon the plains of the merry land,
Eternal eyes, on joy for ever whole :
Return with tidings I shall understand,
　　　Eyes of my soul.

The soul has eyes : alas, she has no tongue,
She has no word of all the mysteries,
No syllable that may be said or sung.
　　　Close, mortal eyes.

Ruth Pitter

HEAVEN AND HELL

*From the Screwtape Letters, written by an experienced demon
to a younger one, whom he instructs in the art of temptation,
and the destruction of souls. Screwtape has referred to a
description of heaven as ' the regions where there is only life
and therefore all that is not music is silence '.*

My dear Wormwood . . .

Music and silence—how I detest them both ! How thankful
we should be that ever since our Father entered Hell—though
longer ago than humans, reckoning in light years, could
express—no square inch of infernal space and no moment of
infernal time has been surrendered to either of those abomin-
able forces, but all has been occupied by Noise—Noise, the
grand dynamism, the audible expression of all that is exultant,
ruthless, and virile—Noise which alone defends us from
silly qualms, despairing scruples, and impossible desires. We
will make the whole universe a noise in the end. We have
already made great strides in this direction as regards the
Earth. The melodies and silences of Heaven will be shouted
down in the end. But I admit we are not yet loud enough, or
anything like it. Research is in progress.

*Yet, in the tumult of an air raid, Wormwood has the mis-
fortune to lose a soul in the moment of death. Screwtape
expresses himself upon this subject.*

My dear Wormwood . . .

You have let a soul slip through your fingers. The howl of
sharpened famine for that loss re-echoes at this moment
through all the levels of the Kingdom of Noise down to the
very Throne itself. It makes me mad to think of it. How well
I know what happened at the instant when they snatched him
from you! There was a sudden clearing of his eyes (was there
not?) as he saw you for the first time, and recognised the part
you had in him and knew that you had it no longer. Just
think (and let it be the beginning of your agony) what he felt
at that moment; as if a scab had fallen from an old sore,
as if he were emerging from a hideous, shell-like tetter, as if
he shuffled off for good and all a defiled, wet, clinging garment. By Hell, it is misery enough to see them in their mortal
days taking off dirtied and uncomfortable clothes and splash-
ing in hot water and giving little grunts of pleasure—stretching their eased limbs. What, then, of this final stripping, this
complete cleansing?

The more one thinks about it, the worse it becomes. He got
through so easily! No gradual misgivings, no doctor's sentence, no nursing home, no operating theatre, no false hopes
of life; sheer, instantaneous liberation. One moment it
seemed to be all our world, the scream of bombs, the fall of
houses, the stink and taste of high explosive on the lips and
in the lungs, the feet burning with weariness, the heart cold
with horrors, the brain reeling, the legs aching; next
moment all this was gone, gone like a bad dream, never again
to be of any account. Defeated, out-manœuvred fool! Did
you mark how naturally—as if he'd been born for it—the
earth-born vermin entered the new life? How all his doubts
became, in the twinkling of an eye, ridiculous? I know what
the creature was saying to itself! 'Yes. Of course. It always
was like this. All horrors have followed the same course,
getting worse and worse and forcing you into a kind of bottle-
neck till, at the very moment when you thought you must

be crushed, behold! you were out of the narrows and all was suddenly well. The extraction hurt more and more and then the tooth was out. The dream became a nightmare and then you woke. You die and die and then you are beyond death. How could I ever have doubted it?'

As he saw you, he also saw Them. I know how it was. You reeled back dizzy and blinded, more hurt by them than he had ever been by bombs. The degradation of it!—that this thing of earth and slime could stand upright and converse with spirits before whom you, a spirit, could only cower. Perhaps you had hoped that the awe and strangeness of it would dash his joy. But that is the cursed thing; the gods are strange to mortal eyes, and yet they are not strange. He had no faintest conception till that very hour of how they would look, and even doubted their existence. But when he saw them he knew that he had always known them and realised what part each one of them had played at many an hour in his life when he had supposed himself alone, so that now he could say to them, one by one, not 'Who *are* you?' but 'So it was *you* all the time'. All that they were and said at this meeting woke memories. The dim consciousness of friends about him which had haunted his solitudes from infancy was now at last explained; that central music in every pure experience which had always just evaded memory was now at last recovered. Recognition made him free of their company almost before the limbs of his corpse became quiet. Only you were left outside.

He saw not only Them; he saw Him. This animal, this thing begotten in a bed, could look on Him. What is blinding, suffocating fire to you, is now cool·light to him, is clarity itself, and wears the form of a Man. You would like, if you could, to interpret the patient's prostration in the Presence, his self-abhorrence and utter knowledge of his sins (yes, Wormwood, a clearer knowledge even than yours) on the analogy of your own choking and paralysing sensations when you encounter the deadly air that breathes from the heart of Heaven. But it's all nonsense. Pains he may still have to encounter, but they *embrace* those pains. They would not barter them for any earthly pleasure. All the delights of sense,

or heart, or intellect, with which you could once have tempted
him, even the delights of virtue itself, now seem to him in
comparison, but as the half nauseous attractions of a raddled
harlot would seem to a man who hears that his true beloved
whom he has loved all his life and whom he had believed to
be dead is alive and even now at his door. He is caught up
into that world where pain and pleasure take on transfinite
values and all our arithmetic is dismayed. Once more, the in-
explicable meets us. Next to the curse of useless tempters like
yourself the greatest curse upon us is the failure of our
Intelligence Department. If only we could find out what He
is really up to! Alas, alas, that knowledge, in itself so hateful
and mawkish a thing, should yet be necessary for Power!
Sometimes I am almost in despair. All that sustains me is the
conviction that our Realism, our rejection (in the face of all
temptations) of all silly nonsense and claptrap, *must* win in the
end. Meanwhile, I have you to settle with. Most truly do I
sign myself

Your increasingly and ravenously
affectionate uncle
Screwtape

C. S. Lewis   *The Screwtape Letters*

'Well done, thou good and faithful servant'. . . .

. . . . the redeemed soul, beyond all hope and nearly beyond
belief, learns at last that she has pleased Him whom she was
created to please. There will be no room for vanity then.
She will be free from the miserable illusion that it is her doing.
With no taint of what we should now call self-approval she
will most innocently rejoice in the thing that God has made
her to be, and the moment which heals her old inferiority
complex for ever will also drown her pride deeper than
Prospero's book. Perfect humility dispenses with modesty.
If God is satisfied with the work, the work may be satisfied
with itself; 'it is not for her to bandy compliments with her
Sovereign'. I can imagine someone saying that he dislikes
my idea of heaven as a place where we are patted on the

back. But proud misunderstanding is behind that dislike. In the end that Face which is the delight or the terror of the universe must be turned upon each of us either with one expression or with the other, either conferring glory inexpressible or inflicting shame that can never be cured or disguised. I read in a periodical the other day that the fundamental thing is how we think of God. By God Himself, it is not! How God thinks of us is not only more important, but infinitely more important. Indeed, how we think of Him is of no importance except in so far as it is related to how He thinks of us. It is written that we shall ' stand before ' Him, shall appear, shall be inspected. The promise of glory is the promise, almost incredible and only possible by the work of Christ, that some of us, that any of us who really chooses, shall actually survive that examination, shall find approval, shall please God. To please God . . . to be a real ingredient in the divine happiness . . . to be loved by God, not merely pitied, but delighted in as an artist delights in his work or a father in a son—it seems impossible, a weight or burden of glory which our thoughts can hardly sustain. But so it is.

C. S. Lewis
From a sermon called ' The Weight of Glory '

Bring us, O Lord God, at our last awakening, into the house and gate of heaven, to enter into that gate and dwell in that house where there shall be no darkness or dazzling, but one equal light; no noise nor silence, but one equal music; no fears nor hopes, but one equal possession; no ends nor beginnings, but one equal eternity; in the habitations of Thy glory and dominion, world without end. Amen.

John Donne

2 ANGELS

ISAIAH'S ANGELS

In the year that king Uzziah died I saw the Lord sitting upon
a throne, high and lifted up, and his train filled the temple.
Above him stood the seraphim: each one had six wings;
with twain he covered his face, and with twain he covered
his feet, and with twain he did fly. And one cried unto
another, and said, Holy, holy, holy, is the Lord of hosts: the
whole earth is full of his glory. And the foundations of the
thresholds were moved at the voice of him that cried, and the
house was filled with smoke. Then said I, Woe is me! for I
am undone; because I am a man of unclean lips, and I dwell
in the midst of a people of unclean lips: for mine eyes have
seen the King, the Lord of hosts. Then flew one of the
seraphim unto me, having a live coal in his hand, which he
had taken with the tongs from off the altar: and he touched
my mouth with it, and said Lo, this hath touched thy lips;
and thine iniquity is taken away, and thy sin purged. And I
heard the voice of the Lord, saying, Whom shall I send, and
who will go for us? Then I said, Here am I; send me.

The Book of Isaiah

THE ANGELS OF BETHLEHEM

And there were shepherds in the same country abiding in the
field, and keeping watch by night over their flock. And an
angel of the Lord stood by them, and the glory of the Lord
shone round about them: and they were sore afraid. And the
angel said unto them, Be not afraid; for behold, I bring you
good tidings of great joy which shall be to all the people:
for there is born to you this day in the city of David a Saviour,
which is Christ the Lord. And this is the sign unto you; Ye

shall find a babe wrapped in swaddling clothes, and lying in a
manger. And suddenly there was with the angel a multitude
of the heavenly host praising God, and saying,

> Glory to God in the highest,
> And on earth peace among men
> in whom he is well pleased.

And it came to pass, when the angels went away from them
into heaven, the shepherds said one to another, Let us now
go even unto Bethlehem, and see this thing that is come to
pass, which the Lord hath made known to us. And they
came with haste, and found both Mary and Joseph, and the
babe lying in the manger.

St. Luke's Gospel

DANTE'S ANGELS
THE ANGELS OF PROTECTION

Two angels are sent to guard the vale where departed spirits
are resting on their journey to Purgatory

'Now—in the hour that melts with homesick yearning
  The hearts of seafarers who've had to say
  Farewell to those they love, that very morning—

'Hour when the new-made pilgrim on his way
  Feels a sweet pang go through him, if he hears
  Far chimes that seem to knell the dying day—

'Did I suspend the office of my ears,
  And turn to watch a spirit rising there,
  And beckoning with his hand for listeners.

'Folding his palms, he lifted them in prayer,
  With gaze set eastward, that said visibly
  To God: "For Thee and nothing else I care."

'*Te lucis ante*, so devoutly he
   Breathed forth, so sweet the singing syllables,
   All sense of self was ravished out of me.

'The others joined their sweet, devout appeals
   To his, and sang the whole hymn afterward,
   Fixing their eyes on the eternal wheels.

'Sharpen thy sight now, Reader, to regard
   The truth, for so transparent grows the veil,
   To pass within will surely not be hard.

'I saw that goodly host stand sentinel
   Thereafter, speechless, in expectant love
   Scanning the sky with lowly looks, all pale;

'And then I saw descending from above
   Two angels, bearing fiery swords in hand,
   Broke short and bated at the points thereof.

'Green as fresh leaves new-budded on a wand
   Their raiment was, which billowed out and blew
   Behind, by flutter of green pinions fanned.

'One lit down just above us, and one flew
   To the far bank and poised there in his place,
   So that the folk lay folded 'twixt the two.

'Clearly I saw their bright heads, but the face
   Dazzled the eye beneath the locks of yellow,
   As every sense is vanquished by excess.'

GABRIEL

Dante, looking up to the face of the Virgin in heaven, asks his guide, who is the angel who stands before her?

'"Now to that face which most resembles Christ
   Lift up thy gaze; its radiance alone
   Can grant to thee the power to look on Christ."

' I looked, and on that countenance there shone
    Such bliss, bestowed by sacred minds who soar
    (For this created) through that lofty zone,

' That nothing I had looked on heretofore
    Had held me breathless in such wonderment,
    Or unto God so close a likeness bore.

' The angel who first thither made descent,
    Before her, sang " Hail, Mary, full of grace ",
    His wings spread wide unto their full extent.

' Response to the divine canticle of praise
    Was sung by all that court so blissfully,
    Still more serenely joyful was each face.

' " O holy father, who dost bear for me
    To stay below, quitting thine own dear site
    To which thou'rt destined in eternity,

' " Which angel is it who in such delight
    Looks in Our Lady's eyes with love so burning
    That like a fire he seems, so radiant bright?"

'Thus I deferred once more to the discerning
    Of one whom Mary's loveliness arrayed
    Even as the rising sun the star of morning.

' " All joy and excellence that dwell ", he said,
    " In soul or angel (and 'tis rightly so)
    In him is at its most sublime displayed;

' " For this is he who brought the palm below
    To Mary when the Son of God on high
    Bearing our fleshly burden willed to go." '

                    Dante The Divine Comedy Paradise
Translated by Dorothy L. Sayers and Barbara Reynolds

SAINT TERESA'S ANGEL

Our Lord was pleased that I should have at times a vision of this kind : I saw an angel close by me, on my left side, in bodily form. This I am not accustomed to see, unless very rarely. Though I have visions of angels frequently, yet I see them only by an intellectual vision, such as I have spoken of before. It was our Lord's will that in this vision I should see the angel in this wise. He was not large, but small of stature, and most beautiful—his face burning as if he were one of the highest angels, who seem to be all of fire : they must be those whom we call Cherubim. Their names they never tell me; but I see very well that there is in heaven so great a difference between one angel and another, and between these and the others, that I cannot explain it.

I saw in his hand a long spear of gold, and at the iron's point there seemed to be a little fire. He appeared to me to be thrusting it at times into my heart, and to pierce my very entrails; when he drew it out, he seemed to draw them out also, and to leave me all on fire with a great love of God. The pain was so great, that it made me moan; and yet so surpassing was the sweetness of this excessive pain, that I could not wish to be rid of it. The soul is satisfied now with nothing less than God. The pain is not bodily, but spiritual; though the body has its share in it, even a large one. It is a caressing of love so sweet which now takes place between the soul and God, that I pray God of His goodness to make him experience it who may think that I am lying.

> *The Life of Saint Teresa of Avila by Herself*
> *Translated from the Spanish by David Lewis*

GUARDIAN-ANGELS OF MEN

And is there care in heaven? and is there love
In heavenly spirits to these creatures base,
That may compassion of their evils move?
There is : else much more wretched were the case

Of men, than beasts. But, O! th'exceeding grace
Of highest God, that loves his creatures so,
And all his works with mercy doth embrace,
That blessed angels he sends to and fro,
To serve to wicked man, to serve his wicked foe.
How oft do they their silver bowers leave,
To come to succour us, that succour want?
How oft do they with golden pinions cleave
The flitting skies, like flying pursuivant,
Against foul fiends to aid us militant?
They for us fight, they watch and duly ward,
And their bright squadrons round about us plant,
And all for love, and nothing for reward:
O! why should heavenly God to men have such regard?

Edmund Spenser   The Faerie Queene

GUARDIAN ANGELS OF THE CREATURES

The sun descending in the west,
The evening star does shine;
The birds are silent in their nest,
And I must seek for mine.
The moon, like a flower,
In heaven's high bower,
With silent delight
Sits and smiles on the night.

Farewell, green fields and happy groves,
Where flocks have took delight.
Where lambs have nibbled, silent moves
The feet of angels bright;
Unseen they pour blessing,
And joy without ceasing,
On each bud and blossom,
And each sleeping bosom.

They look in every thoughtless nest,
Where birds are cover'd warm;

They visit caves of every beast,
To keep them all from harm.
If they see any weeping
That should have been sleeping,
They pour sleep on their head,
And sit down by their bed.

When wolves and tigers howl for prey,
They pitying stand and weep:
Seeking to drive their thirst away,
And keep them from the sheep.
But if they rush dreadful,
The angels, most heedful,
Receive each mild spirit,
New worlds to inherit.

And there the lion's ruddy eyes
Shall flow with tears of gold,
And pitying the tender cries,
And walking round the fold,
Saying, ' Wrath, by His meekness,
And, by His health, sickness
Is driven away
From our immortal day.

' And now beside thee, bleating lamb,
I can lie down and sleep;
Or think on Him who bore thy name,
Graze after thee and weep.
For, wash'd in life's river,
My bright mane for ever
Shall shine like the gold
As I guard o'er the fold.'

William Blake ·

TOM'S ANGEL

No one was in the fields
But me and Polly Flint,
When, like a giant across the grass,
The flaming angel went.

It was budding time in May,
And green as green could be,
And all in his height he went along
Past Polly Flint and me.

We'd been playing in the woods,
And Polly up, and ran,
And hid her face, and said,
'Tom! Tom! The Man! The Man!'

And I up-turned; and there,
Like flames across the sky,
With wings all bristling, came
The Angel striding by.

And a chaffinch overhead
Kept whistling in the tree
While the Angel, blue as fire, came on
Past Polly Flint and me.

And I saw his hair, and all
The ruffling of his hem,
As over the clovers his bare feet
Trod without stirring them.

Polly—she cried; and, oh!
We ran, until the lane
Turned by the miller's roaring wheel,
And we were safe again.

Walter de la Mare

THE CHILDREN'S ANGELS

See that ye despise not one of these little ones; for I say unto you, that in heaven their angels do always behold the face of my Father which is in heaven.

St. Matthew's Gospel

Beholding the face of God, in admiration of so great excellency they all adore him; and being rapt with the love of his beauty, they cleave inseparably for ever unto him. Desire to resemble him in goodness maketh them unweariable and even unsatiable in their longing to do by all means all manner good unto all the creatures of God, but especially unto the children of men : in the countenance of whose nature, looking downward, they behold themselves beneath themselves; even as upward, in God, beneath whom themselves are, they see the character which is nowhere but in themselves and us resembled.

Hooker Laws of Ecclesiastical Polity

3 THE WORLD OF THE POET

ODE TO A GRECIAN URN

Thou still unravish'd bride of quietness,
    Thou foster-child of Silence and slow Time,
Sylvan historian, who canst thus express
    A flowery tale more sweetly than our rhyme :
What leaf-fringed legend haunts about thy shape
    Of deities or mortals, or of both,
        In Tempe or the dales of Arcady?
    What men or gods are these? What maidens loth?
What mad pursuit? What struggle to escape?
        What pipes and timbrels? What wild ecstasy?

Heard melodies are sweet, but those unheard
  Are sweeter; therefore, ye soft pipes, play on;
Not to the sensual ear, but, more endear'd,
  Pipe to the spirit ditties of no tone:
Fair youth, beneath the trees, thou canst not leave
  Thy song, nor even can those trees be bare;
    Bold Lover, never, never canst thou kiss,
Though winning near the goal—yet, do not grieve;
    She cannot fade, though thou hast not thy bliss,
  For ever wilt thou love, and she be fair!

Ah, happy, happy boughs! that cannot shed
  Your leaves, nor ever bid the Spring adieu;
And, happy melodies, unwearièd,
  For ever piping songs for ever new;
More happy love! more happy, happy love!
  For ever warm and still to be enjoy'd,
    For ever panting and for ever young;
All breathing human passion far above,
    That leaves a heart high-sorrowful and cloy'd,
    A burning forehead, and a parching tongue.

Who are these coming to the sacrifice?
  To what green altar, O mysterious priest,
Lead'st thou that heifer lowing at the skies,
  And all her silken flanks with garlands drest?
What little town by river or sea-shore,
  Or mountain-built with peaceful citadel,
    Is emptied of its folk, this pious morn?
And, little town, thy streets for evermore
  Will silent be; and not a soul, to tell
    Why thou art desolate, can e'er return.

O Attic shape! fair attitude! with brede
  Of marble men and maidens overwrought,
With forest branches and the trodden weed;
  Thou, silent form! dost tease us out of thought
As doth eternity. Cold Pastoral!

When old age shall this generation waste,
   Thou shalt remain, in midst of other woe
Than ours, a friend to man, to whom thou say'st,
' Beauty is truth, truth beauty,—that is all
   Ye know on earth, and all ye need to know '.

John Keats

KUBLA KHAN : a Fragment

In Xanadu did Kubla Khan
A stately pleasure-dome decree :
Where Alph, the sacred river, ran
Through caverns measureless to man
Down to a sunless sea.
So twice five miles of fertile ground
With walls and towers were girdled round :
And there were gardens bright with sinuous rills
Where blossom'd many an incense-bearing tree;
And here were forests ancient as the hills,
Enfolding sunny spots of greenery.

But O, the deep romantic chasm which slanted
Down the green hill athwart a cedarn cover !
A savage place ! as holy and enchanted
As e'er beneath a waning moon was haunted
By woman wailing for her demon-lover !
And from this chasm, with ceaseless turmoil seething,
As if this earth in fast thick pants were breathing,
A mighty fountain momently was forced;
Amid whose swift half-intermitted burst
Huge fragments vaulted like rebounding hail,
Or chaffy grain beneath the thresher's flail :
And 'mid these dancing rocks at once and ever
It flung up momently the sacred river.
Five miles meandering with a mazy motion
Through wood and dale the sacred river ran,
Then reach'd the caverns measureless to man,
And sank in tumult to a lifeless ocean :

And 'mid this tumult Kubla heard from far
Ancestral voices prophesying war!
The shadow of the dome of pleasure
Floated midway on the waves;
When was heard the mingled measure
From the fountain and the caves.
It was a miracle of rare device,
A sunny pleasure-dome with caves of ice!

A damsel with a dulcimer
In a vision once I saw:
It was an Abyssinian maid,
And on her dulcimer she played,
Singing of Mount Abora.
Could I revive within me
Her symphony and song,
To such a deep delight 'twould win me,
That with music loud and long,
I would build that dome in air,
That sunny dome! those caves of ice!
And all who heard should see them there,
And all should cry, Beware! Beware!
His flashing eyes, his floating hair!
Weave a circle round him thrice,
And close your eyes with holy dread,
For he on honey-dew hath fed,
And drunk the milk of Paradise. . . .

                              Samuel Taylor Coleridge

. . . At that moment the author was unfortunately called out
by a person on business from Porlock and on his return found
to his mortification that though he retained some vague re-
collection of his vision, yet with the exception of eight or ten
scattered lines and images, all the rest had passed away.

                              (*Coleridge's preface to Kubla Khan*)

A PERSON FROM PORLOCK

There came a knocking at the front door,
The eternal, nameless caller at the door;
The sound pierced the still hall,
But not the stillness about his brain.
It came again. He arose, pacing the floor
Strewn with books, his mind big with the poem
Soon to be born, his nerves tense to endure
The long torture of delayed birth.

Delayed birth : the embryo maimed in the womb
By the casual caller, the chance cipher that jogs
The poet's elbow, spilling the cupped dream.
The encounter over, he came, seeking his room;
Seeking the contact with his lost self;
Groping his way endlessly back
On the poem's path, calling by name
The foetus stifling in the mind's gloom.

R. S. Thomas

THE PERSON FROM PORLOCK

Unkind fate sent the Porlock person
To collect fivepence from a poet's house;
Pocketing which old debt he drove away,
Heedless and gay, homeward bound for Porlock.

O Porlock person, habitual scapegoat
Should any masterpiece be marred or scotched,
I wish your burly fist on the front door
Had banged yet oftener in literature!

Robert Graves

THE WORLD OF SLEEP

O soft embalmer of the still midnight!
  Shutting, with careful fingers and benign,
Our gloom-pleased eyes, embower'd from the light,
  Enshaded in forgetfulness divine;
O soothest Sleep! if so it please thee, close,
  In midst of this thine hymn, my willing eyes,
Or wait the amen, ere thy poppy throws
  Around my bed its lulling charities;
  Then save me, or the passed day will shine
Upon my pillow, breeding many woes;
Save me from curious conscience, that still hoards
  Its strength, for darkness burrowing like a mole;
Turn the key softly in the oiled wards,
  And seal the hushed casket of my soul.

Keats

THE SECRET LAND

Every woman of true royalty owns
A secret land more real to her
Than this pale outer world:

At midnight when the house falls quiet
She lays aside needle or book
And visits it unseen.

Shutting her eyes, she improvises
A five-barred gate among tall birches,
Vaults over, takes possession.

Then runs, or flies, or mounts a horse
(A horse will canter up to greet her)
And travels where she will;

Can make grass grow, coax lilies up
From bud to blossom as she watches,
Lets fish eat out of her palm.

Has founded villages, planted groves
And hollowed valleys for brooks running
Cool to a land-locked bay.

I never dared question my muse
About the government of her queendom
Or its geography,

Nor followed her between those birches,
Setting one leg astride the gate,
Spying into the mist.

Yet she has pledged me, when I die,
A lodge beneath her private palace
In a level clearing of the wood
Where gentians grow and gillyflowers
And sometimes we may meet.

Robert Graves

SEEN FROM THE TRAIN

Somewhere between Crewkerne
and Yeovil it was. On the left of the line
Just as the crinkled hills unroll
To the plain. A church on a small green knoll—
A limestone church,
And above the church
Cedar boughs stretched like hands that yearn
To protect or to bless. The whole

Stood up, antique and clear
As a cameo, from the vale. I swear
It was not a dream. Twice, thrice had I found it
Chancing to look as my train wheeled round it.

But this time as I passed,
Though I gaped as I passed
All the way down the valley, the knoll was not there,
Nor the church, nor the trees it mounded.

What came between to unsight me? . . .
But suppose, only suppose there might be
A secret look in a landscape's eye
Following you as you hasten by,
And you have your chance—
Two or three chances
At most— to hold and interpret it rightly,
Or it is gone for aye.

There was a time when men
Would have called it a vision, said that sin
Had blinded me since to a heavenly fact.
Well, I have neither invoked nor faked
Any church in the air,
And little I care
Whether or no I shall see it again.
But blindly my heart is racked

When I think how, not twice or thrice,
But year after year in another's eyes
I have caught the look that I missed to-day
Of the church, the knoll, the cedars—a ray
Of the faith, too, they stood for,
The hope they were food for,
The love they prayed for, facts beyond price—
And turned my eyes away.

                                        C. Day Lewis

THE SECRET MUSE

Between the midnight and the morn,
To share my watches late and lonely,
There dawns a presence such as only
Of perfect silence can be born.

On the blank parchment falls the glow
Of more than daybreak : and one regal
Thought, like the shadow of an eagle,
Grazes the smoothness of its snow.
Though veiled to me that face of faces
And still that form eludes my art,
Yet all the gifts my faith has brought
Along the secret stair of thought
Have come to me on those hushed paces
Whose footfall is my beating heart.

Roy Campbell

To K. M.
*And there was a horse in the king's stables:
and the name of the horse was,*
Genius.

We sat and talked. . . . It was June, and the summer light
Lay fair upon ceiling and wall as the day took flight.
Tranquil the room—with its colours and shadows wan,
Cherries, and china, and flowers : and the hour slid on.
Dark hair, dark eyes, slim fingers—you made the tea,
Pausing with spoon uplifted, to speak to me.
Lulled by our thoughts and our voices, how happy were we!

And, musing, an old, old riddle crept into my head.
'Supposing I just say, *Horse in a field*', I said,
'What do you see?' And we each made answer : 'I—
A roan—long tail, and a red-brick house, near by.'
'I—an old cart-horse and rain!' 'Oh no, not rain;
A mare with a long-legged foal by a pond—oh plain!'
'And I, a hedge—and an elm—and the shadowy green
Sloping gently up to the blue, to the west, I mean!'. . . .

And now : on the field that I see night's darkness lies.
A brook brawls near : there are stars in the empty skies.
The grass is deep, and dense. As I push my way,
From sour-nettled ditch sweeps fragrance of clustering may.

I come to a stile. And lo, on the further side,
With still, umbrageous, night-clad fronds, spread wide,
A giant cedar broods. And in crescent's gleam—
A horse, milk-pale, sleek-shouldered, engendered of dream!
Startled, it lifts its muzzle, deep eyes agaze,
Silk-plaited mane. . . .
      'Whose pastures are thine to graze?
Creature, delicate, lovely, with woman-like head,
Sphinx-like, gazelle-like? Where tarries thy rider?' I said.
And I scanned by that sinking ship's thin twinkling shed
A high-pooped saddle of leather, night-darkened red,
Stamped with a pattern of gilding; and over it thrown
A cloak, chain-buckled, with one great glamorous stone,
Wan as the argent moon when o'er fields of wheat
Like Dian she broods, and steals to Endymion's feet.
Interwoven with silver that cloak from seam to seam.
And at toss of that head from its damascened bridle did beam
Mysterious glare in the dead of the dark. . . .
       'Thy name
Fantastical steed? Thy pedigree?
Peace, out of Storm, is the tale? *Or Beauty, of Jeopardy?*'...
The water grieves. Not a footfall—and midnight here.
Why tarries Darkness's bird? Mounded and clear
Slopes to yon hill with its stars the moorland sweet.
There sigh the airs of far heaven. And the dreamers' feet
Scatter the leagues of paths secret to where at last meet
Roads called Wickedness, Righteousness, broad-flung or strait,
And the third that leads on to the Queen of fair Elfland's
   gate. . . .

This then the horse that I see; swift as the wind;
That none may master or mount; and none may bind—
But she, his Mistress: cloaked, and at throat that gem—
Dark hair, dark eyes, slim shoulder. . . .
      God-speed, K.M.!
          Walter de la Mare

KING'S COLLEGE CHAPEL

When to the music of Byrd or Tallis,
    The ruffed boys singing in the blackened stalls,
The candles lighting the small bones on their faces,
    The Tudors stiff in marble on the walls,

There comes to evensong Elizabeth or Henry,
    Rich with brocade, pearl, golden lilies, at the altar,
The scarlet lions leaping on their bosoms,
    Pale royal hands fingering the crackling psalter,

Henry is thinking of his lute and of backgammon,
    Elizabeth follows the waving song, the mystery,
Proud in her red wig and green jewelled favours;
    They sit in their white lawn sleeves, as cool as history.

Charles Causley

SUNDAY MORNING, KING'S CAMBRIDGE

File into yellow candle light, fair choristers of King's
    Lost in the shadowy silence of canopied Renaissance stalls
In blazing glass above the dark glow skies and thrones and
    wings
    Blue, ruby, gold and green between the whiteness of the
    walls
And with what rich precision the stonework soars and springs
    To fountain out a spreading vault—a shower that never
    falls.
The white of windy Cambridge courts, the cobbles brown and
    dry,
The gold of plaster Gothic with ivy overgrown,
The apple-red, the silver fronts, the wide green flats and high,
The yellowing elm-trees circled out on islands of their own—
Oh, here behold all colours change that catch the flying sky
To waves of pearly light that heave along the shafted stone.

In far East Anglian churches, the clasped hands lying long
Recumbent on sepulchral slabs or effigied in brass
Buttress with prayer this vaulted roof so white and light and
    strong
And countless congregations as the generations pass
Join choir and great crowned organ case, in centuries of song
To praise Eternity contained in Time and coloured glass.

                    John Betjeman

The world of WORK, as a Poet would like it to be.

        There is no point in work
           unless it absorbs you
           like an absorbing game.

        If it doesn't absorb you
        if it's never any fun,
           don't do it.

When a man goes out to work
he is alive like a tree in spring,
he is living, not merely working.

When the hindus weave thin wool into long, long lengths of
    stuff
with their thin dark hands and their wide dark eyes and their
    still souls absorbed
they are like slender trees putting forth leaves, a long white
    web of living leaf,
        the tissue they weave,
and they clothe themselves in white as a tree clothes itself in
    its own foliage,
As with cloth, so with houses, ships, shoes, wagons or cups
    or loaves.

Men might put them forth as a snail its shell, as a bird that
    leans its breast against its nest, to make it round,

as the turnip models his round root, as the bush makes flowers
    and gooseberries,
        putting them forth, not manufacturing them,
and cities might be as once they were, bowers grown out
    from the busy bodies of people.
And so it will be again, men will smash the machines.

At last, for the sake of clothing himself in his own leaf-like
    cloth tissued from his life,
and dwelling in his own bowery house, like a beaver's nibbled
    mansion
And drinking from cups that came off his fingers like flowers
    off their five-fold stem,
he will cancel the machines we have got.

                        D. H. Lawrence   Work

PICTURES

Dora had been in the National Gallery a thousand times and
the pictures were almost as familiar to her as her own face.
Passing between them now, as through a well-loved grove,
she felt a calm descending on her. She wandered a little,
watching with compassion the poor visitors armed with guide
books who were peering anxiously at the masterpieces. Dora
did not need to peer. She could look, as one can at last when
one knows a great thing very well, confronting it with a
dignity which it has itself conferred. She felt that the pictures
belonged to her, and reflected ruefully that they were about
the only thing that did. Vaguely, consoled by the presence of
something welcoming and responding in the place, her footsteps took her to various shrines at which she had worshipped
so often before : the great light spaces of Italian pictures,
more vast and southern than any real South, the angels of
Botticelli, radiant as birds, delighted as gods, and curling like
the tendrils of a vine, the glorious carnal presence of Susanna
Fourment, the tragic presence of Margarethe Trip, the solemn
world of Piero della Francesca with its early-morning colours,
the enclosed and gilded world of Crivelli. Dora stopped at

last in front of Gainsborough's picture of his two daughters. These children step through a wood hand in hand, their garments shimmering, their eyes serious and dark, their two pale heads, round full buds, like yet unlike.

Dora was always moved by the pictures. Today she was moved, but in a new way. She marvelled, with a kind of gratitude, that they were all still here, and her heart was filled with love for the pictures, their authority, their marvellous generosity, their splendour. It occurred to her that here at last was something real and something perfect. Who had said that, about perfection and reality being in the same place? Here was something which her consciousness could not wretchedly devour, and by making it part of her fantasy make it worthless. . . .

The pictures were something real outside herself, which spoke to her kindly and yet in sovereign tones, something superior and good whose presence destroyed the dreary trance-like solipsism of her earlier mood. When the world had seemed to be subjective it had seemed to be without interest or value. But now there was something else in it after all.

These thoughts, not clearly articulated, flitted through Dora's mind. She had never thought about the pictures in this way before; nor did she draw now any very explicit moral. Yet she felt that she had had a revelation. She looked at the radiant, sombre, tender, powerful canvas of Gainsborough and felt a sudden desire to go down on her knees before it, embracing it, shedding tears.

Dora looked anxiously about her, wondering if anyone had noticed her transports. Although she had not actually prostrated herself, her face must have looked unusually ecstatic, and the tears were in fact starting into her eyes. She found that she was alone in the room, and smiled, restored to a more calm enjoyment of her wisdom. She gave a last look at the painting, still smiling, as one might smile in a temple, favoured, encouraged, and loved. Then she turned and began to leave the building.

Iris Murdoch   The Bell

4 THE WORLD OF SHIPS AND THE SEA

SHIP'S BELL

On cliffs against the sky
I stood with a cedar tree
That grew the way of the wind,
And looked down on the sea.

A ship was passing near
The coast. I could not tell
From lights lost in the mist—
But I heard a ship's bell.

Above the sea on the rocks
And the night closing around,
Above the wind on the cliffs—
A brave, lonely sound!

Fading out to the vast
Where the late splendours fell. . . .
Muffled and slow from the mist. . . .
The sound of a ship's bell!

Glenn Ward Dresbach

THE CHIME OF THE SEA

Consider the sea's listless chime:
Time's self it is, made audible,
The murmur of the earth's own shell.
Secret continuance sublime
Is the sea's end: our sight may pass
No furlong further. Since time was,
This sound hath told the lapse of time.

No quiet, which is death's,—it hath
The mournfulness of ancient life,
Enduring always at dull strife.
As the world's heart of rest and wrath,
Its painful pulse is in the sands.
Last utterly, the whole sky stands,
Grey and not known, along its path. . . .

Gather a shell from the strown beach
And listen at its lips : they sigh
The same desire and mystery,
The echo of the whole sea's speech.
And all mankind is thus at heart
Not anything but what thou art :
And Earth, Sea, Man, are all in each.

Dante Gabriel Rossetti

CHOOSING A MAST

This mast, new-shaved, through whom I rive the ropes
Says she was once an oread of the slopes,
Graceful and tall upon the rocky highlands,
A slender tree as vertical as noon,
And her low voice was lovely as the silence
Through which a fountain whistles to the moon,
Who now of the white spray must take the veil
And, for her songs, the thunder of the sail.

I chose her for her fragrance, when the spring
With sweetest resins swelled her fourteenth ring
And with live amber welded her young thews :
I chose her for the glory of the Muse,
Smoother of forms, that her hard-knotted grain,
Grazed by the chisel, shaven by the plane,
Might from the steel as cool a burnish take
As from the bladed moon a windless lake.

I chose her for her eagerness of flight
Where she stood tiptoe on the rocky height

Lifted by her own perfume to the sun,
While through her rustling plumes with eager sound
Her eagle spirit, with the gale at one,
Spreading wide pinions, would have spurned the ground
And her own sleeping shadow, had they not
With thymy fragrance charmed her to the spot.

Lover of song, I chose this mountain pine
Not only for the straightness of her spine
But for her songs : for there she loved to sing
Through a long noon's repose of wave and wing,
The fluvial swirling of her scented hair
Sole rill of song in all that windless air,
And her slim form the naiad of the stream
Afloat upon the languor of its theme;

And for the soldier's fare on which she fed :
Her wine the azure, and the snow her bread;
And for her stormy watches on the height,
For only out of solitude or strife
Are born the sons of valour and delight;
And lastly for her rich, exulting life,
That with the wind stopped not its singing breath
But carolled on, the louder for its death.

Under a pine, when summer days were deep,
We loved the most to lie in love or sleep :
And when in long hexameters the west
Rolled his grey surge, the forest for his lyre,
It was the pines that sang us to our rest,
Loud in the wind and fragrant in the fire,
With legioned voices swelling all night long,
From Pelion to Provence, their storm of song.

It was the pines that fanned us in the heat,
The pines, that cheered us in the time of sleet,
From which sweet gifts I set one dryad free;
No longer to the wind a rooted foe,
This nymph shall wander where she longs to be
And with the blue north wind arise and go,

A silver huntress with the moon to run
And fly through rainbows with the rising sun;

And when to pasture in the glittering shoals
The guardian mistral drives his thundering foals,
And when like Tartar horsemen racing free
We ride the snorting fillies of the sea,
My pine shall be the archer of the gale
While on the bending willow curves the sail
From whose great bow the long keel shooting home
Shall fly, the feathered arrow of the foam.

Roy Campbell

A PASSER BY

Whither, O splendid ship, thy white sails crowding,
Leaning across the bosom of the urgent West,
That fearest nor sea rising, nor sky clouding,
Whither away, fair rover, and what thy quest?
Ah! soon, when Winter has all our vales opprest,
When skies are cold and misty, and hail is hurling,
Wilt thou glide on the blue Pacific, or rest
In a summer haven asleep, thy white sails furling.

I then before thee, in the country that well thou knowest,
Already arrived am inhaling the odorous air:
I watch thee enter unerringly where thou goest,
And anchor queen of the strange shipping there,
Thy sails for awnings spread, thy masts bare:
Nor is aught from the foaming reef to the snow-capp'd
    grandest
Peak, that is over the feathery palms, more fair
Than thou, so upright, so stately and still thou standest.

And yet, O splendid ship, unhail'd and nameless,
I know not if, aiming a fancy, I rightly divine
That thou hast a purpose joyful, a courage blameless,
Thy port assured in a happier land than mine.

But for all I have given thee, beauty enough is thine,
As thou, aslant with trim tackle and shrouding,
From the proud nostril curve of a prow's line
In the offing scatterest foam, thy white sails crowding.

Robert Bridges

THE FISH

In a cool curving world he lies
And ripples with dark ecstasies.
The kind luxurious lapse and steal
Shapes all his universe to feel
And know and be; the clinging stream
Closes his memory, glooms his dream,
Who lips the roots o' the shore, and glides
Superb on unreturning tides.
Those silent waters weave for him
A fluctuant mutable world and dim,
When wavering masses bulge and gape
Mysterious, and shape to shape
Dies momently through whorl and hollow,
And form and line and solid follow
Solid and line and form to dream
Fantastic down the eternal stream;
An obscure world, a shifting world,
Bulbous, or pulled to thin, or curled,
Or serpentine, or driving arrows,
Or serene slidings, or March narrows.
There slipping wave and shore are one,
And weed and mud. No ray of sun,
But glow to glow fades down the deep
(as dream to unknown dream in sleep);
Shaken translucency illumes
The hyaline of drifting glooms. . . .

Rupert Brooke

FISHING

I will go with the first air of morning
To the land of Palestine.

Once, far from oasis,
Where dates grow costly and fine,
Men gathered the shining shoals,
That rippled up the road to the moon
The road of the moonshine.

Lovely the mercury, the flutter of the sea,
And the squares of the quicksilver nets,
And the drops of the sea divine,
As the fishes took the road to death;
Little waifs, little souls,
Lovely in their living and dying ever,
For luminous are their fins as feathers in the sun,
Sunny their scales as the sheen of the jay,
—When, silly tomboy, in sunshine he screams—
For inwardly lit are they;
Inwardly lit of their own light it seems,
Knowing a clarity ungiven to the day,
As on their branching reefs undersea they alight and sway
To the swell like swarming starlings in a windy tree.
Yet intimate with shadows that in air cannot be,
Dark are they, brooding, knowing, yet gay,
Shaft of sunlight theirs, deeps the lark never knows,
No, nor even the nightingale crucified
On the spine of the rose!

Beautiful their world, having no purpose, being for ever
        unseen.
None know that beauty for beauty's sake made,
Alone, content in the depth for ever it dwells;
Unstable as beech-leaves in May that eternal green,
The shifting, tremulous purple and brown of the rock-shade,

The frail light on the shallows,
And the young travelling shells
Like angels gently moving their wings
Over the dappled wells,
Rising and dipping as they swim in the sunlight;
And the waving, wooing anemones like hedgerow mallows,
And the Horned Iridescent whose life and death is a sleep.

Let me learn the wonder
Of those then who dwelt in the deep,
When Jesus went fishing.
When they by Jesus were lifted from the sea;
From the fast-flowing moonlight with His hands hauled He,
Singing a sailor's tune;
A tune men forgot, having short memory,
Or tired of knowing too well all the handcraft songs:
Potter's plaint or huckster's croon.

But a lilt that He knew
When making cord floats at Madonna's knee,
And singing now where sagged the barque side,
Tumbling black oval in the spate of the moon;
With Matthew, Mark, Luke, and the little John behind Him,
While gaped the rest of the crew;
While broke in hissing bubbles the eternal road of fire,
So the eyes were dazzled looking overside,
From His fingers fled the phosphorus away,
To the road no man may pursue.

For up that road went the feet of the Messiah,
Out of the horizon walked He,
Slim between the fishing smacks glancing not aside,
Gentle in His going, borne slightly on the tide,
Preaching gravely as He went to the groups of gaping fishes,
In the waters of Galilee.

Dorothy Wellesley

5 THE FAIRY WORLD

QUEEN MAB

O, then I see Queen Mab hath been
      with you.
She is the fairies' midwife, and she comes
In shape no bigger than an agate-stone
On the fore-finger of an alderman,
Drawn with a team of little atomies
Athwart men's noses as they lie asleep;
Her waggon-spokes made of long spinners' legs,
The cover of the wings of grasshoppers,
The traces of the smallest spider's web,
The collars of the moonshine's watery beams,
Her whip of cricket's bone, the lash of film,
Her waggoner a small grey-coated gnat,
Not half so big as a round little worm
Prick'd from the lazy finger of a maid;
Her chariot is an empty hazel-nut
Made by the joiner squirrel or old grub,
Time out o' mind the fairies' coachmakers.
And in this state she gallops night by night
Through lovers' brains, and then they dream of love.
                Shakespeare Romeo and Juliet

THE ELFIN WIFE

Gravely she goes about her little duties:
Smiling to show them she does not mind them:
Gravely she genuflects to small gnome beauties
Wheresoever she may find them.

She pauses in her sweeping to make herself some wishes:
She sits on her legs and thinks about the grate:
She feels a dear well-being when she does the dishes
Because of the smoothness of a china plate.

Whether it is linens, clean-smelling, piled,
Whether it is chairs, or rugs or dresses,
She goes among them like a dreamy child
Playing with the things she loves and possesses.

Can you not see her, cool eyes shady,
Cool hands gentle, cool cheeks white?
Can you not see her, my love's lady,
Doing the duties of her grave delight?

Jake Falstaff The Bulls of Spring

THE FAIRY WOOD

I have grown tired of sorrow and human tears;
Life is a dream in the night, a fear among fears,
A naked runner lost in a storm of spears.

I have grown tired of rapture and love's desire;
Love is a flaming heart, and its flames aspire
Till they cloud the soul in the smoke of a windy fire.

I would wash the dust of the world in a soft green flood;
Here between sea and sea in this fairy wood,
I have found a delicate wave-green solitude.

Here, in the fairy wood, between sea and sea,
I have heard the song of a fairy bird in a tree,
And that peace that is not in the world has flown to me.

Arthur Symons

REFLECTIONS

I saw a little boat lying. So still was the water here, that the boat needed no fastening. It lay as though some one had just stepped ashore, and would in a moment return. But as there were no signs of presence, and no track through the thick bushes; and, moreover, as I was in Fairy Land where one does very much as he pleases, I forced my way to the brink, stepped into the boat, pushed it, with the help of the tree-branches, out into the stream, lay down in the bottom, and let my boat and me float whither the stream would carry us. I seemed to lose myself in the great flow of sky above me unbroken in its infinitude, except when now and then, coming nearer the shore at a bend in the river, a tree would sweep its mighty head silently above mine, and glide away back into the past, never more to fling its shadow over me. I fell asleep in this cradle, in which mother nature was rocking her weary child; and while I slept, the sun slept not, but went round his arched way. When I awoke, he slept in the waters, and I went on my silent path beneath a round silvery moon. And a pale moon looked up from the floor of the great blue cave that lay in the abysmal silver beneath.

Why are all reflections lovelier than what we call the reality?—not so grand or so strong, it may be, but always lovelier? Fair as is the gliding sloop on the shining sea, the wavering, trembling, unresting sail below is fairer still. Yea, the reflecting ocean itself, reflected in the mirror, has a wondrousness about its waters that somewhat vanishes when I turn towards itself. All mirrors are magic mirrors. The commonest room is a room in a poem when I turn to the glass. . . . In whatever way it may be accounted for, of one thing we may be sure, that this feeling is no cheat; for there is no cheating in nature and the simple unsought feelings of the soul. There must be a truth involved in it, though we may but in part lay hold of its meaning. Even the memories of past pain are beautiful; and past delights, though beheld only through clefts in the grey clouds of sorrow, are lovely as

Fairy Land. But how have I wandered into the deeper fairy-land of the soul, while as yet I only float towards the fairy palace of Fairy Land! The moon, which is the lovelier memory or reflex of the down-gone sun, the joyous day seen in the faint mirror of the brooding night, has rapt me away.

I sat up in the boat. Gigantic forest trees were about me; through which, like a silver snake, twisted and twined the great river. The little waves, when I moved in the boat, heaved and fell with a plash as of molten silver, breaking the image of the moon into a thousand morsels, fusing again into one, as the ripples of laughter die into the still face of joy. The sleeping woods, in undefined massiveness; the water that flowed in its sleep; and, above all, the enchantress moon, which had cast them all, with her pale eye, into the charmed slumber, sank into my soul, and I felt as if I had died in a dream, and should never more awake.

George Macdonald   Phantastes

THE CITY OF THE BEES

Let us endeavour to picture it to ourselves—not as it appears to the bees, for we cannot tell in what magical, formidable fashion things may be reflected in the 6 or 7,000 facets of their lateral eyes and the triple cyclopean eye on their brow—but as it would seem to us, were we of their stature. From the height of a dome more colossal than that of St. Peter's at Rome, waxen walls descend to the ground, balanced in the void and the darkness; gigantic and manifold, vertical and parallel geometric constructions, to which, for relative precision, audacity, and vastness, no human structure is comparable. Each of these walls, whose substance still is immaculate and fragrant, of virginal, silvery freshness, contains thousands of cells stored with provisions sufficient to feed the whole people for several weeks. Here, lodged in transparent cells, are the pollens, love-ferment of every flower of spring, making brilliant splashes of red and yellow, of black and mauve. Close by, sealed with a seal to be broken only in days of supreme distress, the honey of April is stored, most limpid and perfumed of all, in twenty thousand reservoirs that form a long and magnificent embroidery of gold, whose borders hang stiff and rigid. Still lower the honey of May matures in great open vats by whose side watchful cohorts maintain an incessant current of air. In the centre, and far from the light whose diamond rays steal in through the only opening, in the warmest part of the hive, there stands the abode of the future; here does it sleep, and wake. For this is the royal domain of the brood-cells, set apart from the queen and her acolytes; about 10,000 cells wherein the eggs repose, 15 or 16,000 chambers tenanted by larvae, 40,000 dwellings inhabited by white nymphs to whom thousands of nurses minister. And finally, in the holy of holies of these parts, are the three, four, six or twelve sealed palaces, vast in size compared with the others, where the adolescent princesses lie who await their hour; wrapped in a kind of shroud, all of them motionless and pale, and fed in the darkness.

THE NUPTIAL FLIGHT

Around the virgin queen, and dwelling with her in the hive, are hundreds of exuberant males, for ever drunk on honey, the sole reason for their existence being one act of love. But, notwithstanding the incessant contact of two desires that elsewhere invariably triumph over every obstacle, the union never takes place in the hive, nor has it been possible to bring about the impregnation of a captive queen. While she lives in their midst the lovers about her know not what she is. They seek her in space, in the remote depths of the horizon, never suspecting that they have but this moment quitted her, have shared the same comb with her, have brushed against her, perhaps, in the eagerness of their departure. One might almost believe that those wonderful eyes of theirs, which cover their head as though with a glittering helmet, do not recognise or desire her save when she soars in the blue. Each day, from noon till three, when the sun shines resplendent, this plumed horde sallies forth in search of the bride, who is indeed more royal, more difficult of conquest, than the most inaccessible princess of fairy legend; for twenty or thirty tribes will hasten from all the neighbouring cities, her court thus consisting of more than ten thousand suitors; and from these ten thousand one alone will be chosen, for the unique kiss of an instant that shall wed him to death no less than to happiness; while the others will fly helplessly round the intertwined pair, and soon will perish without ever again beholding this prodigious and fatal apparition. . . .

Very few, I imagine, have profaned the secret of the queenbee's wedding, which comes to pass in the infinite, radiant circles of a beautiful sky. But we are able to witness the hesitating departure of the bride-elect, and the murderous return of the bride.

However great her impatience, she will yet choose her day and her hour, and linger in the shadow of the portal till a marvellous morning fling open wide the nuptial spaces in the depths of the great azure vault. She loves the moment when drops of dew still moisten the leaves and the flowers, when the last fragrance of dying dawn still wrestles with burning day, like a maiden caught in the arms of a heavy warrior; when through the silence of approaching noon is heard, once and again, a transparent cry that has lingered from sunrise.

Then she appears on the threshold—in the midst of indifferent foragers, if she has left sisters in the hive; or surrounded by a delirious throng of workers, should it be impossible to fill her place. She starts her flight backwards, returns twice or thrice to the alighting-board, and then, having definitely fixed in her mind the exact situation and aspect of the kingdom she has never yet seen from without, she departs like an arrow to the zenith of the blue. She soars to a height, a luminous zone, that other bees attain at no period of their life. Far away, caressing their idleness in the midst of the powers, the males have beheld the apparition, having breathed the magnetic perfume that spreads from group to group, till every apiary near is instinct with it. Immediately crowds collect and follow her into the sea of gladness, whose limpid boundaries ever recede. She, drunk with her wings, obeying the magnificent law of the race that chooses her lover, and enacts that the strongest alone shall attain her

in the solitude of the ether, she rises still; and, for the first
time in her life, the blue morning air rushes into her stigmata,
singing its song, like the blood of heaven, in the myriad tubes
of the tracheal sacs, nourished on space, that fill the centre
of her body. She rises still. A region must be found unhaunted by birds, that else might profane the mystery. She
rises still; and already the ill-assorted troop below are
dwindling and falling asunder. The feeble, infirm, the aged,
unwelcome, ill fed, who have flown from inactive or im-
poverished cities—these renounce the pursuit and disappear in
the void. Only a small, indefatigable cluster remain, sus-
pended in infinite opal. She summons her wings for one final
effort; and now the chosen of incomprehensible forces has
reached her, has seized her, and, bounding aloft with united
impetus, the ascending spiral of their intertwined flight whirls
for one second in the hostile madness of love. . . . She
descends from the azure heights and . . . will never again leave
the hive. . . . Prodigious nuptials these, the most fairylike
that can be conceived, azure and tragic, raised high above
life by the impetus of desire; imperishable and terrible,
unique and bewildering, solitary and infinite. An admirable
ecstasy, wherein death, supervening in all that our sphere has of
most limpid and loveliest, in virginal, limitless space, stamps
the instant of happiness on the sublime transparence of the
great sky; purifying in that immaculate light the something
of wretchedness that always hovers around love, rendering
the kiss one that can never be forgotten; and, content this
time with moderate tithe, proceeding herself, with hands that
are almost maternal, to introduce and unite, on one body, for
a long and inseparable future, two little fragile lives.

Maurice Maeterlinck   The Life of the Bee

FAIRY STORY

If meadow-grass can turn to milk,
And glassy ice to water—
If worms can fashion golden silk
To clothe a royal daughter,

If caterpillars, weaving, first,
A chrysalis, that's made to burst,
Can nibble out their way (head first)
    As butterflies, more splendid
    Than ladies who surround a throne—
Then who would make the silly moan
That fairy tales are ended?

If tiny wheelwrights of the dawn,
(Their silver threads unreeling)
Can decorate a garden's lawn
    With wheels (too fine for wheeling),
    If speckled eggs, as petal-frail
    As caskets in a fairy tale,
    Can hold a chorus, that will scale
    The skies, in rapture chanting,
    Then who on earth will dare to say
    That magic was for yesterday,
    And not for our enchanting?

                    Barbara Euphan Todd

6 THE WORLD OF HOME

THE LAKE ISLE OF INNISFREE

I will arise and go now, and go to Innisfree,
And a small cabin build there, of clay and wattles made;
Nine bean rows will I have there, a hive for the honey bee,
And live alone in the bee-loud glade.

And I shall have some peace there, for peace comes dropping
    slow,
Dropping from the veils of the morning to where the cricket
    sings;
There midnight's all a-glimmer, and noon a purple glow,
And evening full of the linnet's wings.

I will arise and go now, for always night and day
I hear lake water lapping with low sounds by the shore;
While I stand on the roadway, or on the pavements gray,
I hear it in the deep heart's core.

William B. Yeats

THE WISH

Well then! I now do plainly see,
This busy world and I shall ne'er agree.
The very honey of all earthly joy
Does of all meats the soonest cloy;
 And they, methinks, deserve my pity
Who for it can endure the stings,
The crowd and buzz and murmurings,
 Of this great hive, the city.

Ah, yet, ere I descend to the grave
May I a small house and large garden have;
And a few friends, and many books, both true
Both wise, and both delightful too!
 And since love ne'er will from me flee,
A Mistress moderately fair,
And good as guardian angels are,
 Only beloved and loving me.

O fountains! when in you shall I
Myself eased of unpeaceful thoughts espy?
O fields! O woods! when, when shall I be made
The happy tenant of your shade?
 Here's the spring-head of Pleasure's flood:
Here's wealthy Nature's treasury,
Where all the riches lie that she
 Has coin'd and stamp'd for good.

Pride and ambition here
Only in far-fetched metaphors appear;

Here nought but winds can hurtful murmurs scatter
And nought but Echo flatter.
  The gods, when they descended, hither
From heaven did always choose their way:
And therefore we may boldly say
  That 'tis the way too thither.

How happy here should I
And one dear She live, and embracing die!
She who is all the world, and can exclude
In deserts solitude.
  I should have then this only fear:
Lest men, when they my pleasure see,
Should hither throng to live like me,
  And so make a city here.

Abraham Cowley

A THANKSGIVING TO GOD
FOR HIS HOUSE

Lord, Thou hast given me a cell
  Wherein to dwell,
A little house, whose humble roof
  Is weather-proof;
Under the spars of which I lie
  Both soft and dry;
Where Thou my chamber for to ward
  Hast set a guard
Of harmless thoughts, to watch and keep
  Me, while I sleep
Low is my porch, as is my Fate,
  Both void of state;
And yet the threshold of my doore
  Is worn by th'poore,
Who thither come, and freely get
  Good words or meat:
Like as my Parlour, so my Hall
  And Kitchen's small:
A little Butterie, and therein
  A little Bin,

Which keeps my little loafe of Bread
  Unchipt, unflead:
Some little sticks of Thorne or Briar
  Make me a fire,
Close by whose living coale I sit,
  And glow like it.
Lord, I confesse, too, when I dine,
  The Pulse is Thine,
And all those other Bits, that bee
  There plac'd by Thee;
The Worts, the Purslain, and the Messe
  Of Water-cresse,
Which of Thy kindness Thou hast sent;
  And my content
Makes those, and my beloved Beet
  To be more sweet.
'Tis Thou that crown'st my glittering Hearth
  With guiltlesse mirth;
And giv'st me Wassail Bowles to drink,
  Spic'd to the brink.
Lord, 'tis Thy plenty-dropping hand,
  That soile's my land;
And giv'st me, for my Bushel sown,
  Twice ten for one:
Thou mak'st my teeming Hen to lay
  Her egg each day:
Besides my healthful Ewes to beare
  Me twins each yeare,
The while the conduits of my Kine
  Run Creame, (for Wine).
All these, and better, Thou dost send
  Me, to this end,
That I should render, for my part,
  A thankful heart;
    Which, fir'd with incense, I resigne,
    As wholly Thine;
But the acceptance, that must be,
  My Christ, by Thee.

Robert Herrick

AN OLD WOMAN OF THE ROAD

O, to have a little house!
To own the hearth and stool and all!
The heaped-up sods upon the fire,
The pile of turf against the wall!

To have a clock with weights and chains
And pendulum swinging up and down!
A dresser filled with shining delph,
Speckled and white and blue and brown!

I could be busy all the day
Clearing and sweeping hearth and floor,
And fixing on their shelf again
My white and blue and speckled store!

I could be quiet then at night
Beside the fire and by myself,
Sure of a bed, and loth to leave
The ticking clock and the shining delph!

Och! but I'm weary of mist and dark,
And roads where there's never a house or bush
And tired I am of bog and road
And the crying wind and the lonesome hush.

And I am praying to God on high,
And I am praying Him night and day,
For a little house—a house of my own—
Out of the wind's and the rain's way.

Padraic Colum

AT HOME, ALONE WITH THE DOG

I want nothing but your fire-side now.
Friend, you are sitting there alone I know,
And the quiet flames are licking up the soot,
Or crackling out of some enormous root :
All the logs on your hearth are four feet long.
Everything in your room is wide and strong
According to the breed of your hard thought.
Now you are leaning forward; you have caught
That great dog by the paw and are holding it,
And he looks sidelong at you, stretching a bit,
Drowsing with open eyes, huge, warm and wide,
The full hearth-length on his slow-breathing side.
Your book has dropped unnoticed : you have read
So long you cannot send your brain to bed.
The low quiet room and all its things are caught
And linger in the meshes of your thought.
(Some people think they know time cannot pause.)
Your eyes are closing now though not because
Of sleep. You are searching something with your brain;
You have let the old dog's paw drop down again. . . .
Now suddenly you hum a little catch,
And pick up the book. The wind rattles the latch;
There's a patter of light cool rain and the curtain shakes;
The silly dog growls, moves, and almost wakes.
The kettle near the fire one moment hums.
Then a long peace upon the whole room comes.
So the sweet evening will draw to its bedtime end.
I want nothing now but your fire-side, friend.

Harold Monro   Hearthstone

AT HOME, ALONE WITH THE CAT

As I mused by the hearthside,
    Puss said to me:
'There burns the fire, man,
    And here sit we.

'Four Walls around us
    Against the cold air;
And the latchet drawn close
    To the draughty Stair.

'A Roof o'er our heads
    Star-proof, moon immune,
And a wind in the chimney
    To wail us a tune.

'What Felicity!' miaowed he,
    'Where none may intrude;
Just Man and Beast—met
    In his Solitude!

'Dear God, what security,
    Comfort and bliss!
And to think, too, what ages
    Have brought us to this!

'You in your sheep's wool coat,
    Buttons of bone,
And me in my fur-about
    On the warm hearthstone.'

                              Walter de la Mare

7 TO END WITH,
A FEW COMIC VERSES

1.

I hate those potent madmen, who keep all
Mankind awake, while they, by their great deeds,
Are drumming hard upon this hollow world,
Only to make a sound to last for ages.

John Crowne

2.

In the City
they sell and buy,
and nobody ever
asks them why.

But since it contents them
to buy and sell,
God forgive them!
They might as well.

3.

You cannot hope
    to bribe or twist,
thank God! the
    British journalist.

But, seeing what
    the man will do
unbribed, there's
    no occasion to.

Humbert Wolfe   The Uncelestial City

AUNT MATILDA

My very strict Aunt Matilda can't
Ever forget that she's an aunt:

Her bracelets jingle like golden bells—
'Never forget what Auntie tells!'

And this is the thing she says for weeks—
'Always listen when Auntie speaks!'

My very strict Aunt Matilda might
Sometimes try to be more polite.

She couldn't be 'Aunt' if it weren't for me,
And this is a thing she'd hate, you see.

She couldn't be anything much at all—
Only Miss M. Matilda Hall.

Barbara Euphan Todd

HYSSOP

Said Judge Jessop, 'The hyssop
You think's in your wall
Correctly and strictly isn't hyssop at all'.
   'Isn't hyssop?' says I; 'Isn't hyssop', says he;
'By no means—not hyssop at all.'

'If my hyssop, Judge Jessop,
Isn't hyssop at all,
Tell me truly and duly why it grows on my wall?'
      'Why it grows on?' says he. 'Yes, it grows on,'
         says I,
'Why it grows and it grows on my wall.'

'On the Bisop', said Judge Jessop,
'(with the h out), we'll call,
And straightly, sedately, we'll resort to your wall.'
    'With a ladder?' says I. 'With a ladder', says he.
'And we'll ask him—"What's that on that wall?"'

So the Bisop, Judge Jessop,
And me—three in all—
Hell and leather together climbed up on my wall.
    'What's that there?' says I. 'What's that where?',
      says he;
'Why, house-leek,' said the Bisop. 'That's all.'
                   Walter de la Mare

A DAY IN SPRING

It was such a bright morning
That the cows, coming out of the cool dark barns feeling a
    good deal better,
Stood for a while and blinked,
And the young heifers said to each other,
'Oh my!
I never saw such a pretty day!
Let's jump over fences!
Let's go running up and down lanes with our tails in the air!'
And the old sisterly Jerseys
Thought to themselves, 'That patch of white clover
Over in the corner where the woodchucks are
Ought to be about ready for a good going over'.
Well, you never saw anything in your life like the way the
    young ducks were acting.
They were tearing in and out of the water
Making enough noise to be heard all over the township;
Even the robins were scandalized
And sat around in the trees looking sideways and one-eyed at
    them.
All the crawdads in that part of the creek
Picked up and moved, and the sober old snake
Slipped off his rock and went for a walk in the briars.

The ghosts of dead spiders
Had been busy all night, and every few feet along the road
There was a rope of gossamer.
The old white horse taking two gray people to meeting
Held up his head and said to himself,
' Look at those ropes!
Watch me bust them!
Whammy, there goes another one!
Doggone, I'll bet there isn't another horse in 42 counties
Can run along a road pulling a buggy and busting ropes and
        cables.'
And all of a sudden he felt so good
That he threw up his hindquarters and gave a twolegged kick.
And the old gray woman said, ' Well, I swan to gracious '.
And the old gray man got all tangled up in the lines
And nearly fell out of the buggy reaching for the whip.
' Whoa, there ', he said. ' Whoa, there, Roosevelt!
Hold on now! What in the Sam Hill is into you?'

About fourteen hundred Mayapple stems,
With their parasols up, marched down the hill,
And all the spring beauties turned up their pale, peaked noses
And said, ' Don't them Mayapples
Think they're somebody
With their bumbershoots up!'

Oh, it was a grand day, a specially grand day,
And all the flowers were so sweet
That the butterflies sneezed,
And the young goats and the lambs
Couldn't think of anything special enough
In the way of capers and didoes,
So they just stood still and looked wise.

                            Jake Falstaff   The Bulls of Spring

THE HEADLESS GARDENER

A Gardener, Tobias Baird,
Sent his head to be repaired;
He thought, as nothing much was wrong,
He wouldn't be without it long.

Ten years he's weeded path and plot,
A headless gardener, God wot,
Always hoping (hope is vain)
To see his noddle back again.

Don't pity him for his distress—
He never sent up his address.

Ian Serraillier

DUCKS

I

From troubles of the world
  I turn to ducks,
Beautiful comic things
Sleeping or curled
Their heads beneath white wings
By water cool,
Or finding curious things
To eat in various mucks
Beneath the pool,
Tails uppermost, or waddling
Sailor-like on the shores
Of ponds, or paddling
—Left! right—with fanlike feet
Which are for steady oars
When they (white galleys) float
Each bird a boat

Rippling at will the sweet
Wide waterway . . .
When night is fallen *you* creep
Upstairs, but drakes and dillies
Nest with pale water-stars,
Moonbeams and shadow bars,
And water-lilies :
Fearful too much to sleep
Since they've no locks
To click against the teeth
Of weasel and fox.
And warm beneath
Are eggs of cloudy green
Whence hungry rats and lean
Would stealthily suck
New life, but for the mien,
The bold ferocious mien
Of the mother-duck.

II

Yes, ducks are valiant things
On nests of twigs and straws,
And ducks are soothy things
And lovely on the lake
When that the sunlight draws
Thereon their pictures dim
In colours cool.
And when beneath the pool
They dabble, and when they swim
And make their rippling rings,
O ducks are beautiful things!

But ducks are comical things :—
As comical as you.
Quack !
They waddle round, they do.

They eat all sorts of things,
And then they quack.
By barn and stable and stack
They wander at their will,
But if you go too near
They look at you through black
Small topaz-tinted eyes
And wish you ill.
Triangular and clear
They leave their curious track
In mud at the water's edge,
And there amid the sedge
And slime they gobble and peer
Saying ' Quack ! quack !'

III

When God had finished the stars and whirl of coloured suns—
He turned His mind from big things to fashion little ones,
Beautiful tiny things (like daisies) He made, and then
He made the comical ones in case the minds of men
    Should stiffen and become
    Dull, humourless and glum :
And so forgetful of their Maker be
As to take even themselves—*quite seriously*.
Caterpillars and cats are lively and excellent puns.
All God's jokes are good—even the practical ones !
And as for the duck, I think God must have smiled a bit
Seeing those bright eyes blink on the day he fashioned it.
And He's probably laughing still at the sound that came out
  of its bill.

Frederick William Harvey

TO A FISH

You strange, astonished-looking, angle-faced,
　　Dreary-mouthed, gaping wretches of the sea,
　　Gulping salt water everlastingly,
Cold-blooded, though with red your blood be graced,

And mute, though dwellers, in the roaring waste;
　　And you, all shapes beside, that fishy be,—
　　Some round, some flat, some long, all devilry,
Legless, unloving, infamously chaste :—

O scaly, slippery, wet, swift, staring wights,
　　What is't ye do? What life lead? eh, dull goggles?
How do ye vary your vile days and nights?
　　How pass your Sundays? Are ye still but joggles
In ceaseless wash? Still nought but gapes, and bites,
　　And drinks, and stares, diversified with boggles?

A FISH ANSWERS

Amazing monster! that, for aught I know,
　　With the first sight of thee didst make our race
　　For ever stare! O flat and shocking face
Grimly divided from the breast below!
Thou that on dry land horribly dost go,
　　With a split body and most ridiculous pace,
　　Prong after prong, disgracer of all grace,
Long-useless-finned, haired, upright, unwet, slow!

O breather of unbreathable, sword-sharp air,
　　How canst exist? How bear thyself, thou dry
And dreary sloth? What particle canst share
　　Of the only blessed life, the watery?
I sometimes see of ye an actual *pair*
　　Go by! linked fin by fin! most odiously.
Leigh Hunt From 'The Fish, the Man, and the Spirit'

WELSH INCIDENT

‘ But that was nothing to what things came out
From the sea-caves of Criccieth yonder.’
‘ What were they? Mermaids? dragons? ghosts?’
‘ Nothing at all of any things like that.’
‘ What were they then?’
                 ‘ All sorts of queer things,
Things never seen or heard or written about,
Very strange, un-Welsh, utterly peculiar
Things. Oh, solid enough they seemed to touch,
Had anyone dared it. Marvellous creation,
All various shapes and sizes, and no sizes,
All new, each perfectly unlike his neighbour,
Though all came moving slowly out together.’
‘ Describe just one of them.’
               ‘ I am unable.’
‘ What were their colours?’
               ‘ Mostly nameless colours,
Colours you’d like to see; but one was puce
Or perhaps more like crimson, but not purplish.
Some had no colour.’
               ‘ Tell me, had they legs?’
‘ Not a leg nor foot among them that I saw.’
‘ But did these things come out in any order?
What o’clock was it? What was the day of the week?
Who else was present? How was the weather?’
‘ I was coming to that. It was half-past three
On Easter Tuesday last. The sun was shining.
The Harlech Silver Band played *Marchog Jesu*
On thirty-seven shimmering instruments,
Collecting for Caernarvon’s (Fever) Hospital Fund.
The populations of Pwllheli, Criccieth,
Portmadoc, Borth, Tremadoc, Penrhyndeudraeth,
Were all assembled. Criccieth’s mayor addressed them
First in good Welsh and then in fluent English,
Twisting his fingers in his chain of office,
Welcoming the things. They came out on the sand,

Not keeping time to the band, moving seaward
Silently at a snail's pace. But at last
The most odd, indescribable thing of all,
Which hardly one man there could see for wonder,
Did something recognizably a something.'
'Well, what?'
       'It made a noise.'
               'A frightening noise?'
'No, no.'
       'A musical noise? A noise of scuffling?'
'No, but a very loud, respectable noise—
Like groaning to oneself on Sunday morning
In Chapel, close before the second psalm.'
'What did the mayor do?"
          'I was coming to that.'

Robert Graves

DIARY OF A CHURCH MOUSE

(Lines, written to order on a set subject, to be spoken on the
wireless.)

Here among long-discarded cassocks,
Damp stools, and half-split open hassocks,
Here where the Vicar never looks
I nibble through old service books.
Lean and alone I spend my days
Behind this Church of England baize.
I share my dark forgotten room
With two oil-lamps and half a broom.
The cleaner never bothers me,
So here I eat my frugal tea.
My bread is sawdust mixed with straw
My jam is polish for the floor.

Christmas and Easter may be feasts
For congregations and for priests,

And so may Whitsun. All the same,
They do not fill my meagre frame,
For me the only feast at all
Is Autumn's Harvest Festival,
Where I can satisfy my want
With ears of corn around the font.
I climb the eagle's brazen head
To burrow through a loaf of bread.
I scramble up the pulpit stair
And gnaw the marrows hanging there.

It is enjoyable to taste
These items ere they go to waste,
But how annoying when one finds
That other mice with pagan minds
Come into church my food to share
Who have no proper business there.
Two field mice who have no desire
To be baptised, invade the choir.
A large and most unfriendly rat
Comes in to see what we are at.
He says he thinks there is no God
And yet he comes . . . . it's rather odd.
This year he stole a sheaf of wheat
(It screened our special preacher's seat),
And prosperous mice from fields away
Come in to hear the organ play,
And under cover of its notes
Ate through the altar's sheaf of oats.
A Low Church mouse, who thinks that I
Am too papistical, and High,
Yet somehow doesn't think it wrong
To munch through Harvest Evensong,
While I, who starve the whole year through,
Must share my food with rodents who
Except at this time of the year
Not once inside the church appear.

Within the human world I know
Such goings-on could not be so,
For human beings only do
What their religion tells them to.
They read the Bible every day
And always, night and morning, pray,
And just like me, the good church mouse,
Worship each week in God's own house.

But all the same it's strange to me
How very full the church can be
With people I don't see at all
Except at Harvest Festival.

John Betjeman

ACKNOWLEDGMENTS

Acknowledgment is gratefully made for permission to include the following works or extracts from them:

Ana, Marcos: *To the Faithful* (from FROM BURGOS JAIL, translated from the Spanish by Chloe Vulliamy and Stephen Sedley, published by Appeal for Amnesty in Spain).

Saint Augustine: THE CONFESSIONS OF SAINT AUGUSTINE, translated by E. J. Sheed (published by Sheed & Ward Ltd.).

Barker, George: *To My Mother* (from COLLECTED POEMS, published by Faber & Faber Ltd.).

The Venerable Bede: lines translated by Helen Waddell (by permission of Constable & Co. Ltd.).

Belloc, Hilaire: *Courtesy* (from SONNETS AND VERSE, published by Gerald Duckworth & Co. Ltd.).

Betjeman, John: *In A Bath Teashop, Christmas, Sunday Morning King's Cambridge, Diary of a Church Mouse* (from COLLECTED POEMS, published by John Murray Ltd.).

Bonhoeffer, Dietrich: *Prayer for his Fellow Prisoners, Christmas 1943* (from LETTERS AND PAPERS FROM PRISON, published by SCM Press Ltd.).

Bradby, H.C.: *Comfort for the Sleepless* (by permission of the author's family).

Bridges, Robert: *A Passer By* (by permission of The Clarendon Press).

Brooke, Rupert: *Clouds, The Soldier, The Fish* (from THE COLLECTED POEMS OF RUPERT BROOKE, published by Sidgwick & Jackson Ltd. and McClelland & Stewart Ltd. in Canada).

Bryant, Arthur (editor): *Postman's Horn* (from ANTHOLOGY OF SEVENTEENTH CENTURY LETTERS, published by Home & Van Thal).

Campbell, Roy: *Horses on the Camargue* (from ADAMASTOR, published by Faber & Faber Ltd. by permission of the estate of Roy Campbell) and *Christ in Hospital, The Secret Muse, Choosing a Mast* (from COLLECTED POEMS, published by The Bodley Head Ltd.).

Causley, Charles: *Timothy Winters, King's College Chapel* (by permission of Rupert Hart-Davis Ltd.).

Chardin, Pierre Teilhard de: LE MILIEU DIVIN (published by Collins & Sons Co. Ltd.).

Chesterton, G. K.: *The Donkey* (from THE WILD KNIGHT AND OTHER POEMS, published by J. M. Dent & Sons Ltd. by permission of Miss D. E. Collins) and *A Prayer in Darkness* (by permission of Miss D. E. Collins).

Colum, Padraic: *An Old Woman of the Roads* (from POEMS, published by Macmillan & Co. Ltd.).

Congreve, Father: FATHER CONGREVE OF COWLEY by Mildred Woodgate (published by S.P.C.K.).

Cornford, Frances: *Féri Bekassy* (from COLLECTED POEMS, published by The Cresset Press).

Dante: THE DIVINE COMEDY translated by Dorothy L. Sayers (published by Victor Gollancz Ltd.).

Davies, William Henry: *School's Out* (from THE COMPLETE POEMS OF W. H. DAVIES, published by Jonathan Cape Ltd., by permission of Mrs. H. M. Davies). ‘

de la Mare, Walter: *The Quartette, Tom's Angel, To K. M., At Home Alone with the Cat, Hyssop* (by permission of the Literary Trustees of Walter de la Mare and the Society of Authors as their representative).

Dresbach, Glenn Ward: *Through the Blowing Leaves, Ship's Bell* (from COLLECTED POEMS, published by the Caxton Printers Ltd., Caldwell, Idaho).

Eliot, T. S.: *Little Gidding*, Part IV (from FOUR QUARTETS, published by Faber & Faber Ltd.) and *Journey of the Magi* (from COLLECTED POEMS 1909-62, published by Faber & Faber Ltd.).

Falstaff, Jake: *The Elfin Wife, A Day in Spring* (from THE BULLS OF SPRING, SELECTED POEMS OF JAKE FALSTAFF, published by G. P. Putnam's Sons).

Saint Francis of Assisi: THE LITTLE FLOWERS OF SAINT FRANCIS, edited by Hugh Martin, (published by SCM Press Ltd.) and *Canticle of the Sun*, translated by Maurice Francis Egan (from THE WORLD'S GREAT RELIGIOUS POETRY, published by the Macmillan Company, N.Y., reprinted by permission of the Baptist Retirement Home, Maywood, Illinois).

Frost, Robert: *The Pasture* (from THE COMPLETE POEMS OF ROBERT FROST, published by Jonathan Cape Ltd. and Holt Rinehart & Winston Inc., Publishers, N.Y. Copyright 1923 by Holt, Rinehart & Winston, Inc. Copyright renewed 1951 by Robert Frost.)

Fry, Christopher: *Rain on dry ground* (from THE BOY WITH THE CART, published by Frederick Muller Ltd.).

Gollancz, Victor: MY DEAR TIMOTHY (published by Victor Gollancz Ltd.).

Graves, Robert: *The Person from Porlock, Turn of the Moon, In the Wilderness, The Secret Land* (from MORE POEMS 1961, published by Cassell & Co. Ltd., by permission of International Authors N.V.) and *Welsh Incident* (from COLLECTED POEMS 1959, published by Cassell & Co. Ltd., by permission of International Authors N.V.).

Harvey, Frederick William: *Ducks* (from DUCKS AND OTHER POEMS, published by Sidgwick & Jackson Ltd.).

Higgins, Frederick Robert: *Father and Son* (published by Macmillan & Co. Ltd., by permission of Mr. Higgins' executors).

Hillary Richard: THE LAST ENEMY (published by Macmillan & Co. Ltd., by permission of the literary executor of Richard Hillary and the publisher).

Houselander, Caryll: *Sœur Marie Emilie* (from THE FLOWERING TREE, published by Sheed & Ward Ltd.) and A ROCKING HORSE CATHOLIC (published by Sheed & Ward Ltd.).

Hughes, Richard: *The Sermon* (from CONFESSIO JUVENIS, published by Chatto & Windus Ltd.).

Hughes, Ted: *An Otter* (from LUPERCAL, published by Faber & Faber Ltd.).

Jennings, Elizabeth: *Fountain, Beyond Possession* (from POEMS, published by André Deutsch Ltd.).

Saint John of the Cross: *Christ and the Soul* and *The Search* from THE SPIRITUAL CANTICLE, translated by E. Allison Peers (published by Burns & Oates Ltd.) and *The Obscure Night of the Soul,* translated by Arthur Symons (from THE POEMS OF ARTHUR SYMONS, published by William Heinemann Ltd.).

Dame Julian of Norwich: REVELATIONS OF DIVINE LOVE edited by Grace Warrack, (published by Methuen & Co. Ltd.).

Kersh, Gerald: *The Soldier* (from POEMS FROM THE DESERT, published by George G. Harrap & Co. Ltd.).

Kipling, Rudyard: *Jane's Marriage* (from DEBITS AND CREDITS, published by Macmillan & Co. Ltd., by permission of Mrs. Bambridge, Macmillan & Co. Ltd., and the Macmillan Co. of Canada Ltd.).

Langland, William: VISIONS FROM PIERS PLOWMAN, translated into modern English by Nevill Coghill (published by Phoenix House).

Lawrence, D. H.: *Work* (from THE COMPLETE POEMS OF D. H. LAWRENCE, published by William Heinemann Ltd., by permission of Laurence Pollinger Ltd. and the Estate of the late Mrs. Frieda Lawrence).

Brother Lawrence: THE PRACTICE OF THE PRESENCE OF GOD edited by Hugh Martin (published by SCM Press Ltd.).

Lee, Laurie: *Autumn Apples, Twelfth Night* (from MY MANY-COATED MAN, published by André Deutsch Ltd.) and *April Rose, Poem for Easter* (from THE BLOOM OF CANDLES, published by John Lehmann Ltd.).

Letts, W. M.: *Tim, an Irish Terrier* (from SONGS OF LEINSTER, published by Dundalgan Press [W. Tempest] Ltd.).

Lewis, C. Day: *In the Shelter, The Misfit, Seen from the Train, O Dreams O Destinations* (from COLLECTED POEMS, published by Jonathan Cape Ltd.).

Lewis, C. S.: THE PROBLEM OF PAIN, MIRACLES, THE PILGRIM'S REGRESS, THE SCREWTAPE LETTERS, *The Weight of Glory* from THEY ASKED FOR A PAPER (all published by Geoffrey Bles Ltd.).

Lindsay, Vachel: *General William Booth Enters Heaven* (from COLLECTED POEMS, published by Macmillan Co., N.Y., Copyright 1913 by the Macmillan Company).

MacCaig, Norman: *Spate in Winter Midnight* (from A COMMON GRACE, published by the Hogarth Press Ltd.).

Maeterlinck, Maurice: THE LIFE OF THE BEE (published by George Allen & Unwin Ltd.).

Masefield, John: *The Everlasting Mercy* (reprinted with permission of Dr. John Masefield, the Society of Authors, and the Macmillan Company, N.Y., from POEMS. Copyright 1912 by the Macmillan Company. Renewed 1940 by John Masefield) and *Good Friday* (reprinted by permission of Dr. John Masefield, the Society of Authors and the Macmillan Company, N.Y., from GOOD FRIDAY AND OTHER POEMS. Copyright 1915, 1916 by John Masefield. Renewed 1943, 1944 by John Masefield).

Meynell, Alice: *Or his bestowals there* (from POEMS, published by Burns & Oates Ltd:).

Milne, A. A.: *Happiness* (from WHEN WE WERE VERY YOUNG, published by Methuen & Co. Ltd.).

Monro, Harold: *Hearthstone* (from COLLECTED POEMS, now in preparation, to be published by Gerald Duckworth & Co. Ltd., by permission of Alida Monro and the publisher).

Moorman, John R. H.: SAINT FRANCIS OF ASSISI (published by SCM Press Ltd.).

Murdoch, Iris: THE BELL (published by Chatto & Windus Ltd.).

Neale, J. E.: QUEEN ELIZABETH I (published by Jonathan Cape Ltd.).

Nicolas, Vidal de: *A Wish* (from FROM BURGOS JAIL, translated from the Spanish by Chloe Vulliamy and Stephen Sedley, published by Appeal for Amnesty in Spain).

Noyes, Alfred: *The Butterfly Garden* (from COLLECTED POEMS, published by John Murray Ltd.).

Peers, E. Allison: SPIRIT OF FLAME (published by SCM Press Ltd.).

Pitter, Ruth: *An Old Woman Speaks of the Moon, Stormcock in Elder, The Fishers, Close Mortal Eyes* (from URANIA, published by The Cresset Press).

Plath, Sylvia: *Kindness* (by permission of Mr. Ted Hughes).

Redgrove, Peter: *Early Morning Feed* (from THE COLLECTOR AND OTHER POEMS, published by Routledge & Kegan Paul Ltd.).

Russell, George William (A.E.): *Promise* (by permission of Mr. Diarmuid Russell).

Sayers, Dorothy L.: THE JUST VENGEANCE (published by Victor Gollancz Ltd.).

Serraillier, Ian: *The Headless Gardener* (from THOMAS AND THE SPARROW, published by Oxford University Press).

Sitwell, Sacheverell: *Magnolia Tree in Summer* (from THE THIRTEENTH CAESAR AND OTHER POEMS, published by Gerald Duckworth Ltd.).

Smith, Stevie: *The Singing Cat* (from NOT WAVING BUT DROWNING, published by André Deutsch Ltd.).

Spender, Stephen: *To My Daughter, Missing My Daughter, The Truly Great* (from COLLECTED POEMS, published by Faber & Faber Ltd.).

Stuart, Muriel: *The Seed Shop* (by permission of Jonathan Cape Ltd.).

Symons, Arthur: *The Fairy Wood* (by permission of William Heinemann Ltd. on behalf of the Symons Estate).

Tagore, Rabindranath: *Gitanjali* nos. LXXIX and XCIII (from COLLECTED POEMS AND PLAYS OF RABINDRANATH TAGORE, published by Macmillan & Co. Ltd., by permission of the Trustees of the Tagore Estate and the publisher.).

Saint Teresa of Avila: THE INTERIOR CASTLE, translated by a Benedictine of Stanbrook (published by Thomas Baker, Publisher), *Saint Teresa's Book Mark*, translated by E. Allison Peers in MOTHER OF CARMEL (published by SCM Press Ltd.), THE WAY OF PERFECTION, translated by a Discalced Carmelite (published by Sands & Co. Ltd.).

Thomas, Dylan: *Poems in October, Fern Hill* (from COLLECTED POEMS, published by J. M. Dent & Sons Ltd., by permission of the Dylan Thomas Estate and the publisher).

Thomas, R. S.: *The View from the Window, A Blackbird Singing, Bread* (from POETRY FOR SUPPER, published by Rupert Hart-Davis Ltd.), and *Children's Song, Cynddylan on a Tractor in Spring, A Person from Porlock* (from SONG AT THE YEAR'S TURNING, published by Rupert Hart-Davis Ltd.).

Todd, Barbara Euphan: *Fairy Story, Aunt Matilda* (from THE SEVENTH DAUGHTER, published by Burns & Oates Ltd.).

Tynan, Katharine: *The Childless Woman in Heaven*, (by permission of the Society of Authors and Miss Pamela Hinkson).

Underhill, Evelyn: *The Holy Spirit* (from LETTERS OF EVELYN UNDERHILL, published by Longmans, Green & Co. Ltd.).

Wellesley, Dorothy: *Fishing* (from POEMS, published by Macmillan & Co. Ltd.).

Wenceslas, Duke of Brabant and Luxembourg: *Rondel*, translated by Sir Henry Newbolt (from POEMS NEW AND OLD, published by John Murray Ltd., by permission of Captain Francis Newbolt, C.M.G.).

Wolfe, Humbert: THE UNCELESTIAL CITY (published by Victor Gollancz Ltd., by permission of Miss Anne Wolfe).

Woodgate, M. V.: JACQELINE PASCAL AND HER BROTHER (published by Browne & Nolan Ltd.).

Woods, Margaret: *I've heard, I've heard* (from THE COLLECTED POEMS, published by The Bodley Head Ltd.).

Yeats, W. B.: *The Ragged Wood, To A Friend Whose Work Has Come to Nothing, The Lake Isle of Innisfree* (from THE COLLECTED POEMS OF W. B. YEATS, published by Macmillan & Co. Ltd., by permission of Mrs. W. B. Yeats and the publisher).

INDEX OF FIRST LINES

'A cold coming we had of it, 154
A Gardener, Tobias Baird, 329
A gift is properly an unreturnable giving, 175
A shepherd-boy his grief is brooding o'er, 159
A thing of beauty is a joy for ever, 239
A voice, loud in that light, to Lucifer crying, 167
Abu Ben Adhem (may his tribe increase), 180
Ah, see the fair chivalry come, the companions of Christ, 106
Ah, you should see Cynddylan on a tractor, 123
All appeared new and strange at first, 70
All is best, though we oft doubt, 219
All the paths of the Lord are loving-kindness and truth, 248
Almighty Father, Thy love is like a great sea, 236
Also in this He showed me a little thing, 66
And art Thou come, dear Saviour, 148
And as he went on his way, 49
And, as it seems, I appear to you to be inferior to swans, 45
And God said . . . I do not set my bow in the cloud, 20
And he said, A certain man had two sons, 250
And is there care in heaven? and is there love, 286
And one of the malefactors which were hanged railed on him, 224
And there were shepherds in the same country, 282
And when he was twelve years old, 68
As I mused by the hearthside, 324
As the hart panteth after the water brooks, 187
Ask, and it shall be given you, 187
At St. Mary of the Angels, 50
At the training depot that first morning, 120

Bad I am, but yet thy child, 254
Behold the apples' rounded worlds, 35
Beholding the face of God, 290
Be not so desolate, 275
Between the midnight and the morn, 297
Beyond the shadow of the ship, 259
Bid me to live, and I will live, 99
Booth led boldly with his big bass drum, 270
Bright clasp of her whole hand around my finger, 87
Bring us, O Lord God, at our last awakening, 281
But lo, what think you; suddenly, 21
But our life came down to this our earth, 171
But that was nothing to what things came out, 333
But yet one thought has often stayed by me, 214
By his commandment he maketh the snow to fall apace, 25

Cat! who has pass'd thy grand climacteric, 62

345